Investigating Chromosomes

Adrian F. Dyer D. PHIL.

Senior Lecturer in Botany, University of Edinburgh

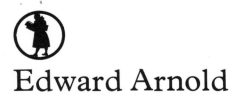

Edward Arnold

© Adrian F. Dyer, 1979

First published 1979
by Edward Arnold (Publishers) Ltd.,
41 Bedford Square,
London, WC1 3DP

British Library Cataloguing in Publication Data

Dyer, Adrian F
    Investigating chromosomes.
        1. Chromosomes   2. Cytology – Technique
        I. Title
574.8'732   QH600

ISBN 0–7131–2722–8

Filmset by Keyspools Ltd., Golborne, Lancs.
Printed in Great Britain by
Whitstable Litho Ltd, Whitstable, Kent.

Contents

Introduction

Many fascinating features of chromosome structure and behaviour are clearly described in the books now available for students at school, college and university. These accounts describe how the chromosome accommodates the genetic information, releases this information according to a predetermined sequence during development and transmits it to the next generation while maintaining combinations of genes which interact functionally in an adaptive way. Some who read about these events will wish to investigate them for themselves. Indeed, at a time when there is an increasing demand for cytogeneticists in plant breeding, human clinical genetics and veterinary medicine, such investigations may be for many a necessary component of their practical training or employment. Unfortunately, all too many are defeated by the technique before facing the challenge of interpreting the chromosomes they see. Some become discouraged by the experience of complex and empirical methods with little to show at the end but a murky glimpse of mitosis. For others, too daunted even to try their hand, chromosomes remain as lifeless microscopic components of a bought slide or as photographs or line drawings in a book. Even those who have some success with their preparations could achieve more if encouraged to think beyond the named stages of mitosis and meiosis.

The purpose of this book is to encourage student and teacher to demonstrate and investigate for themselves the structure and behaviour of the chromosome complement as seen down a light microscope. This purpose partly accounts for the bias in selection of material for inclusion. In the first place, the emphasis throughout is on the chromosomes rather than the techniques. Only one basic technique will be described in detail even though many alternatives exist, some of which may be better or even essential for certain specialized purposes. Much can be achieved by relatively inexperienced cytologists, even those with limited time or facilities, by the imaginative use of a simple versatile technique which becomes more familiar with every successful investigation. Little can be expected if every observation requires the selection of the appropriate method from a daunting array of alternatives. The simple method given here has proved successful with complete beginners at school and university, in classes of over 200, under 'field' conditions away from a laboratory, and with plant, animal and human cells.

At least as important as the choice of method is the selection of suitable living material. The second bias in this book is in the choice of this material, which comes mainly from among the flowering plants. There are sound practical reasons for choosing angiosperm material for introductory chromosome studies: a) they are generally easier than animals to maintain alive under laboratory, or at least greenhouse and garden plot, conditions; b) dividing cells of higher plants are often easier to obtain and process, and the chromosomes themselves often larger, than those of animals and lower plants while most of the basic characteristics of chromosome structure and behaviour are equally well represented; and c) when a particular chromosome condition is accompanied by sexual sterility it can only be maintained in asexually reproducing organisms such as vegetatively propagated plants. For these reasons, plant chromosomes are more often used in teaching and, at least in the past, have been more widely studied, yielding a more extensive literature. Nevertheless, when animal material has an important contribution to make, instructions necessary for its study are included.

This book is also biased in its treatment of the cell because it is concerned only with the chromosome complement and the visible events of nuclear divisions. Although division and segregation of chromosomes are only two of the visible components of cell division (organelle replication and distribution, and cytokinesis or cleavage are equally important for successful cell replication), the additional techniques necessary to study the cytoplasm are beyond the scope of this book.

Finally, the treatment is biased in its emphasis on the practical aspects of material, method and approach. In a book intended to be used primarily in the laboratory, a general outline of each topic is included as background information only to ensure recognition of significant features. For detailed treatment of the underlying explanations and implications of these features in a wider range of material, reference should be made to the reading lists accompanying each section.

Four aspects of the investigation of chromosomes are dealt with in separate chapters. Chapter 1 describes simple techniques for obtaining preparations and recording observations of chromosomes; techniques which with only minor modification are sufficient for all the subsequent sections. Chapter 2 introduces the basic features of chromosome morphology and behaviour to be observed during the mitotic cycle at different stages of the life cycle and during meiosis, together with the methods and materials required to reveal them. Chapter 3 is concerned with cytogenetics, the study of the chromosome complement in relation to the flow of genes between individuals and generations. In particular, this involves application of information from the preceding chapter to the study of the various effects of changes in the size, number or structure of

chromosomes on their behaviour at meiosis. In Chapter 4, a change of approach from one of demonstration to one of enquiry is encouraged by outlining several projects selected to indicate the variety of investigations made possible by using the knowledge gained from Chapters 1 to 3.

Thus the chapters are arranged in order of increasing scope and complexity, each building on the content of the one before. By following them in sequence, the beginner can first learn the basic technique and then proceed towards progressively more sophisticated studies of his own preparations. For those requiring information on specific aspects of chromosome structure or behaviour, the contents are listed in detail.

Chapters and sections dealing exclusively with instructions on technique or lists of material for specific purposes are indicated by a tinted box covering the page number. This applies to the whole of Chapter 1 and Appendices 1 and 2. Within Chapters 2 and 3, information on methods and materials relating to each major topic is placed at the end of the sub-section introducing that topic and presented in a sequence which corresponds to the content of the introduction. Thus, for example, chromosome coiling is described in Section 2.2.2 on pages 17–20 while the relevant information on material and techniques to demonstrate it is given on pages 27–28 at the start of the Section 2.2.5. Similarly, aneuploids are described on pages 103–105 in Section 3.4.2h while the examples are listed on page 110 within Section 3.4.4.

Acknowledgements

I would like to thank all those who have helped me to enjoy an interest in chromosomes since my introduction to the subject as a student. I am also grateful to everyone who has assisted me in the preparation of this book and in particular to Miss Julia Boardman of Edward Arnold (Publishers) Ltd. for her skill in bringing order out of chaos.

1 Finding chromosomes – a matter of method

1.1 Introduction

Every cytologist has his favourite technique for chromosome preparations. This may be one of the many published methods or, more likely, an empirically derived minor variation of it. None is ideal for all purposes and many, though successful in practised hands, require considerable experience before they give consistently good results. The secret for success is a simple, reliable technique and practice.

All techniques are designed to fix, stain and preserve the chromosomes so that they can be profitably studied. *Fixation* is an attempt to kill the material rapidly in such a way that the internal structures are preserved in a life-like form. Because fixation involves such processes as denaturation of proteins, some alteration of structure is always induced and care has to be taken in interpretation to recognize artefacts (those features which are induced by the treatment and not present in the living cell). Because the various cell components differ in their fixation properties, methods are chosen for their ability to achieve good fixation of the particular structures being studied, in this case the chromosomes, even though they may not give equally good fixation of other cytoplasmic structures. Good fixation is a rather subjective assessment indicating that the appearance after treatment suggests a structure similar to that deduced from phase contrast images of living cells and from cells fixed by other techniques. The fixative described in Section 1.5 is based on the long known and widely used acetic-alcohol fixative, which causes some chromosome shrinkage but is otherwise acceptable. The

inclusion of formalin counteracts the tendency to form 'bubbles' along the arms of large chromosomes, and chloroform helps to remove chlorophyll from green tissues and is claimed to make penetration by the fixative more rapid. In certain cases, the acid solvent of the dye used for staining can act satisfactorily as a simultaneous fixative without prior fixation.

After fixation, material can be stored until required, usually in alcohol, or immediately stained for observation. Storage rarely, if ever, improves the final preparation, frequently accentuating the artefacts and sometimes reducing the staining. A disadvantage of orcein, the dye recommended here, is that staining is sometimes less effective after storage in alcohol. However, for teaching purposes, it is desirable that the student makes his preparation directly from the living organism, rather than from excised fixed tissues, so this property of orcein is rarely a drawback. In any case, the finished preparation can be kept for examination on a later occasion if time is limited. Temporary orcein preparations made by the technique described will keep satisfactorily for days, and sometimes for weeks or even months, while permanent preparations show little or no change after 15 years.

Staining is necessary because without it the colourless chromosomes are difficult to distinguish from the equally colourless cytoplasm. A number of dyes have been used by methods, again usually derived empirically, to give preferential staining of chromosomes by adsorption, taking advantage of their characteristic surface properties. Several naturally occurring dyes, such as carmine and orcein, dissolved in simple organic acids have been used successfully although they induce some swelling of the chromosomes.

Orcein in propionic acid gives better differential staining than other solutions because, while the chromosomes are deep purple, the cytoplasm shows little or no staining. Counter-staining of the rest of the cell using a second dye with appropriately different adsorption properties is possible, but rarely beneficial for chromosome studies as it inevitably reduces the contrast between the chromosomes and their background.

Stained chromosomes have to be examined by transmitted light using the most highly magnifying objective of the microscope. The preparation must therefore be thin, to transmit sufficient light and to accommodate the shallow depth of focus of these lenses. For a clear image of chromosomes the material must be only one cell thick on the slide, even though most dividing cells occur in relatively massive tissues. There are two main ways of separating cells of such tissues for examination. Thin sections can be cut, but this involves the lengthy and laborious process of wax embedding and microtome sectioning, and while this preserves cells and organelles in their correct relative positions, the chromosomes may be indistinct or, when cut by the knife, even incomplete. A simpler and quicker alternative which is better suited to most chromosome investigations is to treat the cells so that they no longer adhere to one another, and can be separated and spread over a slide. One method is to warm in dilute acid for a short time before breaking up the tissue mechanically to produce a cell suspension. The alternative treatment in concentrated acid at room temperature is more hazardous and unreliable and tends to give very uneven results within the thickness of the tissue. This maceration inevitably destroys the arrangement of cells within tissues and the technique is unsuitable for anatomical investigations. Carefully restricted pressure on the cover slip will however give a clear image of the cell with its chromosomes

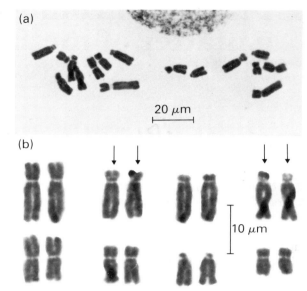

Fig. 1.1 The chromosome complement of the wild hyacinth or bluebell, *Endymion nonscriptus* ($2n = 2x = 16$). **a**, Colchicine pretreated root tip mitosis at metaphase. **b**, Idiogram derived from a second cell showing eight distinguishable chromosomes each represented twice. Two pairs of acrocentric chromosomes (arrowed) have nucleolar organizers in the short arms.

in their natural position, with no more distortion of the organelles than in a section, but with the whole cell intact. Greater pressure, as in the *squash* technique (Section 1.4) will distort their arrangement, but make the individual chromosomes more clearly visible in a complement flattened at one focal level.

The resulting temporary preparation can be made permanent. The decision has to be made, balancing the need for a long-lasting preparation against the risk of losing some cells, at the outset of the preparation, because the slide or coverslip has to be suitably coated with an adhesive. The cell preparation, stuck to a slide or coverslip, is taken through a graded series of alcohol concentrations to a suitable mountant.

The chromosome preparation is then ready for examination. Apart from some basic rules for recording observations, the problems of interpretation, which depend very much on the species and tissue used, will be covered in subsequent sections. However, there is an additional step, often referred to as *pre-treatment*, which can be inserted into the preparative technique to facilitate the subsequent interpretation of many features of the chromosomal complement in the finished slide. Pre-treatment involves the exposure of living material before fixation to the effects of one of a number of chemicals or physical treatments which inhibit the activity of the spindle during division, resulting in the accumulation of cells with chromosomes scattered through the cytoplasm instead of aggregated on the spindle equator and shorter and straighter than normal due to overcontraction. The result after fixing, staining and squashing is a cell in which the number and morphology of the chromosomes is particularly clear (Fig. 1.1).

The rest of this section describes in detail the equipment and operations required for the technique just outlined.

1.2 Equipment and reagents

The full list of requirements is given in Table 1.1, but some additional comments may be helpful.

Dividing cells can usually be recognized under ×10 objectives, and some rather superficial investigations are possible using a ×40 objective, but any detailed examination of chromosomes requires a ×90 to ×105 oil immersion objective. Much of the preliminary work of preparing and scanning preparations can be done at a lower magnification, so, with careful planning, useful work can be carried out with oil immersion objectives being shared between students although ideally each should have his own. Obviously, the better the optical system, the clearer the chromosomes in a good preparation. However, a typical student microscope is perfectly adequate, the critical

factor being that it is correctly set up for maximum optical resolution and illumination according to the manufacturer's instructions. The use of a green filter is often helpful if sufficiently intense illumination is available. The red-purple stained chromosomes will appear black against a green background. Many lenses show least aberration in green light, and the eye is most sensitive to wavelengths in this part of the visible spectrum.

The rod used for separating the cells of the macerated tissue (Section 1.5) should be a piece of 3 mm brass or aluminium rod about 7 cm long, with the cut ends filed and polished. Pieces of plastic knitting needles of comparable size are a tolerable alternative.

An oven or waterbath is required to maintain material for maceration in dilute acid at about 60°C. The waterbath is less convenient than the oven because immersed tubes and bottles tend to float. Most laboratories will have at least one of these items of controlled temperature equipment, but the temperature is not critical and adequate results are possible, though laborious, using mixtures of hot and cold water and a thermometer.

The ridged separating dish is used to float the coverslip away from the inverted slide when making a preparation permanent. While less convenient, any flat container for the diluted acetic acid, with two pieces of glass rod to support the slide above the bottom of the dish, will serve the same purpose.

Species differ in their sensitivity to the pre-treatment chemicals used to clarify the chromosome complements. Colchicine is usually the most successful, but is also unfortunately by far the most expensive and as a possible carcinogen must be handled with care. In many cases saturated solutions of para-dichloro-benzene or alpha-bromo-naphthalene are acceptable substitutes and, in those cases where colchicine is found to be inactive or over-active, necessary alternatives. The former is claimed to be parti-

Table 1.1 Equipment and reagents for chromosome preparations. Key: *Required for every student, **required for every 1–6 students, ***required for every 1–20 students.

	Pretreatment	Fixation and Storage	Maceration	Staining	Permanent Mounting
Glass-ware	***100 ml beaker ***Aquarium aerator	*Two 50 mm × 25 mm stoppered specimen tubes **100 ml measuring cylinder	*Two 50 mm × 25 mm stoppered specimen tubes	*Slides and coverslips	**Four solid watch-glasses
Reagents	***200 mls colchicine or p-dichloro-benzene or α-bromo-naphalene or 8-hydroxyquinoline	***200 ml abs. ethanol ***200 ml 70% ethanol ***100 ml formalin ***100 ml chloroform ***100 ml glacial acetic acid	**100 ml 1M HCl at 60°C *Distilled water	**Working strength lactopropionic orcein in bottle with bottle pipette	**200 ml abs. ethanol **200 ml 95% ethanol **200 ml 70% ethanol **200 ml euparal essence **euparal mountant **45% acetic acid
Other equip-ment	**Forceps	**Forceps	***Water bath or oven at 60°C *3" squares of muslin	*Large sheet white paper on bench *Four 6" squares of blotting paper *Paper tissues **1 scalpel and 2 mounted needles *Brass rod, 7 cm × 3 mm *Microscope with ×100 objective, immersion oil, lens tissue and green filter **Spirit lamp or microbunsen **Tube glycerin-albumen adhesive *xylol for lens cleaning	**5" square ridged separating dish

A basic kit for temporary preparations is available from Philip Harris Biological Ltd.

cularly good for leaf material. During the pre-treatment of living material in one of these solutions, bubbling with an aquarium pump is helpful in stirring and aerating the solution. A clean glass tube, with one end drawn out so as to restrict the opening in order to produce a stream of small bubbles, should be clamped so that this end dips into the solution in a beaker. This tube can be connected at the outer end to the aerator, using polythene, *not rubber*, tubing.

In addition to a range of alcohol dilutions, made up by volume with water to the percentages given in the method, a number of solutions have to be prepared. The instructions for these are given below.

PRE-TREATING AGENTS:

Colchicine: Usually used as solutions of 0.01% to 0.2% w/v in water. Batches differ in their activity. Store in a fridge.

8-hydroxyquinoline: 0.002 M solution in water (0.29 g l^{-1}).

p-dichlorobenzene: Used as a saturated solution in water.

α-bromo-naphthalene: As for *p*-dichlorobenzene or 1% aqueous solution of stock solution of 1 ml bromo-naphthalene dissolved in 100 ml absolute ethanol for $\frac{1}{2}$ hour.

FIXATIVE:

Fixative should be freshly prepared for each fixation. It consists of:

Absolute ethanol	10 parts
Chloroform	2 parts
Glacial acetic acid	2 parts
Formalin	1 part

    (40% formaldehyde in water)

STAIN:

Lacto-propionic orcein: Stock solution: dissolve as far as possible overnight at room temperature 2 g natural orcein (Supplier: George T. Gurr) in a mixture of 50 ml lactic acid and 50 ml propionic acid. Filter.

Working solution: dilute stock solution to between 45% and 60% with water and filter.

It is useful to have both 45% and 60% available, as the stronger stain is better for some material. The solution will keep for many months but may require periodic filtration to remove precipitated particles.

1.3 Material

Detailed consideration of the species and tissues required for particular purposes will be dealt with in later sections. Only general consideration of the plant or animal material will be discussed here.

To show chromosomes, the organism or tissue must be alive and healthy and contain actively dividing cells at the time of fixation. To ensure these conditions requires some understanding of the development, anatomy and life cycle of the organism, and of its cultural requirements. If there is any doubt about these, expert advice should be sought.

Organisms which are easy to keep in culture include many of the flowering plants and the most frequently used material for demonstrating dividing chromosomes is the permanently embryonic tissue of growing root tips. These root tips are frequently broken off and lost when plants are dug out of the ground, so it is usually necessary to cultivate the plants in suitable soil or compost in pots. All plants should be re-potted at least one month before material is required so that new roots can grow. They are most easily accessible with minimum disturbance to the plant when the root tips have reached the sides of the pot and can be collected from the surface when the plant is tipped out. To obtain younger roots the plant must be washed clean after removing most of the soil by gentle shaking. For most plants, cells are most active if the pot is liberally watered 24 to 48 hours before taking the roots, provided that drainage is good. Alternatively, where a species is most readily obtained as seeds, these can be germinated in pots or on moist blotting paper in Petri dishes. A number of lateral root tips can usually be obtained from each seed if the emerging radicle is decapitated. Sometimes roots can be obtained from cuttings in aerated mineral culture solution. Healthy growing roots are brittle, translucent and white, with opaque cream to white, gently tapered tips.

When roots are not available, other tissues such as young leaves can sometimes be used. When plants are flowering, the mitotically active ovary or ovule wall of developing flowers or fruits provides a useful substitute which can be treated in the same way as roots after dissecting out appropriately sized pieces of tissue (Section 2.4).

Access to other sources of dividing cells is described in subsequent sections. However, it cannot be over-emphasized that no cell will yield a good preparation unless it is in a healthy condition, and it is a waste of time persisting with any technique if the material is sickly. Correct cultural management of the material up to the time of fixation is at least as important as the subsequent preparative method, and all too often neglected.

1.4 Pre-treatment

Pre-treatment may be required for some investigations, to clarify the morphology of the chromosome complement in the final preparation. This is unnecessary for certain divisions, such as meiosis, mitosis in pollen grains and mitosis during insect spermatogenesis, when chromosomes are normally well contracted and dispersed, but very helpful for root tip mitoses and with other meristematic tissues in plants. Low temperature treatment (e.g. 2°C for 24 hours) of intact tissue is sometimes an adequate alternative.

Washed root tips, either intact on seeds or cut off about 1 cm behind the tip, or other appropriate excised tissues, are immersed in the solution of colchicine or one of its alternatives (Section 1.2) for 4 to 6 hours at room temperatures not exceeding about 18°C. The material has to remain alive and active during this time, and it is important that the glassware and solution used is entirely free from detergent and other noxious chemicals. Continuous agitation and aeration by the bubbles from an aquarium aerator is recommended, particularly if large amounts of material, such as 100 root tips, are being processed simultaneously. At the least, the solution should be shallow with a relatively large surface and periodic stirring should take place throughout the treatment. The material is subsequently transferred to a clean tube for fixation, using forceps in order to leave behind as much as possible of the solution, grit and debris.

1.5 Basic technique

The steps in the technique are summarized in Table 1.2 and Fig. 1.2, and described in more detail below.

Fixation

Start here for smears and squash preparations of all somatic plant tissues. For squash preparations of divisions in fresh material of plant spores and animal cells start at 5.

1) Choose brittle, translucent roots with cream to white tips, or an equivalent healthy meristematic tissue. Immerse 1 cm root tips, or other tissue pieces of comparable volume, for 5 minutes in an excess of freshly prepared fixative in a specimen tube.

   The material can be washed briefly in 70% ethanol in a clean tube if it is thought necessary to remove all traces of formalin before immersion in HCl. Formaldehyde can react with HCl vapour to produce a toxic chloromethyl ester. It is therefore also advisable to keep the formalin bottle at a distance from the heated HCl. Formalin can be omitted from the fixative but inferior fixation, particularly of large chromosomes, may result.

For storage after fixation, the fixative can be subsequently replaced by 70% ethanol, but this may reduce the effectiveness of later orcein staining.

Maceration

2) Transfer the tissue with forceps to M HCl for 5 minutes at a maintained temperature of about 60°C. Any grit or debris should be left behind in the fixative.

3) Transfer the tissue to water. If several tissue pieces are involved, a convenient way to change solutions is to cover the mouth of the tube with a sheet of muslin, and shake the solution of HCl through into a sink with the tap running, leaving behind the plant material. Then, without removing the muslin, pour the water in, washing the tissue pieces back to the bottom of the tube in 2–3 cm of water. Material can be stored for a day or two in water.

Table 1.2   Summary of technique. See pp. 6–11 for details.

PRE-TREATMENT – for karyotype studies of plants only	4–6 hours in aerated pre-treatment solution (e.g. 0.05% colchicine) at room temperature, preferably below 18°C
FIXATION – for all chromosome studies of plant tissues and smears	5 mins in fixative: Absolute ethanol – 10 parts Chloroform – 2 parts Glacial acetic acid – 2 parts Formalin – 1 part Wash briefly in 70% ethanol in a clean tube
MACERATION – for all chromosome studies of plant tissues and smears	5 mins 1M HCl at 60°C. Transfer to water
CELL SUSPENSION – for all material	Tap or tease 1 mm piece of tissue in 5 mm drop of lacto-propionic orcein. Remove visible particles
COATING COVERSLIP – only necessary for intended permanent preparations	Thinly coat coverslip on lower surface with glycerin albumen and dry over a small flame
STAINING – for all material	Add further stain, spread and lower a coverslip. Tap gently on coverslip with needle point to disperse material if necessary. Leave for 10 mins – 24 hrs
SQUASHING – for plant material and perhaps to a lesser extent for animal material	Press down on coverslip, without lateral movement, through blotting paper
Temporary preparation completed	Examine and repeat, or make permanent as required
MAKING PERMANENT	Float off coverslip in 45% acetic acid 5–10 mins 75% ethanol 5–10 mins 90% ethanol 5–10 mins 100% ethanol
Permanent preparation completed	Mount in euparal

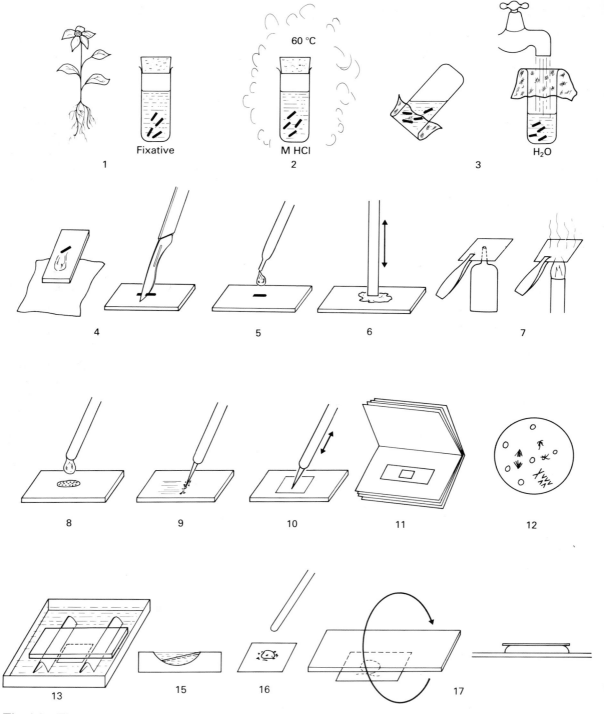

1   Fixative

2   60 °C   M HCl

3

H₂O

4   5   6   7

8   9   10   11   12

13   15   16   17

Fig. 1.2   The technique for making preparations of root tip mitosis. The numbered stages refer to those described in Section 1.5.

Preparing the cell suspension

4) Remove one piece of tissue and place it on a slide, sloped to allow excess water to drain on to blotting paper. Cut off the terminal 1 mm of the root tip, or excise an equivalent volume of other meristematic tissue, and discard the rest. Most beginners use too much material.

5) Begin here for squash preparations of plant spores and animal tissues.

   Onto one root tip, anther, ovule, insect testis follicle or equivalent piece of tissue, place one small drop (c. 5 mm diameter) of lacto-propionic orcein.

6) Gently tap the tissue in the stain/fixative with the end of the brass rod held like a pen in a vertical position. There should be enough stain to produce a thick suspension, but not enough to allow the material to escape from under the descending rod. Animal material requires little or none of this treatment, teasing out the tissues with needles being sometimes better.

   Plant anthers require only enough pressure to burst the walls and release the pollen cells, which are naturally separated from each other as they develop. Even more massive plant tissues such as root tips, with adhering thick cellulose walls, should, if correctly prepared, only require 10–20 taps, each time lifting the rod 1–2 cm above the slide, to produce a suspension of very small particles, ideally of single, separated cells. Great feats of strength or endurance are not required.

Coating the Coverslip

For intended permanent preparations only. Temporary preparations do not require this step, and the method proceeds direct from 6 to 8.

7) If permanent preparations are required, the coverslip to be used must be first coated with an adhesive. A clean coverslip is given a thin coating of glycerin-albumen which is then dried over a small flame. This is best done by putting a small drop of adhesive on the middle of the *underside* of a horizontally held coverslip from the nozzle of the tube, held upright. With a finger tip this drop is then smeared over the coverslip surface as if in an attempt to remove it all. On drying it over the flame, the albumen will smoke slightly and go cloudy, but a thin layer will be almost invisible. The coverslip should not be obscured by a layer of charred meringue!

Staining

8) Add another drop or two of orcein stain so that the suspension can be uniformly spread over the area to be occupied by the coverslip, but not so much that most of the material is lost when the excess stain is squashed out from under the coverslip when it is lowered. A common fault is to add too much stain, although when this is impressed upon beginners, a few in their zeal will work with an almost completely dry preparation. At no time should the cells dry out. With experience, it is often possible to tell from low power examination at this stage whether the material is good enough to warrant proceeding further with the preparation.

9) Remove any tissue particles large enough to see individually, and ensure that no pieces of grit are on the slide.

10) Lower a clean coverslip, or one coated with adhesive on the lower surface. Any small clumps of cells can be dispersed by gentle tapping on the coverslip with the tip of a mounted needle. Leave for at least 10 minutes to stain. The progress of staining can be followed at low power under the microscope, and it may improve for anything up to 24 hours. In most cases a usable preparation will be available

Table 1.3   Technique faults and remedies.

Symptoms	Possible causes and cures
TEMPORARY PREPARATION	
1) No cells present	Too little material, too much liquid, poor maceration – refer to detailed instruction
2) No divisions present	Unhealthy material – check cultural conditions. Wrong tissue; not meristematic – check anatomy. Wrong development stage; not dividing – check development. Wrong division stage in synchronous system – repeat
3) No divisons seen	As 1 or 2, or divisions present but missed through lack of experience – examine under × 40
4) Anaphase and telophase seen after pretreatment	Material dividing very slowly – check material or increase duration of treatment. Pretreatment ineffective – check temperature, concentration or change chemical
5) Chromosome clumped or sticky	Unhealthy material – check cultural conditions. Pre-treatment ineffective – check temperature and solution or change chemical. Poor fixation – renew fixative, check recipe, cut up tissue into smaller pieces. Wrong maceration treatment – check solutions, temperature, time
6) Cells not sufficiently squashed	Too little pressure – press harder Too much material. ⎫ Material not spread out. ⎬ Refer to detailed instructions Grit or debris under coverslip. ⎭ Poor maceration – use smaller pieces and if necessary give up to 20 mins treatment
7) Cells not sufficiently stained	Squashing too soon – leave longer. Poor penetration – check maceration and suspension of cells, and anatomy of tissue. Stain too weak – check recipe or increase concentration
8) Nuclei distorted, fragmented or 'rolled'	Lateral movement of slide during squashing
9) Broken slide or coverslip	Uneven bench surface. Grit under slide or coverslip
PERMANENT PREPARATIONS	
1 to 9 plus:	
10) Coverslip will not float off slide	Too much material, too much adhesive, adhesive not dried off – check detailed instructions
11) Cells lost during dehydration	As 8, or too little adhesive
12) Cells distorted	Cells dried out during processing. Wrong alcohol concentrations or sequence
13) Cloudy mountant	Water in absolute ethanol, possibly from atmosphere – renew

within minutes, but sometimes staining will improve if the preparation is left overnight.

Squashing

11) When examination confirms that staining is adequate, place the slide carefully on a sheet of blotting paper on a completely flat surface and then cover it with two more layers of blotting paper. Avoiding any lateral movement, press the coverslip straight downwards by pushing with the thumbs through the upper layers of blotting paper. Excess stain will be expelled and absorbed and the cells flattened. Well prepared material should not need great pressure, and spores and animal cells usually need very little.

12) Examine again. The most flattened and spread cells are likely to be round the periphery, where the cells were flattened as they moved with the stain to the

outside of the coverslip. If the preparation is successful, it can be examined immediately, stored as it is for examination within a week or two, or made more permanent (see 13 below). If it is unsuccessful, repeat 4–12 and consult the list of faults and remedies in Table 1.3.

Making permanent

13) Invert the slide with coverslip in a separating dish so that it is covered with 45% acetic acid and supported at each end with the coverslip raised a few millimetres above the bottom of the dish. In time, the acetic acid will penetrate under the coverslip, which will then fall to the bottom of the dish with the squashed cells attached to its upper surface. Gentle pressure on the back of the slide can accelerate this if necessary, at the risk of dislodging some cells. Squashes with well flattened cells tend to take longer for coverslip separation than bad preparations with solid lumps of tissue and air spaces.

14) Remove the slide, clean and dry it. Lift the coverslip, holding it at one corner with forceps, and drain off excess liquid by touching the lower edge against filter paper. Invert the coverslip and place it in a solid watch glass containing 70% ethanol so that the cells are covered. Leave for 5–10 minutes. Remember that the cells are now on the lower surface of the coverslip which should be kept the same way up through subsequent transfers.

15) Transfer the coverslip to another solid watch glass, containing 95% ethanol for 5–10 minutes, and then to two watch glasses in turn, each containing absolute ethanol. These watch glasses should be kept covered as much as possible. Do not let the preparation dry out at any stage.

16) Lay the coverslip, tissue side upwards, on blotting paper, and before it dries out place a drop of Euparal mountant on the centre large enough, if spread flat, to cover the whole area.

17) Carefully lower a clean slide held horizontally onto the preparation until the drop of Euparal firmly touches the middle of the slide. By quickly lifting and inverting the slide, allow the weight of the coverslip to flatten the mountant until it spreads over the whole coverslip area. Excess mountant can be expelled if necessary by *gentle* pressure under blotting paper. This procedure is made much easier if the Euparal has the correct consistency. It may be necessary to thin it with the solvent, Euparal essence.

18) Examine again to ensure that the preparation is still in good condition.

19) Successful permanent preparations should be left for an hour or two to dry out a little, then cleaned as far as possible, and then labelled. Leave for a few days to harden before examining under the oil immersion objective.

There are a number of common faults which trouble beginners. These can often be diagnosed from the particular symptoms shown by the unsuccessful preparations. A brief guide to these is given in Table 1.3.

1.6 Recording and interpreting

A vital part of all scientific investigations is the proper recording of results both as an 'aide memoir' for future reference and as a means of communication with others. The prime requirements are accuracy and conciseness. An individual style in presentation may be welcomed by the reader but should not be at the expense of clarity and precision. In chromosome studies, all investigations depend on detailed observation of one or more individual cells. These observations may be recorded as written descriptions, photographic or drawn illustrations, or tables of quantitative data on, for example, the frequency of occurrence of a particular event. Usually a combination of all or several of these is required. Clearly, the accuracy of this descriptive record depends on the correct interpretation of the chromosomal activities in each cell. This interpretation will be considered in more detail in later sections when specific situations involving the chromosome complement are introduced. However, the correctly labelled and captioned drawing of a chromosome complement occupies a central position in all such studies and some general points can be made here. The basic rules are the same whether for a careful free-hand drawing, which will suffice for most teaching purposes, or an accurate scale drawing using a projection eyepiece or camera lucida, which is required when dimensions are critical.

Assuming clean paper and a sharp pencil, the first consideration is the size of drawing. As with photographs, the drawing should be large enough to reveal clearly all the significant structural features, but no larger, as 'empty' magnification conveys no additional information. This usually means a minimum size of half an A4 page for each drawing, and the rest of the page may well be occupied by the legend and descriptive notes.

The drawing should then be made as far as possible accurate to scale, taking care to preserve the same scale throughout the drawing. For some purposes, it is as important to show accurately the relative positions of chromosomes within the cell as it is the morphology of each chromosome. In other cases, such as colchicine-treated metaphase complements which are rarely entirely free from overlap of chromosomes, it is legitimate, for clarity, to 'separate' the overlapping chromosomes in the drawing if they can be clearly distinguished by appropriate changes in focal level, provided that this is stated in the legend.

Every line should be essential to the purpose of the drawing, and unambiguous, and will usually link precisely at each end with other lines. Every outline will thus be represented by a single, clean line with a clear point of origin and termination. Lines should rarely cross and never end in 'space'. There is no excuse for vague, inconspicuous or 'sketchy' outlines and rarely any need for shading. Furthermore every line should represent a feature actually seen down the microscope, and not one which is expected but not visible. It is of course, equally important not to omit from the drawing significant features which are visible.

Certain features of chromosomes are extremely difficult and time consuming to represent accurately. A typical example is the irregular outline of long tangled prophase chromosomes. An accurate drawing of the whole nucleus is usually impossible in the time available. An acceptable alternative is to indicate accurately the distribution of the chromosomes within the cell in a line diagram, and draw in detail a short segment of one chromosome. Even the line diagram can present problems, because an accurate drawing of the lengths of chromosome visible at a fixed level of focus does not convey the impression of a prophase nucleus, but rather, when complete with nucleoli, a frying pan of sausages and eggs. This diagram, commonly met with in class, is correct in its way, but misleading. It is preferable to draw in only two or three chromosomes, followed then as far as possible along their lengths by focussing up and down with the fine adjustment, and amplify this with descriptive notes. This illustrates the necessity in all cytological microscopy to continually focus up and down throughout the examination in order to build up an accurate picture of the cell in three dimensions.

When recording the karyotype – the number, size and morphology of the chromosomes of the whole complement – the easiest diagram for the reader to assimilate is the *idiogram*. In this the metaphase chromosomes are represented in a simple diagramatic way, drawn to scale with the main

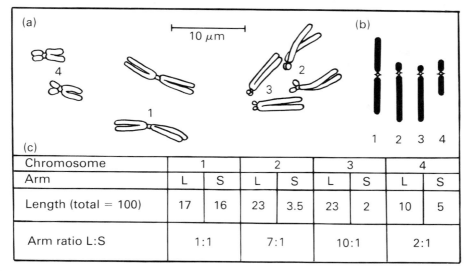

(c) Chromosome	1		2		3		4	
Arm	L	S	L	S	L	S	L	S
Length (total = 100)	17	16	23	3.5	23	2	10	5
Arm ratio L:S	1:1		7:1		10:1		2:1	

Fig. 1.3 Description of a chromosome complement. *Crepis pulchra* ($2n = 2x = 8$). **a**, Drawing of the colchicine – pretreated complement at mitotic metaphase in a squash preparation. In this cell, homologous chromosomes are aligned. Somatic association of homologues has been described sporadically in a variety of organisms over the last 70 years. It is only clear in species with few, distinguishable chromosomes and is often lost in squashing, but it is seen relatively frequently in *Crepis* species. The mechanism of somatic pairing is presumably allied to the similar process at meiosis and will result from and lead to a non-random arrangement of chromosomes in the interphase nucleus. **b**, Haploid idiogram derived from a structurally homozygous diploid sporophyte. **c**, Chromosome dimensions given as arm ratios and lengths as a percentage of the total. (See also Fig. 2.3.)

morphological features indicated but only one chromatid shown, and arranged vertically with their centromeres aligned in order of decreasing overall length with their shorter arms uppermost (Fig. 1.3). If two or more identical chromosome sets are present in the cell, only one is shown. If the sets differ, all the chromosomes are represented. The idiogram is derived from measurements taken from a photograph or accurate drawing, or preferably averaged from several illustrations. The most accurate idiograms derive from ten or twenty camera lucida drawings or photographs. Even then, the absolute lengths of the chromosomes are less meaningful than the relative lengths of individual arms, because even with a standard technique with minimum errors of measurement the degree of chromosome contraction varies from cell to cell depending on the tissue and length of time that the cell was held at metaphase by the pre-treatment. It is sometimes useful to express the arm lengths as percentages of the total length of the chromosome complement when making comparisons. Chromatid width is also a characteristic feature of a complement, and should be correctly represented in relation to length.

In idiograms, a variety of conventions have been used to represent features such as centromeres and nucleolar organizers. Some of these conventions, for example those with centromeres represented as gaps or structures wider than the arms, convey such a distorted image of a chromosome that they are unacceptable, but many others are acceptable and there is little to choose between them.

A drawing of a pre-treated mitotic metaphase complement should show clearly:
a) That each chromosome consists of two chromatids, in most species held together at the localized centromere, as yet undivided.

b) That the chromatid width is more or less constant within and between chromatids.

c) That sister chromatids may be side by side, or partially or completely over-lapping, or coiled round each other.

d) The number and relative sizes of all the chromosomes in the cell.

e) The position of the localized centromere (primary constriction), where present, in each chromosome.

f) The number, size and position of any nucleolar constrictions which may be present, and of nucleoli if visible.

g) The number, size and position of any other segments more or less stained or contracted than the remainder.

Drawings of stages of mitosis, with or without pre-treatment, should show, in addition to any of the features above, the following which are visible:

h) The outline of the parent cell wall.

i) The position of the nuclear membrane if present.

j) The arrangement of the chromosomes, if visible.

Drawings of meiosis should show at appropriate stages:

a) That pre-pachytene chromosomes are single stranded, but from pachytene to metaphase II each has two chromatids.

b) That chromosomes from zygotene to metaphase I are normally paired.

c) That chromomeres are most conspicuous at pachytene, but visible for a while both before and after this stage.

d) That centromere positions may be visible earlier than metaphase I, but are certainly recognizable from that stage onwards, and that each bivalent until anaphase I has two undivided centromeres, normally one on each side of the spindle equator at metaphase I.

e) The position and size of nucleoli and presence of a nuclear membrane during prophase I and II and interphase.

f) The number and position of chiasmata

Centromere position	Anaphase I	Anaphase II
Terminal	< >	/ \
Median	⟨⟨ ⟩⟩	< >

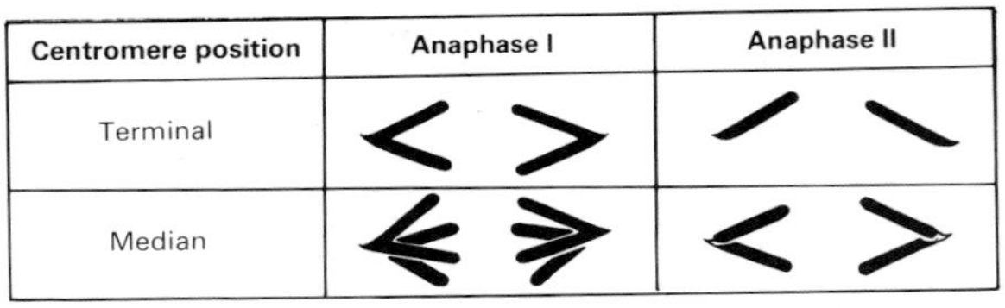

Fig. 1.4 Diagnostic features of meiotic anaphase. Without reference to other cytological features, cells at Anaphase I can be distinguished by the four chromatid arms in chromosomes with interstitial centromeres, while Anaphase II cells can be recognized by the single chromatid arm of telocentric chromosomes.

shown more or less clearly from diplotene until the end of metaphase I.

g) That chromosomes from metaphase I or earlier until telophase II are conspicuously coiled.

h) That whole chromosomes with un-divided centromeres separating at anaphase I will have two chromatids, each with two arms unless the centromere is terminal, while daughter chromosomes separate at anaphase II and only show one arm if the centromere is terminal (Fig. 1.4).

i) That the long axes of the spindles of the two sister cells at meiosis II are not necessarily parallel to the preceding meiosis I spindle axis or to each other.

j) That cytokinesis may or may not occur between meiosis I and II, and that in plant microspores the new tetrad walls are formed within and distinct from the surrounding mother cell wall.

All these features, described in Chapter 2, should be visible in good preparations of cells at the appropriate stages. However, inadequacies of preparation or observation must not be masked in the drawing by the inclusion of details which have not been seen.

All drawings should contain the following information in the legend:

a) Species name (underlined if in Latin).

b) The gametic ('n') or zygotic ('2n') chromosome number.

c) Type and stage of division.

d) Fixation and staining method used.

e) Magnification of 5µm scale line where possible.

f) Chiasma frequency and localization where appropriate.

g) Length of each chromosome as a percentage of total, mean and individual long arm:short arm ratios, and length ratio of longest to shortest chromosome, as appropriate.

Much of what has been said applies equally to photographic illustrations, although photomicrographs are rarely a direct substitute for a drawing. In a few studies, an adequate record can be obtained on photomicrographs for subsequent analysis, but for most work the basic observations have to be made directly on the original preparations and recorded as written data, perhaps with a drawing. Also, because the requirements for a successful photomicrograph, taken at a single fixed level of focus, are much more demanding than for a cell suitable for observation and drawing with continuous changes in focal level, there are usually many fewer cells available for photography. The commonest use of photomicrographs of chromosome preparations is as supplementary illustrations of events and structures described in the text and diagrams, particularly when a report is formally presented, as in this book. As such, good photomicrographs can make the presentation more attractive, generate confidence in the author's observations and, in that they help the reader to visualize more accurately the material described, convey additional information. However, for preliminary investigations and student projects they are rarely essential. This may be some consolation to those who find photomicroscopy with a simple camera and microscope laborious and unpredictable but have no access to the complex and very expensive photomicroscopes designed to make the process routinely simple. It should not, however, discourage those with a particular interest from trying photomicrography, because the results can be very satisfying.

If photomicrographs are to be presented, as they should whenever possible and always at the research level, the rule to observe is 'Good ones only, and if in doubt, leave it out'. Poor photographic illustrations can destroy the confidence of the reader in the quality of the preparations and validity of the observations. He will assume, usually correctly, that the photographs represent the best cells available rather than typical or average ones, and that any visible faults lie with the preparation rather than the photography. He is also likely to assume, sometimes incorrectly, that the complete absence of photographs, like the presence of bad photographs, means that only inferior preparations were obtained.

1.7 Further reading

BRADBURY, S. (Revisor) (1972). *Peacocks Elementary Microtechnique*. 4th Edition. Edward Arnold, London.

DARLINGTON, C. D. and LA COUR, L. F. (1976). *The Handling of Chromosomes*. 6th Edition. George Allen and Unwin, London.

HALL, D. and HAWKINS, S. (1975). *Laboratory Manual of Cell Biology*. English Universities Press, Sevenoaks.

HASKELL, G and WILLS, A. B. (1968). *Primer of Chromosome Practice*. Oliver and Boyd, Edinburgh.

LEWIS, K. R. and JOHN, B. (1964). *The Matter of Mendelian Heredity*. J. A. Churchill Ltd., Edinburgh.

LÖVE, A. and LÖVE, D. (1974). *Plant Chromosomes*. J. B. Cramer, London.

SHARMA, A. K. and SHARMA, A. (1965). *Chromosome Techniques : Theory and practice*. Butterworths, London.

SHAW, G. W. (1973). *Chromosome Studies*. Heinemann Educational Books Ltd., London.

2 Learning about chromosomes – a matter of observation

2.1 Introduction

The internal organization of the chromosome is one of the current mysteries in biology. Although much has been discovered by molecular biologists about the structure and activity of the essential hereditary material, DNA, there is no general agreement as to how this is incorporated in the macromolecular architecture of the chromosome, along with the protein and perhaps RNA and lipids which can comprise up to 85% of its dry weight. The basic structural unit of the eukaryotic chromosome, the *chromonema*, is massive in relation to its component macromolecules. As an illustration of the extent of the problem facing us in understanding the structural organization of the chromosome, a model of the smallest chromosome in the bluebell or wild hyacinth (see Fig. 1.1) made to the same scale as a 2 cm wide model of the DNA helix would be about 60 metres long and as large as the Concorde supersonic airliner. To put this problem another way, a metaphase chromosome 10 μm long contains about 10 cm of DNA, indicating a packing ratio of 10 000:1, but we don't know how this packing is achieved. We can guess that it involves some sort of molecular cross-linkage, and we know that contraction during division involves coiling of the early prophase chromosome, but there is not even any general agreement as to whether an unreplicated anaphase chromosome consists of one chromonema or many.

Light microscopy can resolve few of these problems and electron microscopy is beyond the scope of this book. However, light microscope observations of chromosomes can tell us much about their role in inheritance, adaptation and evolution and a little about their role in differentiation and development. Anyone intending to investigate these aspects of chromosomes must first become thoroughly familiar with chromosome structure and behaviour during nuclear division and the variations which occur within and between organisms during normal growth and reproduction. The purpose of this chapter is to introduce these features and the material and techniques necessary to demonstrate them.

2.2 Chromosome structure under the light microscope

In nearly all organisms it is impossible to examine the structure of individual chromosomes except during division. The features then visible are determined by lateral replication, coiling and longitudinal differentiation.

2.2.1 Lateral replication

Chromosomes at anaphase and telophase of mitosis consist of a single contracted unit (Figs. 2.6, 2.7). When the same chromosome enters prophase of the succeeding division, it has replicated and two such units, called *chromatids* or half-chromosomes, are visible, attached to each other only at the *centromere*. As replication in normal mitosis is always followed by separation at anaphase, no more than two replicates are seen attached to the same centromere. Exceptions to this occur after modified mitotic cycles accompanying the early stages of differentiation in some cells (Section 2.4.2).

During meiosis, replication to form two chromatids is delayed until later in prophase, and separation of daughter chromosomes is delayed until anaphase of the second division. Consequently at meiosis I, unlike all other divisions, early prophase chromosomes are unreplicated and at anaphase it is whole chromosomes which separate and not daughter chromosomes (Section 2.5.1).

2.2.2 Coiling and allocyclic chromosome condensation

At mitosis, a metaphase chromatid or anaphase chromosome is, as a result of contraction by coiling, a more or less solid cylinder usually considerably longer than wide and of constant diameter along most of its length. This *standard coil*, which can sometimes be revealed more clearly after special pre-treatments, arises independently in the two chromatids allowing them to separate once the relational coil of one

chromatid round the other has unwound. The number of gyres seems to be constant for the corresponding chromosome of different cells throughout the individual. The direction of the standard coil appears to be random and can change along the length of the chromosome, and particularly at the uncoiled nucleolar organizer. The direction of coiling of sister chromatids is usually independent but 'mirror-images' are sometimes seen. The width of the coiled chromosome thread suggests lower orders of coiling or some other condensation mechanism. The standard coil usually reaches a maximum at the end of metaphase, although there may be variation in coiling at localized points along the chromosome. This variation provides most of the morphological features of the chromosome (Section 2.2.3).

During meiosis, the coiling is more highly developed and the *major coil* at metaphase I and anaphase I is particularly conspicuous (Fig. 2.1a). A lower order of coiling, the *minor coil* can occasionally be distinguished.

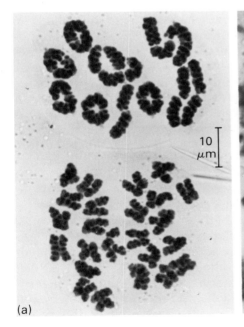

(a)

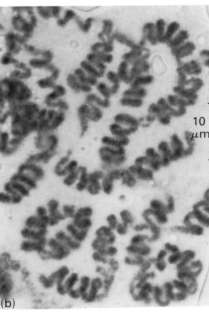

(b)

Fig. 2.1 Coiling in meiotic chromosomes of *Tradescantia virginiana* ($2n = 4x = 24$). **a**, Metaphase I and Anaphase I in a normal orcein stained preparation. **b**, Part of a similar cell at Metaphase I after pre-treatment to relax the major coil.

The major and minor coils of meiosis I become the loose *relic coil* and the standard coil respectively of Meiosis II, because the chromosomes do not completely extend between these divisions. The direction of the major coil can change several times along the chromosome and frequently across the centromere, but not necessarily at a chiasma nor at corresponding positions in homologous chromosomes. As at mitosis, the coiling can be examined more easily after the chromosome has been treated with certain chemicals (Fig. 2.1b).

It is a striking feature of a dividing cell at least at metaphase that in most regions the coiling is uniform in timing and degree along each chromosome arm, throughout the cell and in all other similar cells at the same stage of division. For example, the number and diameter of gyres at meiosis metaphase I is constant for a particular chromosome arm in all pollen mother cells of an individual, even though the direction at a given point may be clockwise or anti-clockwise.

At both meiosis and mitosis, chromosomes which are incompletely contracted have a 'fuzzy' outline. This appears to be caused by thin strands, which in clear examples like amphibian oocyte lampbrush chromosomes are seen to be loops, extending laterally from chromomeres. These strands are most conspicuous at mid-prophase of meiosis but are in general less clear in plant cells (Fig. 2.18a).

In many cells, segments of chromosomes, whole chromosomes or rarely whole complements are *allocyclic*; that is, in contrast to the *eucyclic* chromatin, they reach maximum condensation, if at all, at some stage other than or in addition to late metaphase and/or they may not be at maximum extension throughout interphase. As a result, they show *differential contraction* and are then *heterochromatic* (= *heteropycnotic*) after staining (Table 2.1). Allocycly may accompany or perhaps even result from differences in nucleo-protein composition or organization in some examples, but in others chromo-somes which are allocyclic at one stage of development are eucyclic at another, indicating that differential contraction can be brought about by distortion of the coiling cycle superimposed on a normal structure. In several cases, allocyclic chromatin appears to be condensed throughout the cell cycle but a more detailed study of this chromatin in some species has revealed a brief period of chromosome extension, *the Z-phase*, during interphase, presumably to facilitate replication and chromatid separation. Further research may reveal that a Z-phase occurs commonly in species with heterochromatic chromatin at interphase. It is therefore not always possible to classify heterochromatic regions with precision as either *constitutive heterochromatin* or *facultative heterochromatin*, terms widely used to distinguish between regions which are considered to be permanently condensed due to modification of the basic chromatin organization and those in which intermittent allocycly occurs in the absence of any such structural differentiation.

Chromatin which remains condensed in interphase forms *chromocentres*. Chromocentre formation is at least sometimes associated with the suppression of gene transcription which appears to be restricted to extended chromatin. A further feature of many chromocentres is that their DNA replication does not occur throughout the S phase of the cell cycle but is completed before or, more often, commences after replication in the euchromatic regions. Chromocentres which represent allocyclic segments of chromosomes are considered further in Section 2.2.3d as manifestations of longitudinal differentiation of the chromosome but there are several conspicuous examples of uniformly allocyclic chromosomes which form chromocentres. These include heterochromatic sex chromosomes, autosomes and supernumerary B chromosomes. These are discussed further below, but in considering the significance of differential contraction it has to be remembered that in many or-

Table 2.1 Key to the main types of heterochromatic chromatin. Some of the bands revealed by Giemsa or quinacrine correspond to certain regions revealed by standard techniques as indicated by similar symbols. °†★

DIFFERENTIATED CHROMATIN — Differentially stained (heterochromatic) ± differential contraction and function			
DIFFERENTIAL CONTRACTION (ALLOCYCLY) — visible after standard staining techniques	**NON-CHROMOCENTRIC**	In every chromosome of most complements	Localized centromere
		In at least one chromosome of all complements	Nucleolar organizer
		In all chromosomes at prophase	*Chromomeres
	CHROMOCENTRIC	Apparently permanently contracted at all stages of development — Segments of specialised structure and composition ('constitutive heterochromatin')	°†Centromeric (Pro-chromosomes), †Telomeric, °†Interstitial
		Apparently permanently contracted at all stages of development — Chromosomes derived from euchromatic chromosomes	Allocyclic B chromosomes
		Dispersed at some stage of development — Chromocentres in all interphase cells – allocycly accented by cold treatment	†H-segments
		Dispersed at some stage of development — Chromocentres in some interphase cells only ('facultative heterochromatin')	Allocyclic sex chromosomes and autosomes
Uniformly contracted metaphase chromosomes	GIEMSA BANDING – reflects differential protein denaturation?	Animal cells — After mild alkaline denaturation	★'G' bands
		Animal cells — After stringent alkaline denaturation	°'C' bands
		Plant cells after stringent alkaline denaturation	†Giemsa bands.
	QUINACRINE STAINING – DNA specific banding reflects differential access to DNA?		*†'Q' bands

ganisms, particularly plants with large chromosomes, there are no chromocentres.

2.2.2a Allocyclic sex chromosomes

In most animals and dioecious plants some or all the sex chromosomes are at least partially heterochromatic at certain stages of development and division. Many of them form interphase chromocentres. In some liverworts the X chromosome does not form chromocentres until mid-interphase, after its DNA has been replicated. In female mammals with two X chromosomes, neither is heterochromatic in young embryos but later one of them, not necessarily the same one in every cell, becomes allocyclic and forms what is known in man as the *Barr body*. In marsupials it is always the paternal X which forms the conspicuous chromocentre. The allocycly is associated with suppressed gene activity and with changes in the proteins associated with the DNA.

In other examples, the sex chromatin which forms condensed chromocentres at interphase appears as relatively under-condensed segments at other stages. The single X chromosome of normal male locusts appears as a chromocentre at interphase but at meiosis metaphase I is long thin and weakly stained compared with the normally contracted paired autosomes. The typical allocycly of this chromosome is maintained even when a segment is translocated to an autosome.

2.2.2b Allocyclic autosomes

In the pseudo-haploid males of several species of coccid bugs, including the widespread mealy bug, *Planococcus* (=*Pseudococcus*) *citri*, the entire paternal complement becomes allocyclic from the blastula stage of the embryo onwards. The chromosomes are permanently condensed throughout the cell cycle but normal replication and disjunction is maintained until meiosis, when the paternal complement separates from the rest and degenerates. One of the smallest auto-somal bivalents of the grass-hopper, *Chorthippus*, is relatively over-contracted from pachytene to late diakinesis.

2.2.2c Allocyclic supernumerary B chromosomes

In many of the several hundred species in which supernumerary chromosomes have been found, the additional chromosomes are consistently allocyclic, forming chromocentres, although otherwise very similar to the eucyclic supernumeraries of other species. There is some evidence to suggest that heterochromatic B chromosomes have usually evolved from eucyclic supernumeraries in turn derived from chromosomes of the standard complement (Sections 3.3.1, 3.4.6 and 3.5.5). The metaphase condition has presumably been extended through the cell cycle by genetically controlled modifications of the normal condensation cycle, perhaps as a mechanism for suppressing gene activity. It is not known if these B chromosomes are eucyclic in young embryos like mammalian X chromosomes and the paternal complement of mealy bugs.

2.2.3 Longitudinal differentiation

Few chromosomes are uniform throughout their length. Most show localized regions of different width or staining intensity. (Table 2.1, Section 2.2.2). The terminology and classification of the many more or less distinct types of behaviour which give rise to this visible differentiation are notoriously difficult. The situation is becoming more confused as additional material and new techniques reveal more examples without providing much further insight into their significance. Although, for simplicity, the main recognizable types of differentiated segments will be introduced here under a number of headings according to their visible characteristics, this is an arbitrary and probably artificial classification and it must not be assumed that all chromosome regions included within the same category are more than superficially similar or that those separated into different categories are necessarily fundamentally different. Indeed, until more, much needed, information is available on the structural organization of the chromosome, no classification or terminology should be adhered to rigidly. Instead, it should be recognised that i) differentiation of the chromatin along the chromosome exists; ii) this differentiation may reflect differences in macromolecular configuration of the nucleoprotein complex at least sometimes associated with differences in the composition and degree of repetition of DNA base sequences; iii) these differences may have a functional significance in determining the specialized nature or specified timing of gene activity in the affected regions; iv) some structural and functional differences result in differential condensation visible after simple staining methods as regions of different width and staining intensity; v) further chromatin differentiation can be revealed by other methods involving certain pretreatments; and vi) additional, and as yet, cryptic, chromatin differentiation may be exposed when techniques are developed to show more subtle features of nucleoprotein.

Recognition of the underlying differentiation of the chromatin may be complicated by effects of the cellular or external environment which may modify or suppress the allocyclic behaviour of specialized segments, such as the nucleolar organizer in some hybrids, or superimpose allocycly, irrespective of structure, as in mammalian X chromosomes (Section 2.2.2). Consequently, it may not be possible to determine whether differential staining along a chromosome arm has a structural basis or to conclude from uniform staining that the structure is homogeneous.

2.2.3a The centromere

In most species, every mitotic metaphase chromosome has a single localized *centromere* revealed as a constriction at which the chromosome is frequently bent, or, in large chromosomes, as a complex region consisting of a replicated under-contracted segment, including the localized spindle fibre attachment points, the *kinetochores*, and sometimes centromeric chromomeres, and two condensed but unreplicated regions at the proximal ends of each arm. The kinetochores are thought to be sites for polarized polymerization in the assembly of the microtubules which make up each fibre. It is presumably the balanced attraction of the two kinetochores to opposite spindle poles while the chromatids are held together by the adjacent undivided regions which causes the chromosome to come to equilibrium on the spindle equator (Fig. 2.2a).

At metaphase of meiosis I, the centromere constriction is usually obscured by the major coil. In a normal bivalent, the centromere of each homologue is attached to only one pole, even though the attachment point can sometimes be seen to be replicated (Fig. 2.2b). It is the balanced attachment of each of the two centromeres to opposite poles of the spindle while the homologous arms are held together by chromatid attraction distal to chiasmata which co-orientates the bivalent on the spindle equator.

A localized centromere, once called the *primary constriction*, may be at any point along a chromosome although it remains constant for a particular chromosome from cell to cell. The centromere may be median (a *mesocentric* chromosome, arm length ratio 1:1), sub-median (arm ratio >1:1, <3:1), sub-terminal (an *acrocentric* chromosome, arm ratio 3:1 or greater) or terminal (a *telocentric* chromosome) (Sections 3.3.3 and 3.4.2b; Fig. 2.3).

In a minority of species, including members of the plant families Juncaceae and Cyperaceae, certain aquatic fungi and algae including *Spirogyra* and *Chlamydomonas* and amoebae, ciliates, nematodes, scorpions and homopteran, heteropteran and lepidopteran insects, the spindle attachment is not localized at one point but dispersed along

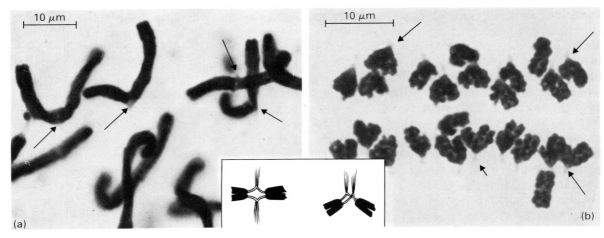

Fig. 2.2 Centromeres (arrowed) at **a**, mitotic metaphase in *Allium cepa* ($2n = 2x = 16$), **b**, meiotic anaphase I in *Tradescantia virginiana* ($2n = 4x = 24$). Inset: diagrams of centromeres at corresponding stages. Amphitelic attachment of a mitotic centromere to both spindle poles results in auto-orientation of individual chromosomes at metaphase. Syntelic attachment of a meiotic centromere to one pole results in co-orientation of bivalents at metaphase. Although centromeres have not divided at meiotic anaphase I, the spindle attachment points appear to have replicated before that stage.

much or all of each chromosome. Where many small but distinct attachment points can be recognized, the chromosome is said to be *polycentric*. Where the attachment is apparently uniform along the chromosome, it is described as *holokinetic* but there may be no fundamental difference between the two types. These chromosomes, in contrast to those with localized centromeres, have no centromeric constriction and remain straight and approximately perpendicular to the polar axis of the spindle throughout division. The pattern of karyotype evolution is also different in these species, because unstable acentric fragments are rarely formed (Section 3.2). Chiasmata are always few and terminal.

Occasionally in species with localized centromeres, spindle attachment and movement occurs also at points along the chromosome arms. Although examined in some detail in maize where it is associated with a structurally abnormal chromosome, the basis for this neocentric activity is not known.

2.2.3b The nucleolar organizer

On at least one of the chromosomes of each

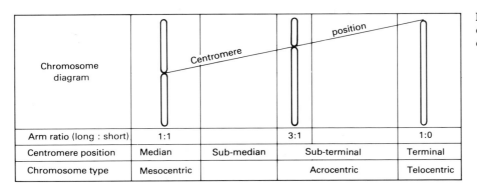

Chromosome diagram				
Arm ratio (long : short)	1:1		3:1	1:0
Centromere position	Median	Sub-median	Sub-terminal	Terminal
Chromosome type	Mesocentric		Acrocentric	Telocentric

Fig. 2.3 The classification of centromere position.

complement is a second segment, in addition to the localized centromere, which is recognizable by its activity and is almost always under-contracted throughout mitosis (Section 3.3.3). It is similar in appearance to the centromere though frequently more extended, but during prophase it is attached laterally to a nucleolus and at no stage is it attached to the spindle. Such segments are *nucleolar organizers* (N.O.) and the site of the multiple repeats (up to 8000 in hyacinth) of the DNA unit coding for the ribosomal RNA which forms a major component of nucleoli. Nucleolar material disperses entirely at the end of prophase and re-forms at each N.O. at late telophase although, where two or more organizers are close, nucleoli may fuse later in interphase.

Very small organizers may be obscured as the chromosome contracts and if, as in certain hybrids, an organizer is inactive in transcription during interphase, it does not produce a nucleolus or an under-contracted segment during mitosis. Nucleolar organizers are not usually visible as constrictions during meiosis, being apparently masked by the major coil, but their position is revealed by attached nucleoli until diakinesis. Occasionally, segments are seen which are similar in appearance to nucleolar organizers but have no associated nucleoli. Their function is unknown.

2.2.3c Chromomeres

These are small regions of denser material arranged at short intervals along prophase and similarly extended chromosomes (Fig. 2.4). They are probably present in all the chromatin of all eukaryotes and are most conspicuous at meiosis (Section 2.5). In comparable cells, the pattern of size, shape and position of the chromomeres is characteristic of the individual, confirming that they reflect differentiation along the chromosome. Pachytene chromomere maps in lily, rye, *Agapanthus* and tomato have revealed small and otherwise undetectable structural differences between homologous chromosomes within a population and even within a single individual. Similar analyses are possible in polytene chromosomes (Section 2.4.2).

Chromomeres appear to be regions of denser coiling. It has been suggested that they are the discrete sites of controlled, precocious formation of the standard or major coil which enlarge and fuse until they are obscured as coiling becomes uniform throughout. An alternative interpretation is that each one represents the coiled lateral loops of multiple repeats (*slaves*) of a particular locus (*master*).

2.2.3d Chromocentric segments

Segments with a variety of different types of behaviour during division are associated with similar interphase chromocentres. In at least some species the chromocentres disperse briefly during interphase. They are also at least superficially similar to the chromocentres formed by wholly allocyclic chromosomes (Section 2.2.2) and they may have important features in common. The following categories of chromocentric segment are distinguished somewhat arbitrarily on the basis of their position and behaviour.

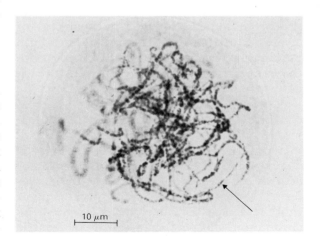

10 μm

Fig. 2.4 Chromomeres at pachytene of meiosis in a pollen mother cell of *Lilium auratum* ($2n = 2x = 24$). Occasional unpaired segments are visible (arrow).

Centromeric and telomeric chromocentres

Plants with small chromosomes, less than about 3 μm long and with less than about 2.5×10^{-13} g DNA per nucleus, show chromocentric or *prochromosomal* organization, where in interphase and early prophase nuclei chromocentres contrast strikingly with the almost chromatin-free areas of the rest of the nucleus. These chromocentres frequently occur in close pairs. These pairs, or prochromosomes, correspond to over-contracted regions on either side of the centromere of each chromosome. These proximal regions merge gradually during prophase with the contracting distal region. Plants with larger chromosomes have more or less *reticulate* nuclei in which the chromatin is more evenly dispersed. Most, if not all plants contain repetitive DNA and it has been suggested that it is larger amounts of this (up to 90% in the lily) which explain the greater size of some chromosomes and, whereas in small chromosomes any repetitive DNA is concentrated near the centromere and imparts different characteristics to that region, in bigger chromosomes the larger amounts of this DNA are distributed in small segments along the chromosome to form chromatin of even and intermediate staining intensity. It has also been suggested that prochromosomes provide a mechanism for localized restriction of crossing over to form *super-genes* because they are often found in the more specialized relatives of plants which lack them.

At least superficially similar hetero-chromatic regions are found near the centromeres of many animal species. In several, including *Drosophila* and mouse, it has been confirmed that these centromeric chromocentres contain repetitive DNA with characteristic base ratios. In some organisms, a short region at the distal end of some or all chromosome arms form similar telocentric chromocentres. It has been claimed that the characteristic properties of the ends of chromosome arms, such as inability to fuse with broken chromosomes, attachment to the nuclear envelope and attraction by terminalized chiasmata to a homologue at meiosis, indicate the presence of a specialized structure, the *telomere*. Chromocentres frequently fuse if brought into contact within the nucleus, and fusion of centromeric or telomeric chromocentres and their attachment to differentiated regions of the nuclear envelope have been implicated in the initiation of meiotic pairing at telomeres or centromeres (Section 2.5.1).

Interstitial chromocentres

Some plants and animals, including species with no centromeric or telomeric chromocentres, form interphase chromocentres from interstitial regions of the chromosome arms which are still over-condensed during prophase. Although frequently formed in sex chromosomes or associated with nucleolar organizers, these interstitial bands also occur in autosomes away from any recognizable morphological feature. Their size and position on a prophase chromosome form a characteristic pattern which is repeated in other dividing cells of that individual but may differ from that of an homologous chromosome in the same cell or different individuals. Population analyses of these polymorphisms can provide valuable information on the genetic system of the species.

While the interphase chromocentres are clear in all preparations, the position of the corresponding segments in the chromosomes during division can rarely be seen clearly, even with phase contrast, beyond late prophase without additional specialized treatments. In many cases the segments corresponding to the chromocentres stain differentially at metaphase after a Giemsa banding procedure involving nucleoprotein denaturation or after staining with certain DNA specific fluorochromes, (Section 2.2.3e; Table 2.1) but superficially similar heterochromatic regions can have different responses to the same treatment, even within the same cell, indicating that these chromocentres should not be thought of as a homogenous category of chromatin.

One distinguishable type, the so-called *H-segments*, can be revealed by any staining technique because of their characteristic response to a previous low temperature treatment. At 10°C or higher, the segments appear to be fully contracted during most or all of the mitotic cycle and distinguishable as spherical chromocentres during interphase and early prophase but indistinguishable, unless Giemsa or fluorochrome techniques (Section 2.2.3c) are used, from eucyclic regions between late prophase and the end of telophase. However, during the slow divisions at lower temperatures, a stable pattern of under-contracted segments appears in the chromosomes throughout mitosis (Fig. 2.5) and the chromocentres, which in the absence of fusion correspond in number and relative size to the H-segments, may become less pronounced. The segments are frequently interrupted by small eucyclic regions except where the distribution of segments is distinct from that of chiasmata.

The patterns of H-segments in homologues frequently reveal heterozygosity within individuals and polymorphism within species (Fig. 2.5c). They have been used as chromosome markers to study the consequences of chiasmata, population polymorphism and species evolution, particularly in the lily-like genus *Trillium*, but their function is unknown. All of the species known to have H-segments have reticulate nuclei and most have unusually large chromosomes and thus long division cycles (e.g. *Trillium grandiflorum* Table 2.2). It has also been noted that most of them are among the organisms which in nature do not merely survive but actually undergo cell division at unusually low temperatures, down to 0°C, the very conditions which induce the differential response of the segments. Whether or not H-segments are of significance in the adaptation of organisms with long

mitotic cycles for cell division at low temperature is not known.

2.2.3e Giemsa and fluorochrome banding

Although the techniques are outside the scope of this book it should be mentioned that in recent years important new staining methods have been developed which in some plants and animals reveal differentiation along metaphase chromosomes which was not previously detectable. In human and crop-plant cytogenetics particularly they have provided a valuable new tool for karyotype analysis. The techniques fall into two distinct groups, although it is often the same chromosome regions which respond to both (Table 2.1). One group involves staining with Giemsa solution after pre-treatments which denature the chromatin. The other group includes the use of one of several different DNA specific fluorescent dyes, such as quinacrine, without pre-treatment. Differential response to these techniques is thought to reflect differences in the degree of repetition of the DNA, in the base ratio of the DNA and in the associated protein.

After the appropriate pre-treatment, Giemsa stain produces complex patterns of so-called '*G*' *bands* in the uniformly contracted metaphase chromosomes of a variety of animals including insects, amphibia, reptiles, birds and mammals but the same technique does not induce differential staining of plant chromosomes. Metaphase banding patterns are however revealed in some plants by the alternative Giemsa pre-treatments involving more severe denaturation used to reveal '*C*' *band* patterns in mammalian complements, and by fluorochromes. In these plants, the differentially stained metaphase segments are usually accompanied by corresponding interphase chromocentres but only the latter are visible in standard orcein preparations. In a few species orcein will produce the same banding

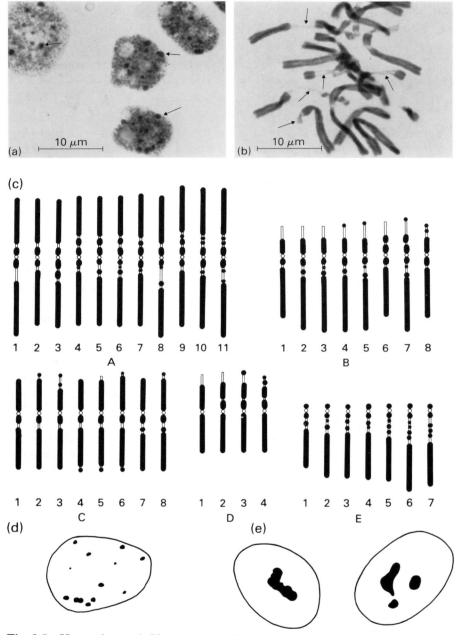

Fig. 2.5 Heterochromatic H-segments. **a,** Interphase nuclei with chromocentres in *Trillium grandiflorum*. **b,** H-segments in metaphase chromosomes of *Trillium grandiflorum* endosperm mitosis dividing at 2°C. **c,** Polymorphism for H-patterns in the chromosomes of the root tip complement of 16 individuals of *Trillium erectum* ($2n = 2x = 10$). Several individuals were heterozygous for H-patterns of one or more chromosomes. **d,** Unfused chromocentres in root-tip nuclei of *Tulbaghia fragrans* with 12 distal H-segments. **e,** Fused chromocentres in root tip nuclei of *Trillium kamtschaticum* with several large proximal H-segments.

as Giemsa stain after the appropriate denaturation treatment (see p. 29).

2.2.4 The complement

A eukaryotic chromosome is structurally independent, but not functionally so. It forms an indispensable and integral part of a complement of chromosomes, a *genome*. A complete set of genes is dispersed over two or more structural units, the chromosomes, in contrast to the situation in prokaryotes, where the chromosome is not only much simpler and less massive in structure, but is also a single unit which includes every gene of the organism. Dispersal of the gene complement over several chromosomes creates the possibility of an additional recombination mechanism, that of the independent assortment of chromosomes at meiosis, while maintaining recombination within a chromosome by crossing over. This no doubt provides a greater potential for adaptation, but at the same time requires a precise mechanism to ensure regular disjunction of balanced, entire gene complements. Eukaryotes have a complex mechanism of spindle organization, centromere activity and chromosome contraction during chromosome division. Prokaryotes, with one chromosome per genome, have no comparable mechanism. Overall control of the whole chromosome complement during division to ensure regular disjunction is clearly indicated by the synchronous division of centromeres, synchronous and uniform coiling, cooperation between chromosomes in producing a single coordinated spindle and uniform rate of anaphase separation of chromosomes.

The necessity for regular disjunction of a genome consisting of several chromosomes does not explain why the eukaryotic chromosome is so consistently massive and complex. However, although some eukaryotes are small and unicellular, all are more complex than prokaryotes, so the eukaryotic chromosome complexity may be associated with the precise regulation of gene activity necessary in a complex organism. The necessity to replicate and reorganize chromosome material other than DNA may explain why in a eukaryote cell the DNA replication period occupies only part of the interval between cell divisions while in a prokaryote the process is continuous.

2.2.5 Materials and Methods

Lateral replication (Section 2.2.1). For chromatids at mitosis see page 35. For chromatids at meiosis see page 66.

Coiling and allocyclic chromosome condensation (Section 2.2.2). Chromosome coiling can be made more clearly visible at mitosis and meiosis.

A pre-treatment of 90–120 minutes at 21–23°C with a 4:2:0.8 mixture of 0.055 M KCl, $NaNO_3$ and CH_3COONa reveals clear standard mitotic coils in chromosomes of human tissue culture cells. This method has proved ineffective on plant root tip mitoses, but a treatment of a few minutes clarifies the major coil and reveals the minor coil at meiosis in pollen mother cells of *Tradescantia virginia* (Fig. 2.1) when crushed anthers are immersed in the mixture before the standard technique.

ALLOCYCLIC SEX CHROMOSOMES (Section 2.2.2a):

Man : Barr bodies, 1 µm chromocentres corresponding to X chromosomes in excess of one, can be seen in stained preparations of cells from buccal smears. Scrape the inside of the cheek firmly with the edge of a wooden spatula, spread the mucoid deposit thickly on a clean slide and immerse immediately in fixative. Do not allow the smear to dry. Proceed with the standard technique. Normal males have no Barr body, while in normal females it can be seen in 30–40% of nuclei examined. Abnormal numbers or size of Barr bodies may indicate sex chromosome abnormalities, but diagnosis by inexperienced cytologists is unreliable.

Insects : In preparations of meiosis from male grasshoppers or locusts such as *Chorthippus, Locusta, Schistocerca* (Section 2.5) the unpaired X chromosome appears under-contracted from pro-metaphase I to early anaphase I and over-contracted throughout interphase and prophase I.

ALLOCYCLIC AUTOSOMES (Section 2.2.b): The small bivalent, M_6, is heterochromatic at pachytene in male *Chorthippus* species (Section 2.5). The paternal genome is wholly heterochromatic at mitosis and meiosis in adult male mealy bugs and some stick insects.

ALLOCYCLIC SUPERNUMERARY B CHROMOSOMES (Section 2.2.2c): These are found in some individuals of the plants *Dactylis glomerata, Festuca ovina, Narcissus bulbocodium, Ornithogalum umbellatum, Puschkinia libanotica* (Fig. 4.2c), *Secale cereale* and *Zea mays* and the locust, *Locusta migratoria* (Section 3.4.2g).

Supernumerary chromosomes in *Allium, Lilium, Trillium, Tradescantia* and *Ranunculus* species are eucyclic (Section 3.4.2g).

Longitudinal differentiation (Section 2.2.3)

CENTROMERE (Section 2.2.3a):

Clear localized centromeres at mitosis and meiosis: *Allium cepa* (Fig. 2.2a), *Tradescantia virginiana* (Fig. 2.2b), *T. paludosa, T. bracteata* (Fig. 3.1), *Nothoscordum inodorum* (*N. fragrans*) (Fig. 3.2c) and many other species with large chromosomes.

Centromere position: (Section 3.3.5c).

Dispersed centromere: *Luzula purpurea*.

NUCLEOLAR ORGANIZER (Section 2.2.3b):

Conspicuous interstitial N.O.: *Hyacinthus orientalis* (Fig. 3.2a), *Vicia Faba, Hordeum vulgare*.

Near terminal N.O. with small *satellite*: *Bellevalia romana* (Fig. 3.2b), *Trillium* spp.

N.O. number: (Section 3.3.5c)

N.O. position: (Section 3.3.5c).

Suppression of N.O.: *Allium, Crepis* and *Tulbaghia* species hybrids; *Allium proliferum* (*A. cepa* × *A. fistulosum*), *Crepis capillaris* × *C. rubra, Tulbaghia violacea* × *T. verdoornia* (N.O. of first named species in each case suppressed).

CHROMOMERES (Section 2.2.3c): Clear at zygotene/pachytene in *Lilium* (Fig. 2.4) and the grass-hopper *Chorthippus*. Not clear in *Tradescantia* (Section 2.5.2).

CHROMOCENTRIC SEGMENTS (Section 2.2.3d):

Centromeric chromocentres: *Epilobium* spp. *Lycopersicum esculentum, Phaseolus vulgaris, Rhoes discolor*.

Telomeric chromocentres: pachytene bivalents in male meiosis in grasshoppers and locusts, *Secale cereale* mitosis.

Interstitial chromocentres:

Autosomes: *Rumex acetosa, Allium carinatum, Anemone blanda*.

Sex chromosomes: *Rumex acetosa* (XX/XY_1Y_2, sex chromosomes conspicuously larger than acrocentric autosomes), *Humulus japonicus* (XX/XY_1Y_2, allocyclic Y smaller than X, larger than autosomes), *Humulus lupulus* (XX/XY, X and Y with under-contracted segments at male meiotic and mitotic prophase; *Melandrium album* probably similar), bryophytes with dioecious gametophytes.

H-segments: Pre-treat plant for 96 hours at 2–5°C before fixing roots (-12°C for 4 weeks for *Scilla sibirica*). Proximal H-segments: *Fritillaria recurva, Trillium kamtschaticum* (Fig. 2.5e); Distal H-segments: *Paris polyphylla, Tulbaghia fragrans* (Fig. 2.5d); Non-localized H-segments: *Trillium erectum, Trillium grandiflorum* (Fig. 2.5a,b,c). Small H-segments also in *Vicia faba, Secale cereale, Adoxa moschatellina* and *Cestrum elegans*. The clearest animal examples are the newts, *Triturus* spp.

GIEMSA BANDS (Section 2.2.3e): The following Giemsa pretreatment will reveal the same pattern of differential staining in *Scilla sibirica* whether orcein or Giemsa stain is used.

1) Immerse root tips for 5 hours in 0.05% colchicine.
2) Fix overnight in a mixture of 3 parts ethanol to 1 part acetic acid. The fixative must not contain formalin.
3) Soften in 45% acetic acid for about 1 hour.
4) Tap out and squash in 45% acetic acid on a slide under a coverslip previously coated with glycerin albumen. Warm gently.
5) Float off coverslip with cells attached in absolute ethanol. Wash coverslip in absolute ethanol and dry in air.
6) Treat for 5–6 minutes at 45°C in a *fresh* saturated solution of barium hydroxide, $Ba(OH)_2.8H_2O$, before rinsing several times in distilled water.
7) Incubate in '2 × SSC' (double strength saline sodium citrate = 0.30 M NaCl + 0.03 M Na citrate) at 60°C for 30–60 minutes.
8) Wash coverslip in distilled water and dry in air before staining for a short period in orcein until optimum differentiation of segments is achieved (as an alternative to 1% fresh Giemsa (Gurr's R66 improved) solution at pH 6.8).
9) Air dry and mount in Euparal.

2.3 The visible events of mitosis

The first point to emphasize is the smooth continuity of the events of the division cycle. Students being introduced to mitosis should if possible first watch a film of living cells in division (Appendix 3), or even examine living and dividing cells under the microscope (Section 4.2.1). At least they should read a continuous description of the events which take place without any reference to named stages. The latter are convenient for reference to a particular point in the cycle, but they are quite arbitrary and their boundaries are not precise. When the named stages dominate the description, a false impression of discontinuity in mitosis is given. Even when the events are speeded up 100 × on film, there is only one clearly defined event, the timing of which can be closely specified. That event is the abrupt and simultaneous division of all the centromeres. Even then, other events are taking place within the cell without interruption. The phases of division are defined almost entirely by reference to only one of the many cell components, the chromosomes.

The mitotic cycle is like steeplechasing. Relatively long periods of steady preparation are interrupted by relatively short bursts of conspicuous activity. Prophase, metaphase, anaphase and telophase are no more easily defined in terms of chromosome behaviour than are the run-up, take off, flight and landing of the steeplechaser in terms of the position of his legs. The cells seen in a fixed preparation of a meristematic tissue are like a disordered set of 'stills' from a film of the steeplechaser in action. Most, corresponding to cells in interphase, will show him running steadily round the track. A minority of photographs, corresponding to cells in division, will show him apparently stationary in a variety of striking poses which can only be interpreted as the situation at a particular instant in a dynamic process. Examination of very few such photographs chosen to illustrate the run up, take off, flight and landing would give an impression of jerky movement which the cinefilm would show to be quite false. In the same way, the customary practice of illustrating or studying cells chosen at the midpoint of each arbitrarily defined stage of mitosis gives an equally false impression of the continuity of events in cell division (Fig. 2.6).

It is also important, when generalizing about mitosis, to remember that there are differences, sometimes quite substantial

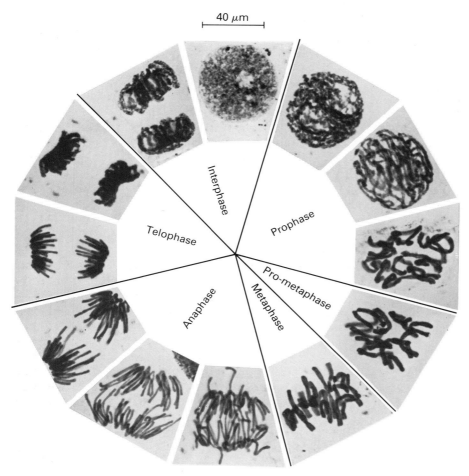

40 μm

Interphase
Prophase
Pro-metaphase
Metaphase
Anaphase
Telophase

Fig. 2.6 The visible events of mitosis in *Allium cepa* ($2n = 2x = 16$). The sizes of the sectors are not proportional to the duration of the phases. Interphase is the longest phase and anaphase the shortest (see Table 2.3).

ones, in the process as it occurs in animal cells, higher and lower plant cells, and cells of different tissues, such as root meristem and pollen grain. Most of these differences concern the spindle and separation of the daughter cells.

Sophisticated techniques like polarized light and electron microscopy have still not elucidated the mechanism of spindle action, organelle distribution or cytokinesis although much new information has been obtained. The standard technique described in this book only stains chromosome material, but the spindle, which is intimately involved in

mitosis, can sometimes be seen if the contrast is increased by de-focussing the condenser. The fibrous appearance results from the many parallel protein microtubules of which it is composed. It is the active and directed movement of microtubules in relation to each other which is thought to provide the basis of anaphase movement of the chromosomes. While the following outline of mitosis, which is strictly the division of the nucleus only, will concentrate on the chromosomes, it is worth commenting on the spindle characteristics which are often considered to differentiate from plant mitoses. A typical dividing animal cell has an *aster* of fibres radiating from each pole in addition to the spindle and these are most highly developed during division but may remain through interphase. At the centre of the aster, sometimes just visible by light microscopy, is a dense granule which under the electron microscope is revealed as two, or at late interphase four, cylindrical *centrioles*. Asters are also found in dividing cells of certain lower plants, particularly those without a rigid cell wall, and perhaps provide a cytoplasmic skeleton or framework in the absence of a wall, regardless of whether the cell is plant or animal. Centrioles too are found in lower plants. They occur in all plants which have motile cells with cilia or flagella. In higher groups like cycads the only motile cell is the male gamete and centrioles appear at the pole only of the mitosis preceding sperm formation. In view of this, and the fact that centrioles can develop directly into the basal bodies of flagella, it seems likely that they are concerned with flagella formation and that, after self replication, they make use of the spindle for regular disjunction. They do not attach directly to the spindle fibres and there is no direct evidence that they organize the spindle in any cells. Indeed they have been removed experimentally from spermatocytes of a cranefly without affecting spindle function.

While studying mitosis in stained preparations it is necessary to notice the arrangement of the whole complement in undistorted, lightly squashed cells (Fig. 2.6) as well as the detailed appearance of individual chromosomes separated from each other by heavy squashing (Fig. 2.2a).

Many of the important events of the chromosome cycle cannot be distinguished under the light microscope as they occur in the interphase nucleus. Some can be inferred using such techniques as autoradiography with radioactive precursors of chromosome components, but these are beyond the scope of this book. The critical stages in the normal chromosome cycle are DNA replication, chromonema replication and chromatid replication during interphase, and centromere division (chromosome replication) and chromosome separation (nuclear replication) usually followed by cytokinesis or cleavage (cell replication) during the mitotic stages (Fig. 2.7). These complex events must occur in all mitotic cell divisions. Some of the more detailed events described below for higher organisms, concerning the nuclear envelope, nucleolus and chromosome coiling, show variation in lower plants and animals.

2.3.1 Mitosis

1 (*Interphase*) In most interphase cells, the only visible nuclear changes as a cell proceeds towards mitosis are the increasing volumes of the nucleus and nucleolus. In a few plant and animal cells, minor changes have been seen in the distribution of chromatin which characterize the *S period* of the cell cycle when chromosome DNA is being synthesised and the subsequent interval before mitosis begins. The S period usually occupies about half of interphase (Table 2.2).

2 (*Prophase*) The first sign of the onset of division is the contraction by coiling of the chromosomes within the nuclear envelope. Individual chromosomes can then be distinguished and are seen to be already double, with sister chromatids wound relationally round each other. Chromomeres can often be distinguished. As contraction approaches a maximum, the nucleoli, which detach and move amongst the chromosomes, shrink and finally disappear. At the same time, in most cells, the nuclear envelope fragments and becomes indistinguishable from endoplasmic reticulum, although in some algae and fungi the chromosomes divide on a spindle formed within an intact nuclear envelope.

3 (*Prometaphase*) The spindle is then organized. Some fibres run from each pole to one of the daughter attachment points or half-

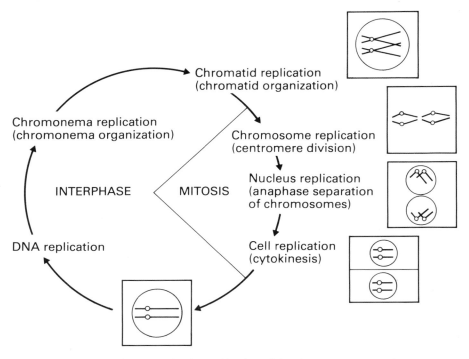

Fig. 2.7 The essential events in the replication of the chromosome complement during the mitotic cell division cycle. The chromonema is the hypothetical fundamental structural unit of the chromosome. Chromonema organization involves the production and assembly of the other structural components and their association with the new DNA. Chromatid replication involves the organization of the chromosome into two structurally, and during mitosis, visibly, distinct equal sub-units. It is not yet known whether an unreplicated chromosome contains two or more DNA molecules or only one. In chromosomes which contain a single DNA helix, or several helices associated within a single nucleoprotein unit, the chromonema and the chromatid are identical. The interphase events shown in the diagram could be almost simultaneous, particularly if each unreplicated chromosome contains a single DNA helix, or the events might occur in a different sequence, in which the organization into new structural units by separation of DNA molecules precedes DNA replication, if each unreplicated chromosome contains two or more helices.

centromeres of each chromosome. Half-centromeres usually attach to the pole they happen to be facing, even if it is not the nearest. If, as occasionally happens, both sister half-centromeres attach to the same pole, this is soon corrected so that the two half-centromeres of each chromosome are attached to opposite poles. This is known as *amphitelic* centromere attachment. Other fibres do not link with the chromosomes but provide the spindle framework. These fibres appear to run continuously from pole to pole but electron micrographs indicate that at least sometimes the individual microtubules within the fibres extend little more than half way along the spindle, overlapping and interdigitating at the equator with micro-tubules from the opposite pole. The chromosomes move at a rate of about 1 µm per minute towards the equator of the spindle from where they were left after the nuclear envelope dispersed. After *congression* they oscillate to and fro several times across the equator until the two half-centromeres, one

Table 2.2 A selection from the literature of estimates by a variety of techniques of the duration of the cell cycle and some of the identifiable component phases. These data indicate the variation detectable between organisms, between stages of development, between cell types and the influence of internal factors such as genotype and external factors such as temperature and light conditions. (Time in hours unless indicated otherwise.)

Material	Whole Cycle	Inter-phase	G_1	S	G_2	Mitosis	Pro.	Meta.	Ana.	Telo
Animals:										
Strongylocentrotus embryo 15°C	276 mins	236 mins	203 mins	13 mins	20 mins	40 mins				
Xenopus embryo	15 mins	10 mins	—	10 mins	—	5 mins				
Human HeLa cells										
33°C	73.6	60.6	26	22.4	12.2	13.0				
36°C	25.8	24.3	13	7.4	3.9	1.5				
38°C	19.2	18.4	7.5	7.6	3.3	0.8				
Unicells:										
Tetrahymena pyriformis 23°C	225 mins	195 mins	51 mins	39 mins	105 mins	30 mins				
Lower plants:										
Chlamydomonas reinhardtii	23	19	15	4	—	4				
Angiosperms – root tips:										
Vicia faba 20°C	18.0	14.4	2.4	4.0	8.0	3.6				
Trillium grandiflorum 20°C	120	c. 110	c. 50	c. 30	c. 30	c. 10				
Tradescantia paludosa										
13°C	51.4	46.3	15.4	22.5	8.3	5.1	4.11	0.33	0.22	0.18
21°C	20.8	19.1	5.8	10.8	2.5	1.7	1.28	0.12	0.09	0.18
30°C	16.0	14.3	2.4	9.5	2.4	1.7	1.30	0.15	0.09	0.17
Pisum sativum 20°C										
Cultured excised roots { Dark	17.8	13.2	2.0	4.3	6.9	4.6				
White light	17.0	15.5	4.4	4.9	6.2	1.5				
Red light	21.0	18.8	4.2	8.3	6.3	2.2				
Green light	24.6	18.4	10.4	5.7	2.3	6.2				
Blue light	19.8	17.4	6.0	6.8	4.6	2.4				
Zea mays										
Root cap columella	14	13	—	8	5	1				
Quiescent centre (Q.C.)	174	171	151	9	11	3				
Cortex near Q.C.	42	38	22	10	6	4				
Cortex 200 μm from Q.C.	30	27	18	5	4	3				
Cortex 400 μm from Q.C.	25	22	13	4	5	3				
Cortex 700 μm from Q.C.	20	17	9	3	5	3				
Cortex 1000 μm from Q.C.	20	17	9	3	5	3				
Stele near Q.C. – young root	18	16	3	5	8	2				
Stele near Q.C. – old root	35	32	19	6	7	3				
Hordeum vulgare										
$2n = 2x$	11.3	10.2	2.9	3.0	4.3	1.1				
$2n$ = isogenic auto-$4x$	12.4	11.2	2.2	4.9	4.1	1.2				
Angiosperms – other cell types:										
Triticum aestivum										
'Chinese Spring' 20°C										
Pollen mother cell (meiosis)	72	48	33	15	—	24 (Meiosis)				
Pollen grain mitosis	82	58	46	12	—	24	12	7	1.5	2.5
Generative cell mitosis	84	60				24				
Second embryo sac mitosis	12									
Second endosperm mitosis	5.5									
Second zygote mitosis	17									

on each chromatid, come to an equilibrium position. The position of each chromosome is established by *auto-orientation*.

4 (*Metaphase*) There is a short period when the centromeres are more or less aligned along the equator, daughter centromeres are still attached to each other and to opposite poles, and the chromosome arms extend away from the equator in the direction from which the chromosome migrated to the equator. The relational coiling of chromatids now completes the unwinding which leaves the fully contracted chromatids lying side by side. This uncoiling involves considerable rotational movement of the free ends, clearly visible in living cells, but the mechanism is entirely unknown.

5 (*Anaphase*) Suddenly the division of centromeres is simultaneously completed and the two daughter centromeres of each chromosome separate and move apart at 0.2 to 4.0 μm per minute to opposite poles, dragging the arms behind them. Where the chromosome is a long one, one daughter chromosome will have to double back on itself as the centromere moves back past its own arm. Initial movement of chromosomes seems to be primarily due to movement of centromeres along the spindle perhaps by interaction of half-spindle with continuous fibres; later, elongation of the spindle itself contributes to the separation of daughter chromosomes. Movement ceases when all the centromeres are aggregated closely about the poles, with the arms extending back along the spindle. It has been suggested that, in at least some cells, the arrangement of centromeres in the polar group is not random and that homologues tend to lie close together. If so, this would provide a basis for the repeated reports of somatic pairing or association of homologous chromosome at mitosis (Fig. 1.3a).

6 (*Telophase*) The nuclear envelope then reforms, first across the polar side of the group of chromosomes and subsequently round the chromosome arms, closely following their outline. Small pieces of membrane, looking like endoplasmic reticulum, can be seen in electron micrographs to appear over the surface of the chromosome mass and then fuse. At the same time the nucleoli re-form at each nucleolar organizer and adjacent ones may fuse.

7 (*Interphase*) Once the nuclear membrane is complete the nuclei expand to become approximately spherical and nucleoli reach their full size.

It is not usually possible to distinguish interphase nuclei (strictly those between successive mitoses) from post-mitotic nuclei of differentiating cells. Except in some young embryos, interphase is the longest stage, often occupying 90% of the cycle (Table 2.2). Of the rest, prophase usually occupies about half, with anaphase the shortest of the others. These relative durations are reflected in the frequencies with which they are seen in preparations (Section 4.2.2). Although values differ somewhat according to temperature and to the technique used to determine the duration (Table 2.2), it is clear that the total length of the cycle varies widely, even within organisms, mostly due to variation in interphase duration. The cycle tends to be shortest in organisms with small nuclei, in embryos and in the most active meristematic tissues. In plants, the minimum cycle time increases with DNA content at the diploid level but, for a given DNA content, is shorter in dicotyledons, annuals and diploids than in monocotyledons, perennials and polyploids. Thus the shortest cycles are in short lived annuals with small nuclei, and the longest in perennials with large nuclei. In a root tip there can be a $100 \times$ variation in cycle duration between cells in different regions separated only by a few microns. There is some evidence from reciprocal transplantation experiments and hybrid zygotes that the timing is largely determined by the cytoplasm.

If, as is usual, cell division accompanies mitosis, then cytokinesis or cleavage, involving the redistribution of spindle fibres, overlaps with anaphase, telophase and early interphase. Cytokinesis occurs in plant cells with rigid walls. A new cell wall expands, usually centrifugally, to cut the parent cell in two when it reaches the existing cell walls. The new wall, and the two new plasmalemma membranes which line it, are formed by the fusion of membrane bound vesicles produced by Golgi bodies, or perhaps elements of endoplasmic reticulum, situated near the spindle equator after the daughter chromosomes have separated at anaphase. At this stage fibres again become conspicuous, forming a barrel shaped structure, the phragmoplast, at the equator. These fibres appear to be responsible for orientating and aligning the droplets, and the phragmoplast expands outwards just ahead of the growing cell wall.

2.3.2 Material and methods

Mitosis (Section 2.3.1) The standard technique for the examination of dividing cells will reveal many of the significant events of mitosis. The role of the spindle can be further illustrated by comparison with similar cells in which the spindle has been destroyed by pretreatment with colchicine. For easy culture and all-the-year-round availability plant root tips are probably the best. The onion, *Allium cepa*, obtained easily as bulbs or seeds, is very useful (Fig. 2.6). The problems of autumn dormancy of bulbs can be avoided by using varieties like 'Silverskin' which have no dormancy, or overcome by breaking dormancy with 4–6 weeks low temperature treatment.

When available, there are a number of plants which are preferable because of larger or fewer chromosomes with more obvious variation in morphology. Examples include *Crocus balansae*, *Bellevalia romana* (Fig. 3.2b), *Puschkinia libanotica* (Fig. 4.2c),

Tulbaghia violacea, *Tradescantia paludosa*, *Trillium grandiflorum*, *Lilium* spp. and *Hyacinthus orientalis* var. 'Roman Hyacinth'.

In the absence of these, roots from the readily available seeds of *Vicia faba* (broad bean), *Hordeum vulgare* (barley) or *Secale cereale* (rye) germinated in pots or on moist filter paper in Petri dishes are acceptable, though the cereals have hard root-tips.

Common wild plants which are useful alternatives include *Allium ursinum*, *Endymion non-scriptus* (Fig. 1.1) and *Ranunculus ficaria* (Fig. 4.3). Where possible, ripe fruits should be collected and preparations made from seedling root tips to avoid unnecessary disturbance to the plant community.

In the absence of growing root tips, mitoses from developing embryos, enlarging ovary and ovule walls or young leaves and petals are good alternatives (Section 2.4.4). This can be particularly important where the plant is growing outside.

There are a number of sources of mitoses in animals. Very frequently, mitoses are seen in meiotic preparations. Another good source of mitoses in insects is the embryo. The large eggs of *Schistocerca gregaria* are a good example. Puncture the chorion of 3–6 days old eggs of *Schistocerca gregaria* and squeeze contents into 0.75% NaCl. Remove the white transparent embryo from the yellow yolk and make a preparation by the standard method.

Preparations of mitosis can be obtained from the tails of amphibian larvae. Newts of the genus *Triturus* have chromosomes which are among the largest in the animal kingdom. The simplest method, unfortunately restricted to the spring breeding season, is to narcotise young larvae when the forelimbs show two finger buds and remove the tail tip, which will regenerate. The tip is then fixed and prepared by the standard technique. Mitoses not obscured by the pigment cells can be found and chromosome morphology studied.

There are some relatively simple techniques for studying mammalian mitoses but obtaining actively dividing tissues presents problems. All the fundamental features relating to mammalian mitoses can be studied more easily in other material, and it is becoming increasingly easy to obtain unwanted slides of human chromosome preparations to satisfy curiosity about the complement.

2.4 Modifications of mitosis and chromosomes during the life cycle

In a highly differentiated multicellular organism, not all dividing cells are the same in behaviour or appearance (Fig. 2.8a). As some cell differentiation is compatible with continued mitotic activity, dividing cells can differ in respect of size, shape and cytoplasmic contents as well as in the position and orientation of the mitotic spindle and the timing of the cycle. This variation is exemplified by a comparison of dividing cells of the apical root meristem, vascular cambium, leaf palisade, pollen and embryo sac of an angiosperm. Few of the cellular features of dividing root tip cells, frequently described as the *typical* mitotic cell of higher plants, are shared by the other cell types.

In a similar way, the number, structure and behaviour of the chromosomes can also differ between cells of the same individual. Meiosis, which can be considered as an extreme modification of mitosis (Fig. 2.9f), is considered separately (Section 2.5), as are those occasional spontaneous changes in chromosomes which form the basis of karyotype evolution (Chapter 3). However, there are a number of other controlled changes affecting the karyotype during development. These changes result in differences between cells and tissues in chromosome size, in the number of replicates of the genome or in the number of individual chromosomes. Most of these changes occur during the development of somatic tissues.

Those that occur in the germ line, the cell lineage from zygote to zygote (Fig. 2.8b), are usually reversed at some other stage of the life cycle in order to preserve a stable karyotype from one generation to the next.

It is necessary to be able to identify accurately these ontogenetic alterations of the karyotype in order to recognize the significance of any chromosomal variation observed in an organism. Demonstration and investigation of these conditions requires techniques for obtaining mitotic chromosomes at various stages of the life cycle (Section 2.4.4). These same techniques have other important uses. They provide additional material for karyotype analysis if the usual source is unavailable (Section 2.3.2). They provide a means of checking whether a karyotype observed in one somatic tissue is representative of dividing cells throughout the organism. Finally, they are necessary in any detailed cytogenetic investigation for following the transmission of a particular chromosome or genome through the life cycle from one generation to the next and establishing the relationship between gametic, zygotic and somatic complements.

Modifications of mitosis and karyotype related to development are readily accessible in flowering plants. Angiosperms are therefore the main source of material for this section.

2.4.1 Changes in chromosome size with development

Differences in chromosome size, with no differences in DNA content, occur between different tissues of the same plant. Similar variation occurs between cells at different stages of development of the same tissue. Chromosome size appears to be correlated with metabolic activity, and increasing nutrient phosphate levels can increase both. Perhaps changes in the amount of protein associated with the DNA account for the differences.

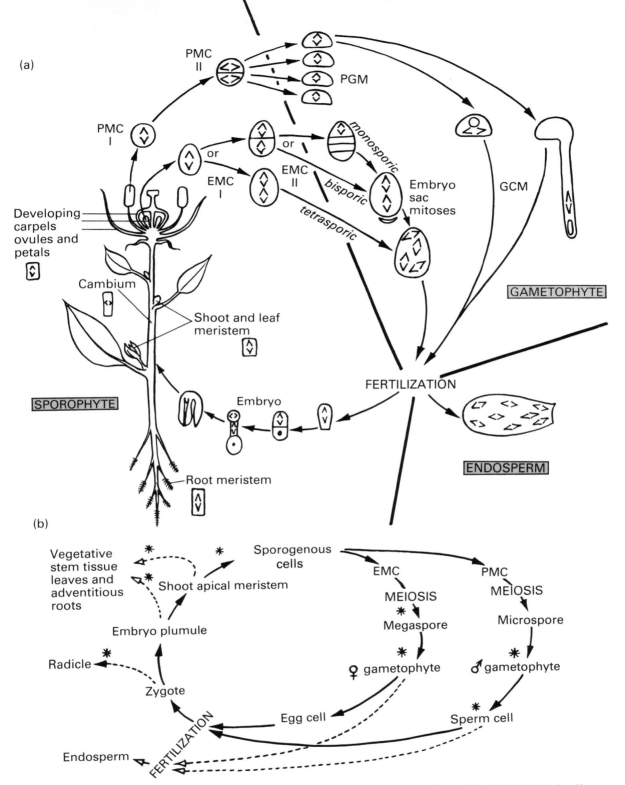

Fig. 2.8 **a**, Dividing cells in the life cycle of an angiosperm. **b**, The angiosperm 'germ line' (solid line), the direct cell lineage through each sexual generation from zygote to zygote. The broken lines indicate the development of ephemeral somatic tissue derived from the germ line. PMC = pollen mother cell; EMC = embryo sac mother cell; I = first meiotic division; II = second meiotic division; PGM = pollen grain mitosis; GCM = generative cell mitosis; and * = stages of development where controlled chromosome non-disjunction leading to karyotype segregation have been found (Section 2.4.3).

2.4.2 Changes in ploidy level with development

Changes in ploidy level accompany the normal alternation of generations by fusion in the zygote and endosperm of the meiotically reduced complements found in the spores and gametes. Similar processes in purely somatic tissues are rare. Nuclear fusion occurs in developing antipodal cells of *Lilium* and *Caltha*. Somatic reduction has only been convincingly demonstrated in highly polyploid cells of specialized tissues and in certain male insects where sex determination depends on the loss of the paternal complement early in the development of the initially diploid embryo.

However, increased levels of ploidy as a result of modified, foreshortened cell cycles are common in differentiating somatic tissues of many plants and animals. The increase in nuclear content takes different forms depending on the point in the cycle at which chromosome replication and segregation is curtailed (Fig. 2.9). The modified cycles may be repeated several times, particularly in large secretory cells, to produce cells with many thousand times the gametic DNA content.

Binucleate cells and, after subsequent cycles, *multinucleate coenocytes* are formed when mitosis proceeds normally but cytokinesis is suppressed. Caffeine treatment of meristemic cells produces a similar result but does not induce differentiation.

Polyploidy, with double the number of chromosomes in the nucleus, results when both cell and nuclear replication are omitted. This is the most frequent cause of enlarged nuclei in differentiated somatic cells of many animal and plant tissues. The increase usually occurs without chromosome condensation within an intact nuclear envelope by a process which is referred to by some as endo-mitosis, producing endo-polyploid nuclei. Only by stimulating mitosis with auxins can it be demonstrated that the large nuclei of root, pith and cortex are 8- or even 16-ploid. Occasionally the reversion to a full mitotic cycle occurs naturally and polyploid and diploid mitoses are found together in a meristem, a condition known as *polysomaty*. In addition, there are rare examples of the controlled induction of polyploidy by suppression of anaphase in modified divisions similar to those induced by colchicine and these are further remarkable in that they occur in the germ line during the formation of unreduced gametophytes of certain apomicts.

Diplochromosomes, chromosomes with four or more chromatids attached by one unreplicated centromere, result when centromere division as well as cell and nuclear replication are suppressed. Diplochromosomes are found infrequently alongside polyploid nuclei in differentiated cells and sometimes appear after colchicine treatment.

Polytene chromosomes, in which the basic chromosome unit, the chromonema, has replicated without the organization of chromatids or any subsequent events of the cycle, are found in a permanently prophase-like condition in certain highly specialized cells. As many as ten repeated cycles of this type can result in giant chromosomes where the chromomeres form conspicuous transverse bands which allow detailed analysis of longitudinal differentiation. The classic examples are the salivary and other gland cells of dipteran flies, where analysis is further aided by the somatic pairing, band by band, of homologues, but similar chromosomes occur in some plant cells within the ovule, including the embryo suspensor and antipodals.

These four cytological conditions represent the results of progressively curtailed modifications of the mechanical events of the chromosome cycle but all retain the part of interphase in which DNA is replicated (Fig. 2.9). They may be functionally equivalent because the corresponding cells of related species may have alternative forms of nuclear doubling and in some cells two or more types of increase may be superimposed, as in the

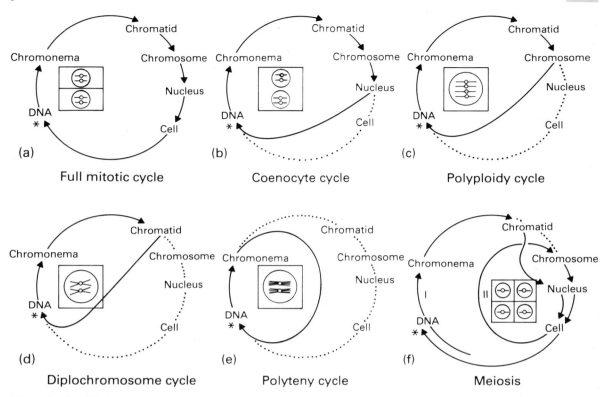

Fig. 2.9 Modified cell cycles occurring during development. **a,** The full mitotic cycle consisting of replication of DNA, chromonema, chromatid, chromosome, nucleus and cell. See Fig. 2.7. **b,** A shortened mitotic cycle, omitting cytokinesis, producing a binucleate cell. Successive similar cycles produce a multinucleate coenocyte as found in young endosperm. **c,** A shortened mitotic cycle, omitting nuclear and cell replication, producing a polyploid nucleus as found in many differentiated plant and animal cells. Repeated cycles produce successively larger nuclei. **d,** A shortened mitotic cycle, omitting nuclear, cell and chromosome replication, to produce diplochromosomes, with two chromatids before replication and four at the next mitosis, as found occasionally among polyploid differentiated cells. **e,** A shortened mitotic cycle, omitting all but DNA and chromonema replication, to produce a polytenic chromosome. Repeated cycles produce successively larger chromosomes as in dipteran gland and angiosperm embryo suspensor cells. **f,** Meiosis, two successive shortened cycles (I and II) after a single DNA replication, to produce four cells each with half the original complement of chromosomes. In each cycle, the inset diagram represents the chromosomes at the point in interphase indicated *, just prior to the next DNA replication, after one complete circuit of the path shown by the continuous line in a cell which was initially mononucleate with one pair of chromosomes.

polytene and polyploid nuclei of some endosperm coenocytes.

The second division of meiosis and the rare somatic reduction cycles can also be considered as curtailed mitotic cycles but ones in which the chromosomal events are retained while DNA replication is omitted (Fig. 2.9).

2.4.3 Karyotype segregation during development

While in most organisms there are changes in the number of genomes in the nuclei in certain tissues, each genome usually remains intact during development. However, in certain plants and animals, controlled non-disjunction at pre-determined stages of development (Fig. 2.8b; Section 2.4.4) results in the gain or loss of specific chromosomes and the production of cell lines with an altered karyotype. This process alters the gene complement of the cells and is at the same time controlled by it.

In some examples the altered complement is found only in purely somatic tissues, a constant karyotype being found throughout the germ line. The classic example of this somatic segregation is in *Parascaris equorum*, a round worm, where the two large polycentric chromosomes found in the zygote are maintained in the germ line but fragment and lose their acentric terminal segments during the embryonic mitoses giving rise to somatic tissues. A related situation occurs in some plants with supernumerary B chromosomes (Section 3.4.2g) in addition to the basic complement. The B chromosomes are maintained from one generation to the next by their retention in the shoot apex and reproductive tissues, but are lost by mitotic non-disjunction during the development of somatic tissues such as lateral or adventitious roots and leaves which do not take part in reproduction. Presumably, if they have a significant effect on development it is expressed only in the young embryo or during preparation for sexual reproduction. In such plants, karyotype analysis based entirely on root tips fails to reveal the presence of B chromosomes in the population.

In a variety of sexually reproducing organisms, similar mechanisms exist in the germ line to alter the number of autosomes, sex chromosomes or even whole genomes. In these the complementary products enter the two types of gametes so that the original zygotic complement is restored by fertilization. Another type of karyotype segregation during sexual reproduction again affects B chromosomes. In several plants and insects, directed non-disjunction increases the number of B chromosomes in the cells of the germ line and thus transmitted to the gamete (Fig. 2.10). In many cases the non-disjunction takes place at a division where only one of the products will continue in the germ line, such as female meiosis and gametophyte mitosis, and the unseparated

Boosting mechanism	♀ Parent (2x + 1B)			♂ Parent (2x + 1B)			Frequency of progeny[1] with					Mean no. B chrom. in progeny
	Sporophyte mitosis	EMC meiosis I	1st gametophyte mitosis	Sporophyte mitosis	1st mitosis in gametophyte PGM	2nd mitosis in gametophyte GCM	2x + 0B	2x + 1B	2x + 2B	2x + 3B	2x + 4B	
None	 [diagram]	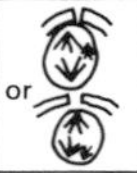 or [diagram]	 or [diagram]	 [diagram]	 [diagram]	 [diagram]	25	50	25	—	—	1·0B
Directed non-disjunction at ♀ meiosis I e.g. *Trillium*	3	 [diagram]	3	3	3	3	—	50	50	—	—	1·5B
Directed non-disjunction at ♂ 1st gametophytic mitosis (PGM) e.g. *Haplopappus gracilis* or 2nd mitosis (GCM)[2] e.g. *Zea mays*	3	3	3	3	 [diagram]	 [diagram] 2	25	25	25	25	—	1·5B
Directed non-disjunction at 1st gametophytic mitosis in ♂ and ♀[2] e.g. *Secale cereale*	3	3	 [diagram] 2	3	 [diagram]	3	25	—	50	—	25	2·0B
Non-disjunction + selection at sporophytic mitosis e.g. *Crepis capillaris*	 [diagram]	3	3	 [diagram]	3	3	—	100	—	—	—	2·0B

1. As expected with random fertilization and no gamete selection and after 100% non-disjunction in boosting mechanisms.
2. Boosting mechanism does not increase number of B chromosomes in endosperm. 3. Normal disjunction.

Fig. 2.10   The effect of B chromosome boosting mechanisms in angiosperms on the frequency of B chromosomes in the progeny.

daughter B chromosomes are preferentially included in the germ-line cell as a result of directed centromere movement on an asymmetric spindle. In the remaining cases non-disjunction occurs at a premeiotic mitosis and if both daughter cells continue for a while in the germ line, selection in time favours the one with the increased number of B chromosomes.

2.4.4 Material and methods

Sporophyte mitoses

Mitotically active cells are found in growing root and shoot apices, young expanding leaves and petals, developing ovary and ovule walls and embryos (Fig. 2.8a). The many dividing cells of vascular and cork cambia are less accessible. The technique used for all tissues is essentially the standard one but one or two points should be remembered. In all cases, small pieces of tissue must be excised to ensure rapid and complete penetration. When a lot of chlorophyll is present, it may help the removal of pigments if the chloroform content of the fixative is doubled or trebled. It is usually possible to obtain a number of active *adventitious buds* containing mitoses if the main shoot is decapitated a few days in advance. The apex should as far as possible be dissected out before fixation. Divisions in the *ovule wall* are less frequent in an old bud or open flower. Ovules should be taken at about half their size in the mature flower or a few days after successful pollination, and they are best handled through the various solutions including colchicine or some equivalent by leaving a number of exposed ovules attached to a piece of placenta. *Leaf meristems* are particularly useful in monocotyledons where they are easily located at the base of the growing leaf. Grass or cereal 'seeds' can be germinated on moist filter paper in a Petri dish or in damp vermiculite. When the first or second leaf is about 2 cm long, remove the basal 2 mm, cut into thin strips and treat as root tips. The squash is made by the standard technique.

The male gametophyte – pollen grain mitosis (PGM)

Preparations of PGM, the first division after meiosis, can be made by two alternative techniques, the squash and the smear. The latter may be preferable when the pollen grain wall is so thick as to interfere with staining. In both cases a bud at the correct stage of development is first found by trial and error, tapping out a single anther in a drop of orcein and briefly examining the temporary preparation when sufficiently stained. Buds containing pollen grains at mitosis are frequently about $\frac{3}{4}$ of their final size and still tightly closed. The anthers have assumed their characteristic mature colour, which is not always yellow, but the petals usually have not. The anthers contain a mixture of uninucleate and binucleate pollen grains which separate readily in the stain except for the few families such as Ericaceae and Cyperaceae where tetrads remain intact. PGM takes place a few days after meiosis in those plants with rapidly developing flowers on aerial stems but it may be weeks or months later in the underground buds of some early flowering perennials with meiosis in the autumn (Appendix 1). PGM is not as synchronous as meiosis, although mitotic indices of up to 80% have been recorded, and often some dividing cells are present in an anther for several days. Anthers which are too young have large pollen mother cells, either separate or in a mass, tetrads or uninucleate pollen; anthers which are too old have only binucleate grains.

Having identified a bud with PGM, the remaining anthers, singly or several at a time depending on size, can be treated as described in the standard technique by tapping them out immediately in lacto-propionic orcein without previous fixation. The chromosomes are sufficiently contracted and well spread for analysis of the gametophytic karyotype without pre-treatment (Fig. 2.11). Staining may take a long time if the wall is thick, and may not be entirely satisfactory even after being left over-night. In such cases, and if the anthers are large enough to handle as in *Tradescantia* or *Lilium*, they can be first fixed and macerated as for root tips. Alternatively, smear preparations can be made as follows. Line up one or more anthers, depending on size, across one end of a clean slide lying flat on the bench.

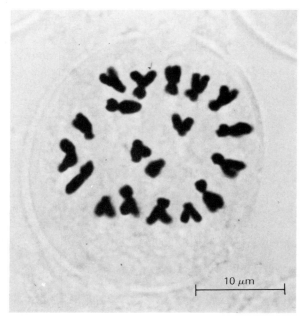

Fig. 2.11   Polar view of pollen grain mitosis at metaphase in *Dichorisandra thyrsiflora* ($n = 19$). See also Figs 3.1 and 4.1.

Then holding a second slide above the first at an angle of forty five degrees to it so that the lower end touches the anthers, first burst the anthers with the upper slide and then smear the contents rapidly along the lower slide using enough pressure to leave a one-cell thick layer along much of its length. As rapidly as possible and certainly before the moist smear dries out, immerse the slide with adhering pollen grains in fixative and then in hot dilute hydrochloric acid before

staining with orcein as in the standard technique. If the pollen grains tend to burst and lose their contents it will be necessary to increase the fixation time. Preparations can be made permanent by dehydrating the slide and attached material and mounting in Euparal as for squashes. For demonstration purposes, plants should be chosen for a low number of chromosomes and for ease of finding the correct stage when required. For this, *Tradescantia virginiana* is better than most even though, being tetraploid ($2n = 4x = 24$), a few of the pollen grains have unbalanced complements (Section 4.4.1). Inflorescences which have a large number of buds and only the oldest one or two flowers open will include all stages of pollen development at close intervals from before meiosis to anther dehiscence (*anthesis*). The buds are usually arranged in two opposing rows and in a sequence of increasing age of bud from bottom to top which alternates from one side of the inflorescence to the other. A quick method of finding the appropriate stage, whether PGM or meiosis, is to use a mounted needle to take one anther from each of four consecutive buds of approximately the right age, two from one side and the alternating two from the other side of the inflorescence. These four anthers are then arranged in order of age at intervals along one slide, and each is tapped out in orcein, taking care to avoid transferring cells from one sample to another. A quick examination after the nuclei have stained will show which pollen sample is at the required stage. This can then be traced back to a bud on the inflorescence and further preparations made. If none of the samples includes the required stage, the process is repeated with the four buds adjacent to the first sample, older or younger as dictated by the stages seen. This same approach can be used on all species, although where the flowers are solitary or the inflorescences compound or irregular, more reliance must be placed on other indicators of bud age, such as bud or anther size.

The male gametophyte – generative cell mitosis (GCM)

In some plants, representing over 50 families including Gramineae, Cruciferae, Ranunculaceae and Compositae, the second and final division of the male gametophyte to form two male gametes from the generative cell occurs within the pollen grain of a still closed bud some time after PGM and when liberated the pollen grain is trinucleate. For these the same technique can be used for GCM as for PGM although the wall will be thicker and stain penetration slower. In the remaining plants, GCM does not take place until after pollen germination and within the growing tube. In these plants it is most easily studied in pollen germinated in culture. The method to be described is effective for many species, including members of the families Amaryllidaceae, Commelinaceae, Iridaceae, Liliaceae, Balsaminaceae, Cruciferae, Papaveraceae, Scrophulariaceae, Solanaceae and Tropaeoleaceae, but germination in culture of several other species has not been achieved at all. The presence of a piece of stylar tissue from *another* plant may promote germination, and make studies of GCM possible, in species where the simple basic medium is inadequate. In Cyperaceae, only one spore of each still intact tetrad is capable of development.

MEDIUM:

Stock mineral solution:

H_3BO_3	0.10 g
$Ca(No_3)_2.4H_2O$	0.30 g
$MgSO_4.7H_2O$	0.20 g
KNO_3	0.10 g
Make up to 100 ml with water.	

Culture solution:

Stock mineral solution	1 ml
Sucrose	0.5–3.0 g
Water	9 ml

The concentration of sucrose is often critical. Too low a concentration induces burst tubes and too high a concentration causes stunted and distorted tubes. The concentration for maximum length and straightness varies with species and with growth conditions; for example, c. 3% is optimal for *Papaver*, 8–10% for *Tradescantia* and 15–20% for *Tulipa*, *Scilla*, *Trillium* and *Prunus*.

METHOD:

Dust dry pollen onto the surface of a drop of medium on a clean slide placed on moist filter paper in a Petri dish. If pollen becomes submerged it will not grow. Cover the Petri dish with a lid to maintain a moist atmosphere to avoid evaporation from the medium. Examine rapidly at intervals, taking care not to allow the medium to evaporate. Pollen tubes will first emerge in 15–45 minutes if the culture is to be successful. They will be more easily seen if the microscope condenser is racked down out of focus to give a pseudo-phase-contrast effect. After the tubes have grown for some hours, nuclei can be seen within the tube by phase contrast or after orcein staining. To stain, remove remaining culture solution with a small piece of filter paper without disturbing the pollen tubes, add a drop of lacto-propionic orcein, and, without disturbing the material, leave to stain under a coverslip. Then proceed by the standard technique, though squashing may not be necessary.

After 12 hours culture or less, vegetative and generative nuclei can be seen growing down the tube. In most species, GCM can be seen after 12 to 30 hours. It is not normally synchronous and occurs in the culture over a period of several hours, all stages being visible. After about 24 hours, vegetative nuclei and male gametes can be seen. More rarely (e.g. *Ornithogalum virens*, $n = 3$) mitosis commences before anthesis and near synchronous division is completed within the first hour or two of culture.

Karyotype analysis is possible at this stage, particularly when the chromosomes are small in relation to the diameter of the pollen tube (Fig. 2.12). Where the chromosomes are large, division in the pollen tube is very congested and the metaphase plate is distor-

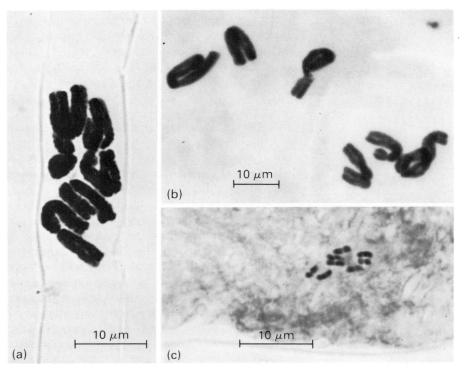

Fig. 2.12 Generative cell mitosis in pollen tubes after acenaphthene treatment. **a**, *Tulbaghia violacea* ($n = x = 6$). **b**, *Tulbaghia natalensis* ($n = x = 6$). The tube has been ruptured by squashing. **c**, *Antirrhinum majus* cv. 'Scarlet Flame' ($n = x = 8$).

ted with centromeres arranged obliquely almost from one pole to the other. In order to inhibit the mitotic spindle and accumulate metaphases in which karyotype analysis can be made, sprinkle a small amount of acenaphthene ($C_{10}H_6.CH_2.CH_2$) crystals on to the filter paper beside the slide when the culture is set up. The vapour does not affect pollen germination or tube growth but has an effect similar to colchicine on spindle organization, accumulating metaphases with over-contracted chromosomes more widely separated than normal. Squashing will probably be needed to clarify the whole complement, even to the extent of bursting the tube when chromosomes are large.

Suitable material for demonstration purposes includes the following species.

Generative cell mitosis in developing pollen grain: *Ranunculus ficaria*, *Secale*

cereale, members of the *Cruciferae* and *Compositae*.

Generative cell mitosis in pollen tubes germinated in culture: *Hyacinthus orientalis* ('Roman hyacinth'), *Bellevalia romana*, *Tulbaghia violacea*, *Tradescantia virginiana* (all large chromosomes, congested division) and *Antirrhinum majus* (small chromosomes).

The female gametophyte

Most angiosperm embryo sacs contain eight nuclei (Fig. 2.8). In those with *monosporic* development, these form by three successive synchronous mitoses, without intervening cytokinesis, from one of the four megaspores resulting from meiosis in the single mother cell in each ovule. In the remaining species, several variations are found. In the so-called *bisporic* and *tetrasporic* species, two or all four megaspores contribute to the embryo sac usually with corresponding reductions in the number of subsequent mitoses. The significance of this variation in development is not known but in most cases the heterozygosity, and occasionally the balance of maternal and paternal complements, of the later formed endosperm will be affected.

Although laborious sectioning techniques have been used to examine embryo sac mitoses, clear preparations can be achieved with little or no modification of the standard orcein technique. Three slightly different ways of extracting embryo sacs for staining are possible. In all cases, ovules attached to a piece of placenta are excised from ovaries at about the same time as PGM and the exposed ovules fixed and macerated in the standard way. In species with very small embryo sacs or, like orchids, with very small undifferentiated ovules, a group of ovules can be treated like a root tip in the standard squash method and the embryo sacs sought amongst the ovule cells after the temporary preparation has been made. In some cases, integuments can be dissected away first. For larger ovules, embryo sacs can be expelled by placing three or four ovules in orcein stain under a coverslip and then tapping gently on the coverslip above them. This is not always successful and the large compact masses of tissue may prevent adequate flattening of the embryo sacs when the coverslip is under pressure. A third alternative, for species with large ovules containing large embryo sacs such as *Trillium, Lilium* and *Hyacinthus* where the mature embryo sac is several hundred micrometres long, involves the dissection of embryo sacs and the removal of much of the unwanted ovule tissue. The ovules are fixed and macerated in the standard way and then, either directly or after immersion for an hour or two in orcein, placed in a drop of dilute stain on a slide on the stage of a binocular dissecting microscope. The stain should be diluted, with the appropriate concentration of lactic and propionic acid mixture, sufficiently to reveal the cells and tissues but still stain the nuclei. The ovules are then burst open with mounted needles at the micropylar end and gently squeezed and teased with minimum disturbance of the outer tissues until the embryo sac is separated from the surrounding cells. In order to distinguish the embryo sac it may be necessary to try a variety of alternative illumination arrangements with transmitted or reflected light against a white or black background. The large, often pear-shaped, embryo sac is quite unlike any other cell in the ovule. The embryo sac is then separated as far as possible from the other material, which is then removed. This procedure is repeated for a number of ovules. When several embryo sacs have been obtained, the water or dilute stain is removed as far as possible before adding normal orcein and lowering a coverslip. When the chromosomes are sufficiently stained, the coverslip may be pressed down, but only gentle squashing is required. The preparations can be made permanent by the standard technique.

For demonstration purposes use species with large chromosomes and embryo sacs such as *Ranunculus* (monosporic), *Allium* and *Trillium* (bisporic) and *Lilium, Hyacinthus* and *Fritillaria* (tetrasporic).

Mitosis in the fertilization products

Preparations from within ovules after fertilization show mitosis in the embryo and, in angiosperms, also in the endosperm, the ephemeral product of the second fertilization. In the zygote the sporophytic complement is restored but most endosperms have three gametic complements with maternal and paternal genomes in the ratio 2:1. Lily endosperm is pentaploid (4:1) and other variants exist. Early mitoses are essentially normal except that in many species they are synchronous (Fig. 2.13a) and not accompanied by cytokinesis. Later mitoses are asynchronous, associated with cytokinesis and sometimes modified to produce polyploid nuclei, particularly at the chalazal end.

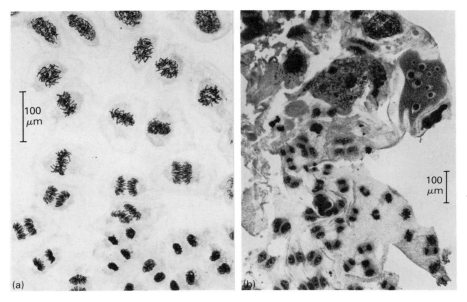

Fig. 2.13 Endosperm mitosis. **a**, A wave of synchronous division passing along the coenocytic endosperm of *Paris quadrifolia* ($3n = 6x = 30$). **b**, Chromosome fragments and bridges and polyploid nuclei resulting from irregular mitosis in hybrid endosperm of *Paris quadrifolia* × *Trillium grandiflorum* (originally $3n = 5x = 25$).

Mitotic errors tend to be more frequent in endosperm than other tissues, particularly after hybrid pollination (Fig. 2.13b).

The methods described for developing embryo sacs are also suitable for dividing endosperms and embryos in older fertilized ovules. It is easier to separate out at least part of the endosperm than it is to obtain the developing embryo sac and with care it can be obtained as an intact multinucleate or multi-cellular sheet or sac of cytoplasm. If it fragments too readily, longer fixation should be tried. Embryos frequently appear in the same preparations. Endosperm tissue is recognized by its large polyploid nuclei and sometimes by the lack of cell walls or by the division synchrony. Young embryos can be distinguished as a compact mass of very small dense cells with asynchronous division.

In addition to the striking preparations of synchronous mitosis possible with some young endosperms, analysis of metaphase complements (Fig. 2.19a) in endosperms reveals the female contribution to the endosperm which varies according to the pattern of embryo sac development (see above). The mononucleate cells with very large nuclei which appear in some preparations are likely to be polyploid synergid, antipodal or suspensor cells while a coenocyte with similar nuclei is probably the chalazal region of the endosperm.

For demonstration purposes, plants with large chromosomes and large ovules, such as *Hyacinthus*, *Lilium*, *Trillium* and *Ranunculus* are best. Endosperm from the large ovules of *Haemanthus katherinae* has been used for phase-contrast cine-micrography of normal and experimentally disturbed mitosis and associated electron microscope studies.

Changes in chromosome size with development (Section 2.4.1)

Compare dividing chromosomes of:
i) Endosperm, root tip, leaves and pollen grain nuclei of the same species (endosperm > root tip > pollen grain, leaves).

ii) 1 week, 3 week and 5 week old roots of onion or rye seeds. (3 week > 1, 5 week).

iii) 1 week old radicle and 3 week old laterals of *Vicia faba* seeds. (3 week > 1 week).

Changes in ploidy level with development (Section 2.4.2)

ALTERNATION OF GENERATIONS: Compare complements of pollen grain, root tip and endosperm of the same plant.

SOMATIC NUCLEAR FUSION: Fusion during mitosis of three haploid megaspore nuclei at the antipodal end of the developing embryo sac of *Lilium* immediately following meiosis.

BINUCLEATE CELLS: Anther wall and tapetum (also polyploid) of *Lilium*, wheat, rye.

COENOCYTE: Young endosperm of *Lilium*, *Trillium*, *Hyacinthus*; suspensor of young embryo of *Pisum*.

POLYPLOID NUCLEI: Polyploidy arises within an intact nuclear envelope in e.g. differentiating xylem vessels behind the root apex in *Vicia faba* $(2x = 12)$, *Hyacinthus* $(2x = 16)$; epidermal hairs as on the anthers of *Bryonia dioica* $(2x = 20)$; and many other differentiated cell types. Examination of differentiating cells of roots 24 hours after 4 hours treatment in 20–50 ppm aqueous indole-3-acetic acid (IAA) solution may reveal polyploid cells of stele and cortex in auxin-induced mitosis. Natural polysomaty occurs sporadically towards the back of apical meristems in root tips of *Tulbaghia* spp. $(2x = 12)$, *Spinacea oleracea* $(2x = 12)$ and *Beta vulgaris* $(2x = 18)$.
Polyploidy due to suppressed anaphase in the mitosis preceding meiosis occurs in EMC of *Allium odorum* $(2x = 16)$, an apomict.

DIPLOCHROMOSOMES: Rare and unpredictable; said to occur more commonly in roots of *Spinacea oleracea* $(2x = 12)$ than in most species.

ABSENCE OF ENDOPOLYPLOID NUCLEI IN DIFFERENTIATED CELLS: In a few species, the root and stem cells which are endopolyploid in most plants retain the diploid sporophytic complement, e.g. *Helianthus annuus*, *H. tuberosus*, *Lactuca sativa*, *Crinum* spp.

POLYTENE CHROMOSOMES: The twelve or more antipodal cells in mature embryo sacs of *Hordeum vulgare* $(2x = 14)$. The four polyploid and polytene endosperm nuclei, 250 µm in diameter, in a common sheet of coenocytic cytoplasm dissected from young developing seeds of *Ipheon uniflorum*. The polytene nuclei of the multicellular embryo suspensor of *Phaseolus vulgaris* dissected from seeds of pods about 10 cm long. Banding in *Phaseolus* is made clearer by keeping the plants at 10°C for 2 weeks before making the preparation. The polytene chromosomes in the salivary glands of the fruit fly *Drosophila* and similar species can be prepared from well-fed last instar larvae taken as they crawl up the side of the culture vessel to pupate. Dissect out the translucent two-lobed gland in a drop of 0.67% NaCl solution by pulling the mouth parts away from the rest of the body with needles. Transfer the glands to a drop of lacto-propionic orcein on a clean slide and gently tease out the gland before lowering a coverslip and leaving to stain. Gentle tapping and pressure is then used to spread the chromosomes in each cell in order to reveal the 3000 to 5000 bands. Mature larvae of the black fly *Eusimulium aureum*, the mosquito *Anopheles* and the midge *Chironomus* are suitable alternatives with large salivary glands.

Karyotype segregation during development (Section 2.4.3)

SEGREGATION OF WHOLE GENOMES: *Rosa canina* $(2n = 5x = 35 = AABCD)$. Non-disjunction of univalent B, C and D genomes at embryo sac meiosis results in tetraploid female gametophytes $(n = 4x = 28 =$

ABCD). After irregular disjunction and exclusion of univalents at pollen meiosis, only balanced haploid pollen grains ($n = x = 7 = A$) are viable.

SEGREGATION OF B CHROMOSOMES:
In each of the following species it is necessary to select individuals with one B chromosome.

SOMATIC SEGREGATION, ELIMINATION FROM ADVENTITIOUS ROOTS: *Haplopappus gracilis* ($2x + 1B = 4 + 1B$), *Aegilops speltoides* ($2x + 1B = 14 + 1B$).

NON-DISJUNCTION FOLLOWED BY SELECTION IN SHOOT APEX AFTER FLORAL INITIATION: *Crepis capillaris* ($2x + 1B = 6 + 1B$). Possibly also *Ranunculus ficaria* ($2x + 1B = 14 + 1B$) and *Caltha palustris* ($2x + 1B = 53 - 60 + 1B$). Comparable segregation occurs during development in *Locusta migratoria*.

DIRECTED NON-DISJUNCTION (DND) AT EMBRYO SAC MEIOSIS I: Directed towards chalazal pole – *Trillium grandiflorum* ($2x + 1B = 10 + 1B$), *Plantago serraria* ($2x + 1B = 10 + 1B$), *Tradescantia virginiana* ($4x + 1B = 24 + 1B$). Directed towards micropylar pole – *Lilium callosum*, *L. medeoloides* ($2x + 1B = 24 + 1B$).
 Comparable boosting mechanisms occur in the female grasshopper, *Myrmeleotettix maculatus*.

DND AT FIRST FEMALE GAMETOPHYTE MITOSIS: *Secale cereale* ($2n = 2x + 1B = 14 + 1B$).

DND AT FIRST MALE GAMETOPHYTE MITOSIS: *Secale cereale* ($2n = 2x + 1B = 14 + 1B$), *Alopecurus pratensis* ($2n = 2x + 1B = 14 + 1B$), *Agrostis canina* ($2n = 2x + 1B = 14 + 1B$), *Dactylis glomerata* ($2n = 4x + 1B = 28 + 1B$), *Festuca pratensis* ($2n = 2x + 1B = 14 + 1B$), *Puschkinia libanotica* ($2n = 2x + 1B = 10 + 1B$). (Fig. 4.2).

NON-DISJUNCTION AT SECOND MALE GAMETOPHYTE MITOSIS: *Zea mays* ($2n = 2x + 1B = 20 + 1B$).

2.5 The visible events of meiosis

Although meiosis is a unique event in the sexual life cycle and differs from mitosis in several complex ways, it has many fundamental features in common with somatic cell division. Although differing in detail, the chromosome coiling, spindle organization and cytokinesis, for example, are essentially the same in meiotic and mitotic cycles. A cell physiologist might, with some justification, consider meiosis merely as an interesting modification of mitosis (Fig. 2.9f). The essential differences are that there is little or no G_2 period so division immediately follows DNA synthesis; there are two divisions following one replication, thus reducing the chromosome number; DNA synthesis and histone replication are disengaged; the bivalent is the mechanical unit at the first division; and the cycle is longer. It is likely that meiosis arose from mitosis as sexual reproduction evolved as a means of generating more genetic variation. Some of the simplest unicellular algae still lack both meiosis and fertilization and reproduce entirely asexually by mitosis. The development of a meiotic cycle in early organisms must have involved changes in timing of critical events such as chromosome replication, changes in the invisible metabolic events such as protein and nucleic acid synthesis, and the introduction of unique mechanical events such as chromosome pairing and disjunction and chiasma formation. It is the genetical consequences of these unique events which give the study of meiosis its central place in cytogenetics (Chapter 3).

Adaptation, speciation and long-term evolution depend on the generation of genotypic, and thus phenotypic, variation. In an asexual life cycle this variation depends entirely on the immediate products of mutation. In a haploid asexual life cycle there will usually be a rapid elimination of new mutants, while in a diploid asexual cycle the mutation will usually not be expressed in the heterozygote produced. Only in a sexual life cycle can the products of mutation be fully exploited. Mutations at different loci will arise independently in different individuals. Fertilization between such individuals can bring these mutations together within one organism of a later generation. Meiosis then releases new allelic combinations by recombining not only alleles on the same chromosome but also those on different chromosomes. Random fertilization of recombinant gametes will then produce individuals with new combinations of phenotypic characters.

An understanding of regular meiosis in a diploid is a necessary preliminary to a study of any aspect of genetics. The purpose of this sub-section is to consider in some detail the visible events of normal meiosis; the genetical consequences are comprehensively discussed in other books. In common with mitosis, the events follow in a smooth sequence with anaphase disjunction the only discontinuity, and the cycles of chromosome contraction and spindle activity are generally similar. As in mitosis, the events of meiosis show some variation between different organisms, but there are only minor differences within an individual because only hermaphrodite invertebrates and higher plants have two types of meiocyte in the same individual. Where separate 'male' and 'female' meiosis occurs in a species, whether in different individuals or in the same hermaphrodite, differences in chiasma frequency (e.g. *Lilium*) or distribution (e.g. *Triturus*) may occur. Occasionally at either male meiosis (e.g. some protozoans, annelids, insects, molluscs and scorpions and certain plant species), or female meiosis (e.g. some copepods and lepidopterans) no chiasmata are formed at all, although bivalents maintain their integrity until anaphase so that meiosis is mechanically normal.

As in mitosis, many crucial events occur in the preceding interphase at the molecular, macromolecular or even organelle level which are not recognizable under the light microscope by any staining technique. For example, the electron microscope has shown that plastids and mitochondria de-differentiate and ribosomes disperse by late-prophase I and then the plastids and mitochondria re-differentiate and ribosomes are regenerated during later stages of meiosis, a phenomenon of considerable interest in relation to the alternation of sporophyte and gametophyte generations and the maintenance of a competent cytoplasm through successive generations.

Meiosis takes much longer than mitosis (Tables 2.2 and 2.4); indeed the visible stages of meiosis from leptotene to telophase II take at least twice as long, and in some plants with large nuclei as much as ten times as long, as the whole mitotic cycle including interphase. This is largely due to a very long prophase I which can occupy over 80% of the time in division (Table 2.3).

There is considerable variation in the duration of meiosis from species to species (Table 2.4). As for mitosis (Section 2.3.1), there is a positive correlation between the length of meiosis and the diploid nuclear DNA content and the rate of division is affected by temperature, increasing up to about 30°C in most cases. In *Endymion nonscriptus*, the visible stages take 864 hours at 0°C, 168 hours at 10°C, 48 hours at 20°C and 20 hours at 30°C. However, for a given temperature and DNA content, meiosis takes longer in animals than in plants and also longer in diploids than in polyploids. Frequently, meiosis in a polyploid is shorter even than in its diploid ancestor, despite the difference in DNA content. Among plants, the shortest meiotic cycles occur in ephemerals and perennials with a short growing season.

Man, who has about half the DNA value of *Locusta*, has a meiotic duration in the male of about 3 weeks. In the female, the developing egg cell is held in an early phase of the first division, at about the stage that chiasmata are formed, from birth until it is released some 12 to 45 years later. A similar developmental pause occurs in *Dactylorhiza* where embryo

Table 2.3   Duration of the visible stages of meiosis (hours).

Stage	PMC				EMC
Plant	2x Tradescantia paludosa	6x Triticum aestivum 'Chinese Spring' 20°C	4x Secale cereale 20°C	2x Secale cereale* 20°C	2x Secale cereale* 20°C
Prophase I	113	17	30	41	33
leptotene	48	10	13	20	12
zygotene	24	4	9	11	9
pachytene	24	2	6	8	9
diplotene	} 17	} 1	} 2	1	2
diakinesis				$\frac{1}{2}$	$\frac{1}{2}$
Metaphase I				2	$1\frac{1}{2}$
Anaphase I				1	$\frac{1}{2}$
Telophase I				1	$\frac{1}{2}$
Interphase, Prophase II	} 13	} 7	} 8	$2\frac{1}{2}$	2
Metaphase II				$1\frac{1}{2}$	1
Anaphase II				1	$\frac{1}{2}$
Telophase II				1	$\frac{1}{2}$
Total	126	24	38	51	$39\frac{1}{2}$

(*Mitotic cell cycle in root tips lasts 13 hours.)

Table 2.4   The total duration of the visible stages of meiosis in some plants and animals.

	Relative DNA content (Haplopappus = 1 = 5.5 pg/G_1 cell)		Duration of visible stages of meiosis in PMC or SMC (days)
Drosophila melanogaster (fruit fly)	0.015		4
Haplopappus gracilis		1	1.5
Locusta migratoria (locust)	2.4		8
Secale cereale		5.2	2.1
Allium cepa		9.9	
Tulbaghia violacea		10.6	4.0
Tradescantia paludosa			5.4
Triturus viridescens (newt)	8.1		12
Lilium longiflorum		19.3	8.0
Trillium erectum		21.8	11.4

sac mother cells are held at an early stage of meiosis until pollination has taken place.

Despite some minor variations in regular meiosis, there is a sequence of major events common to most organisms. The following description of meiosis is a generalized one but particular features visible in lily pollen mother cells (Fig. 2.18), and grasshopper sperm mother cells (Fig. 2.14) are included where relevant. This meiotic material is readily obtainable in quantity, the chromosomes are large and their structure is unusually clear during the unique events of prophase. It would be helpful for those studying meiosis for the first time to see a film of living cells or animated diagrams (see Appendix 3) and the preparation of wire models (see p. 67) is valuable for improving or confirming an understanding of chiasma formation.

2.5.1 Meiosis

1 (*Premeiotic interphase*) In many cases, cells enter meiosis with a degree of synchrony. This has frequently developed over one or more preceding mitotic cycles so that synchronous pre-meiotic mitoses may also be seen. Nuclei entering meiotic prophase are usually considerably larger than other meristematic nuclei, and, in the case of oocytes and embryo sac mother cells, the cells are also unusually large. Most of the nuclear DNA is replicated at the end of premeiotic interphase, shortly before division begins. The S phase is longer than at mitosis. The long G_2 period between DNA synthesis and the onset of prophase typical of most mitoses is absent from the meiotic cycle (Table 2.2).

In plants, the meiotic synchrony may extend throughout an anther and even to other anthers of the same bud. In plants with many anthers, such as paeony, there may be a range of stages from the oldest, outer anthers to the youngest inner ones. At the onset of meiosis the pollen mother cells are still attached to each other to form a compact tissue. In grasshopper testes, the synchrony only extends within one lobule of a follicle. Lobules are successively older down the follicle and many preparations will show all stages from pre-meiotic mitoses to mature sperm. The sperm mother cell nuclei show a dense, heteropycnotic chromocentre which corresponds to a contracted and folded single X chromosome (Section 2.2.2).

2a (*Leptotene*) Extended chromosomes then become visible within the nuclear envelope. They appear to be single both under the light and electron microscope, and are longer and thinner and have clearer chromomeres (Section 2.2.3c) than at mitosis. Only short segments of each chromosome can be distinguished at this stage in the congested nucleus, and some areas still appear as dense masses. The nucleus and nucleolus increase in size as the chromosomes thicken and shorten. In some organisms the chromo-somes take up a polarized arrangement within the nucleus at this stage, probably in conjunction with the onset of pairing.

In some varieties of lily and other species, there is a short phase of partial contraction and relaxation immediately before meiosis begins. Later, as the single chromosomes become clearer, the chromosomes group in a tight compact ball to one side of the nucleus. Some grasshoppers, like many other animals and some plants (e.g. rye), show a *bouquet* stage where the ends of all the chromosomes appear to attach to the nuclear membrane within a restricted area on the circumference, producing a series of loops extending into the nucleus. The electron microscope has confirmed in a range of plants and animals that the ends of chromosomes, like the centromeres, can attach to the nuclear envelope and sometimes, again like the centromeres, they are aggregated at one place. The close association, or even physical linking, of centromeres or telomeres may be an important preliminary step in chromosome pairing. In *Locusta* the centriole lies just outside the nuclear envelope at the point where the chromosomes attach. The single X chromosome is still recognizable as a compact dark mass (Fig. 2.14a).

2b (*Zygotene*) It is at this stage that evidence of *synapsis* (pairing) is first seen. Pairing is not usually instantaneous and may start at one or more 'contact points' before running along the chromosome with a 'zip' like action. These contact points may be near the end of the chromosome arms (as in e.g. *Allium fistulosum*) or near the centromeres (*Campanula* and male newt) or at both points (*Trillium*) or perhaps neither. The initial contact, by an unknown mechanism, is between equivalent segments of *homologous* chromosomes (chromosomes of common evolutionary origin and similar information content) and must involve movements across several micrometres. Presumably it is during this movement that the interlocking of bivalents is normally prevented. The regular

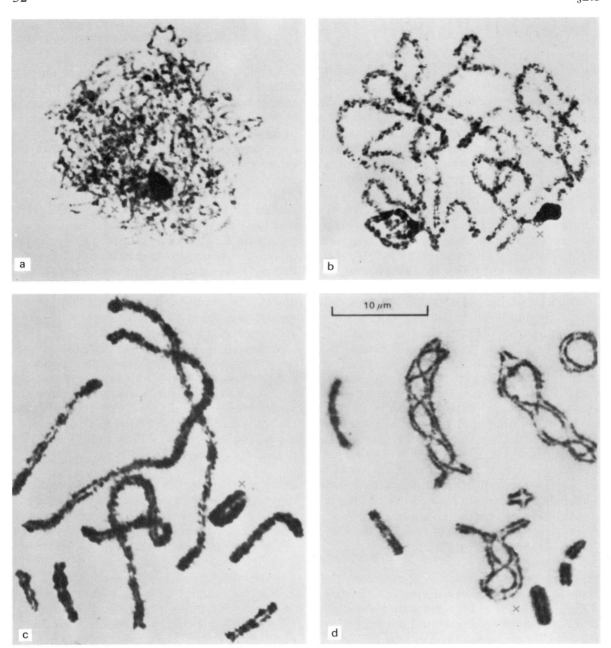

Fig. 2.14 Meiosis in male *Chorthippus brunneus* (grasshopper). (Copied with permission from 'The Meiotic Mechanism' by John, B. and Lewis, K. R., Oxford University Press, 1973.) Preparation stained with lacto-propionic orcein. **a**, Prophase 1, leptotene: all the chromosomes except the single condensed X-chromosome are long, fine, apparently single, threads. **b**, Prophase 1, zygotene: chromomeres are visible along the paired homologous autosomes. The X-chromosome is still condensed. Chromosome ends are congregated in one part of the nucleus (at bottom of photograph) to produce the 'bouquet' arrangement. **c**, Prophase 1, pachytene: paired homologues have condensed further to become shorter and thicker and individual bivalents can be recognized but each appears to be comprised of only two closely associated strands. The unpaired X-chromosome is still relatively

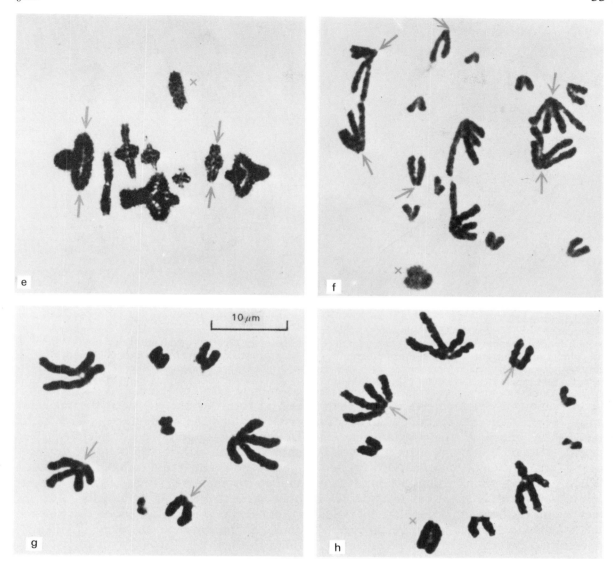

over-condensed. **d**, Prophase 1, diplotene: within each bivalent, four chromatids are visible. The chromosomes have separated except at points where chiasmata have been formed by one chromatid from each homologue. **e**, Metaphase 1: the bivalents have congressed and co-orientated with centromeres at opposite sides of the equator of the spindle. Spindle poles are at top and bottom of photograph. Arrows indicate centromere positions in one bivalent with sub-median centromeres and one with terminal centromeres. The univalent X-chromosome lies off the equator. **f**, Anaphase 1: homologous chromosomes or half-bivalents are separating to opposite spindle poles at top and bottom of photograph. Homologous chromatids are widely separated except at the undivided centromeres. Arrows indicate centromere positions in the homologues of two pairs of chromosomes with submedian centromeres (each showing four chromatid arms) and of one pair with terminal centromeres (each showing two chromatid arms). The single X-chromosome is moving towards the nearest spindle pole and is slightly less condensed than the autosomes. **g** and **h**: polar views of the two products of meiosis I as seen in metaphase II. **g**, contains only autosomes while the sister nucleus in **h** contains also the X-chromosome. Homologous chromatids are widely separated but centromeres (arrowed) are still undivided and the chromosomes, including the X-chromosome, are auto-orientated on the spindle equator. **i** and **j**: side views of the two products of meiosis I as

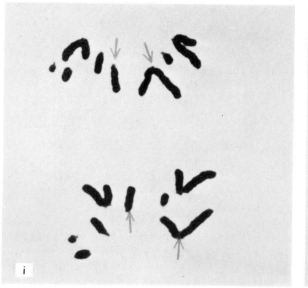 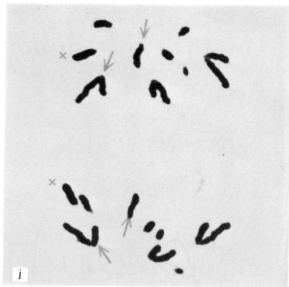

Fig. 2.14 (cont.)
seen at anaphase II. **i**, contains only autosomes while **j** also contains the X-chromosome. All the centromeres having divided, homologous chromatids or daughter chromosomes are separating as in mitosis to opposite poles of the spindle, at the top and bottom of the photographs. Arrows indicate centromere positions in one pair of chromatids with sub-median centromeres (each showing two chromatid arms) and one pair of chromatids with terminal centromeres (each showing 1 chromatid arm).

juxtaposition of chromomeres of like shape and size seen at the contact points can later be seen along most of the chromosome as pairing proceeds, although it frequently fails near a large nucleolus or similar obstruction. When pairing is finished, homologous centromeres are adjacent, as are the telomeres, and the homologues are loosely coiled relationally around each other. Pairing can be interrupted by, for example, temperature shock and frequently seems to have a natural time limit which halts pairing while it is still incomplete even in a homozygous diploid.

In the lily, as the paired segments of chromosomes extend as loops from the compact polarized mass, the association between homologues does not appear to be very intimate. Only chromomeres appear to touch, and the inter-chromomere threads are several hundred nanometres apart. It is difficult to understand from this evidence how individual DNA helices can be intimately associated. The loops continue to extend into the nucleus until the bivalents evenly occupy the whole nucleus once more. In the grasshopper, the completely paired chromosomes, still in the bouquet arrangement, show the same proximity between similar chromomeres (Fig. 2.14b). The bouquet arrangement is gradually lost as chromosome contraction proceeds, but the dense X chromosome univalent is still distinguishable.

2c (*Pachytene*) The paired chromosomes continue to shorten and thicken as coiling proceeds, and simultaneously the chromomeres become fewer, larger and more conspicuous. Chromomere mapping is usually done at this stage in, for example, rye, maize and tomato. There may be several thousand chromomeres in each haploid complement. The individual homologues become less easy to distinguish during this stage and it is impossible to see the two important events which take place at this time. The two chromosomes of each bivalent replicate, each forming two chromatids. At the same time or shortly afterwards, pairs of non-sister chromatids normally form chiasmata.

Another feature of this stage which is implicated in chiasma formation but is also not visible under the light microscope, is the *synaptonemal complex*. This is regularly found in electron micrographs of sections of higher organisms and even diatoms and fungi which include recently paired chromosomes, and appears as a tripartite structure up to 0.2μm wide running the length of the interface between the paired chromosomes. It usually has a slow helical twist along its length. On the pairing face of each chromosome, which appears as a dark granular or fibrillar mass of irregular width, is a lateral *axial element* showing dense transverse striations. These elements first appear at several points along the unpaired chromosomes early in meiosis, and when homologous elements pair alongside each other at a constant distance apart of about 0.10 μm, a third component develops between them. This component has a median, dense *central element* about 0.04 μm wide and a surrounding *central space* across which extend lateral microfibrils or 'bridges'. These bridges run out from the axial elements and meet in the centre to form the central element, which varies in detailed appearance with the species.

The synaptonemal complex seems to be necessary for, but not a guarantee of, chiasma formation, and therefore usually accompanies chromosome pairing. As might be expected, the achiasmate male *Drosophila* has no synaptonemal complex, but complexes are found in some achiasmate cells and, surprisingly, detached complexes are found in some post-meiotic and nurse cells in insects.

It has been suggested that the transverse bridges and the central element provide the intimate molecular contact which is thought to be involved in pairing and chiasma formation. It has been shown that a small

amount of DNA synthesis (c.2% of total and with a characteristically high $G+C:A+T$ base ratio) occurs when the chromosomes are pairing and the central element is being formed and an even smaller further amount is synthesized at about the time that chromatids are organized and chiasmata form. The earlier synthesis, in lily, replicates small segments of unique sequences of about 10 000 base pairs. The later synthesis is a repair replication associated with the appearance of single-strand breaks in the DNA. This suggests that the central element and transverse bridges contain nucleoprotein and that their formation involves a minute amount of DNA synthesis. However, enzyme studies on whole mounts indicate that the central component is composed of protein alone and there is no evidence that it contains any DNA. Other experiments indicate that the central element protein is assembled in the nucleolus and is common to all bivalents. The transverse bridges could thus be a non-specific pairing protein which pulls the chromosomes together into approximate alignment. This leaves open the question of the 'crossing over' of nucleoprotein to form chiasmata. At the molecular level breakage and rejoining of closely associated DNA molecules are presumably involved perhaps by a process related to DNA repair. It is possible that the synaptonemal complex is an independent structure with which chromosome DNA fibrils become intimately involved after pairing.

It is interesting to note that in at least some organisms the central component begins to develop at the inner layer of the nuclear envelope when the corresponding ends of two homologous chromosomes are attached to the envelope close together and the axial elements are therefore more or less aligned. The pairing mechanism thus seems to involve the sliding together on the nuclear envelope of the chromosome ends. When all chromosome ends move towards the same point on the envelope, not just the two members of one pair, the polarized alignment of the bouquet stage results. In other cells, the two ends of a bivalent may be attached to different, even opposite, areas of the nuclear membrane.

In the lily at this stage the chromosomes become increasingly and uniformly condensed and evenly distributed within the nucleus (Fig. 2.4). Occasional unpaired segments can be distinguished. The 2–3000 chromomeres initially visible become indistinguishable as the bivalents contract. At about this stage, pollen mother cells separate from each other in the anther and begin to develop a thick wall. In those grasshoppers with a bouquet stage, the polarized arrangement is lost as the bivalents contract. The X univalent, previously folded, straightens out and, though still relatively over-condensed, can be clearly seen to be double (Fig. 2.14c). The other bivalents are beginning to develop a 'fuzzy' or 'hairy' outline (Section 2.2.2). The ends of chromosome arms are often precociously contracted.

2d (*Diplotene*) By the time the bivalents have contracted to about a quarter of their length when first recognizable, they typically no longer show relational coils of one chromosome around the other, the *lampbrush* condition is more developed and the homologues are beginning to separate from one another, starting near the centromere. At this stage, the synaptonemal complexes are freed from the chromosomes and disperse, or in some cases aggregate in stacks. As the chromosomes separate, each is seen to consist of two chromatids. As meiosis proceeds, the chromosomes become separated throughout their length apart from one or more points where they are brought so close together that they cannot be distinguished. In clear preparations it can be seen that at these points one chromatid of each chromosome crosses over from one side of the bivalent to the other to form a chiasma. These chiasmata are the basis of the genetic exchange in heterozygous genotypes which results in recombination of alleles at different loci on homologous chromosomes. At the level of the

whole chromatid, chiasma formation is relatively straightforward (Fig. 2.15). Examination of the results of chiasma formation in asymmetrical bivalents, where the two chromosomes differ visibly in morphology, shows that breakage of a chromatid from each chromosome at corresponding positions is followed by reunion of broken ends from non-sister chromatids. When a chiasma is first recognized, sister segments of all chromatids are still closely associated, so the reformed chromatids produced by the chiasma run from one side of the bivalent to the other. It is of course not possible to demonstrate the exchange of chromatid material in symmetrical bivalents under the light microscope, nor is it easy to reconcile breakage and rejoining of the relatively massive chromatids with the molecular events which must underlie it.

Later, the chiasmata may move towards the end of the chromosome arm. This is known as *terminalization*, and is a mechanical process whereby the chiasma, but of course not the point of genetic exchange, moves away from the centromere. Although the mechanism is unknown, the separation of homologues seems to be more active in the centromere region and this may be involved in chiasma terminalization. Terminalization must involve relaxation on the side of the chiasma away from the centromere of the unexplained attraction which keeps sister chromatids closely associated while homologous chromosomes are widely separated. At the same time, an apparently similar association, but between segments of non-sister chromatids, must be reconstituted behind the moving chiasma. Whatever the mechanism, in many species no terminalization occurs at all before it is rapidly completed during anaphase separation of chromosomes.

Except in the rare examples of achiasmate meiosis, failure to form a chiasma after pairing will allow the homologues to separate (*desynapsis*) later when the attraction between them lapses and the consequent univalents are likely to show irregular disjunction at

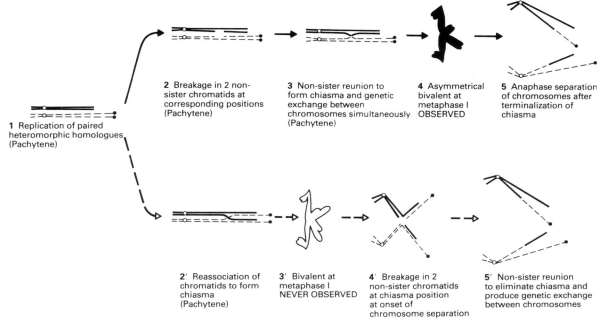

1 Replication of paired heteromorphic homologues (Pachytene)

2 Breakage in 2 non-sister chromatids at corresponding positions (Pachytene)

3 Non-sister reunion to form chiasma and genetic exchange between chromosomes simultaneously (Pachytene)

4 Asymmetrical bivalent at metaphase I OBSERVED

5 Anaphase separation of chromosomes after terminalization of chiasma

2′ Reassociation of chromatids to form chiasma (Pachytene)

3′ Bivalent at metaphase I NEVER OBSERVED

4′ Breakage in 2 non-sister chromatids at chiasma position at onset of chromosome separation

5′ Non-sister reunion to eliminate chiasma and produce genetic exchange between chromosomes

Fig. 2.15 Chiasma formation at the chromatid level. Examination of metaphase I bivalents formed by heteromorphic pairs of homologous chromosomes confirms that chiasmata form as shown in the sequence 1, 2, 3, 4, 5, above. An alternative model for chiasma formation, shown in the sequence 1, 2′, 3′, 4′, 5′, has been shown to be incorrect. Metaphase bivalents of the type shown in 3′ have not been observed.

| Bivalent | **Chiasma frequency per bivalent** | | | | | | | |
	1	2	3	4	5	6	7	8
A			20 μm					
B								
C								
D								
E								

Fig. 2.16 Variation in chiasma frequency and position within and between the five bivalents (A to E) of pollen mother cells of the same flower of *Trillium grandiflorum* ($2x = 10$). In each cell, the five bivalents are distinguishable by their size and morphology, shown diagrammatically in the left-hand column as revealed at root tip mitosis. The mean chiasma frequency for each bivalent (A, 6.8; B, 4.3; C, 4.7; D, 3.7; E, 3.8) is proportional to chromosome length.

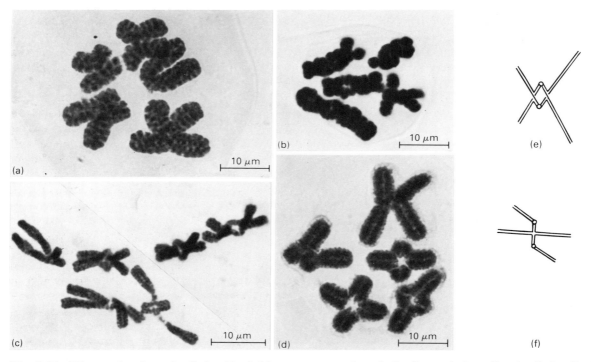

Fig. 2.17 Dispersed and proximally localized chiasmata at metaphase I of pollen meiosis. **a**, Proximally localized chiasmata in *Trillium kamtschaticum* ($n = 5$). **b**, Dispersed chiasmata in *Trillium cernuum* ($n = 5$). **c**, Proximally localized chiasmata in *Tulbaghia violacea* ($n = 6$). **d**, Induced localization of chiasmata in *Trillium grandiflorum* ($n = 5$). Normally dispersed as in *T. cernuum*, they have been restricted to regions close to the centromere following heat shock during prophase. **e**, Diagram of metaphase bivalent with two proximal chiasmata. **f**, Diagram of metaphase bivalent with one proximal chiasma. For distally localized chiasmata see Fig. 3.1b and Fig. 4.1a,e.

anaphase (Fig. 3.3). Thus, for mechanical reasons, even the smallest bivalents must have at least one chiasma for regular meiosis. While only one chiasma is necessary to hold a bivalent together, larger bivalents in many species have several chiasmata, up to nine in the largest bivalent of *Trillium grandiflorum*. In these there is considerable variation in the position and number of chiasmata in the corresponding bivalent of different cells within the same and different individuals (Fig. 2.16). As a result no two meiocytes have exactly the same chiasma distribution. Any two non-sister chromatids can be involved in each chiasma, so that where there are two or more chiasmata in a bivalent the chromatids in adjacent chiasmata may be the same (2-strand double) or one (3-strand) or both (4-strand) may be different. In some organisms,

3-strand doubles appear to occur more frequently than expected on a random basis. The effect on recombination of the additional chiasmata is perhaps misleading. Maximum recombination between two loci at opposite ends of an arm which always has only one chiasma is 50%. To achieve the same level of recombination in an arm which sometimes has no chiasmata and sometimes several, the average chiasma frequency must exceed three.

The distribution of chiasmata in many organisms is apparently random, although it is not known if crossing over is restricted to certain segments at the macromolecular level, and there is evidence of chiasma interference in some organisms where the presence of one chiasma influences the likelihood of another chiasma in the same or a different segment or even another chromosome. In other organisms, the chiasmata are clearly restricted to certain regions of each chromosome arm. Chiasmata may be localized in the proximal region (close to the centromere) of each arm, or the distal region, or both (Fig. 2.17). Localization sometimes reflects the pairing or chiasma initiation points and may result when the time available for pairing is curtailed. For example, high temperature interruption of pairing induces localization. However, chiasmata do not always form in every paired segment and natural localization can follow complete pairing. Localization of chiasmata does not merely reduce the amount of crossing over, but eliminates recombination entirely from large areas of the genome, which are then always inherited as intact linkage groups. Before concluding that these linkage groups occur within a species it is necessary to confirm that 'male' and 'female' meioses are similar. Chiasma distribution may differ between the sexes so that the overall effect of the localization is a general reduction in crossing over, rather than the creation of large permanent linkage groups. Occasionally, groups of cells with noticeably different chiasma distribution occur within one individual.

In the lily there are twelve bivalents, 10 acrocentric and 2 larger ones with submedian centromeres. The bivalents usually form two to five chiasmata with one to three per arm apparently dispersed at random (Fig. 2.18a). There is sometimes a chiasma in the short arm of the acrocentrics. Occasionally, clear chiasmata can be seen where all four chromatids are distinguishable. No detectable chiasma terminalization occurs at this stage. In the males of many grasshopper species there are 8 bivalents and the unpaired X chromosome, now clearly showing two chromatids and an almost terminal centromere though still relatively over-contracted (Fig. 2.14d). The three longest bivalents, L1, L2 and L3, have sub-median centromeres and one to three chiasmata in each arm distributed randomly. The four medium sized bivalents, M4, M5, M6 and M7 and the short bivalent S8 have almost terminal centromeres and usually one interstitial chiasma in the long arm. These smaller bivalents form a cross-shaped configuration, merely by rearrangement of chromatids at the single chiasma as centromeres separate as far as the chiasma will allow. Bivalent M6 is usually more contracted than the rest and is similar in appearance to the X univalent (Section 2.2.2b). In the locusts, *Locusta* and *Schistocerca*, there are 11 bivalents in addition to the

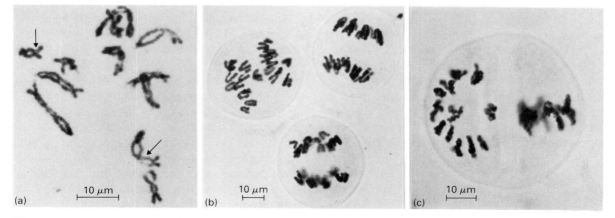

(a) 10 μm (b) 10 μm (c) 10 μm

Fig. 2.18 Meiosis in *Lilium auratum* ($2n = 2x = 24$). **a**, Diplotene. At this stage the twelve bivalents have a lampbrush appearance. The two chromatids of each chromosome are visible in places (arrow). **b**, Anaphase I. A haploid set of twelve chromosomes is moving to each pole. **c**, Metaphase II. Twelve chromosomes at the equator of each of two spindles orientated at right angles to each other and to the first division spindle.

X chromosome, all apparently telocentric. In grasshoppers and locusts, chiasmata begin to terminalize at this stage.

2e (*Diakinesis*) The bivalents then move to the periphery of the nucleus and lie, well separated, on the inside of the nuclear membrane. As the chromosomes further contract and become more rigid, adjacent loops between chiasmata on the same bivalent come to lie at right angles to each other, instead of in the same plane as previously. Nucleoli are still visible, attached to the bivalents with nucleolar organizers, but in most species they become smaller and eventually disappear at the time the nuclear envelope disintegrates.

In the lily, the major coil has almost reached its maximum at this stage, and in the very contracted bivalents the loops between chiasmata are closed, and the position of a chiasma is shown by the constriction in the outline of the bivalent. In grasshoppers, individual chromatids are less clear, but contraction is not yet at a maximum and the open loops between chiasmata are still visible. By the time the nuclear membrane breaks down, all bivalents and the X univalent are equally contracted.

3 (*Prometaphase I*) As the nuclear membrane disintegrates, a spindle forms which is of similar structure to the mitotic spindle, but there is an important difference in the way the centromeres attach. In regular diploid meiosis, the bivalent is the structural unit and each centromere attaches to one pole by means of microtubules. As the two chromosomes of a bivalent are held together by attraction of chromatids distal to the chiasmata, the attachment of the two centromeres to opposite poles brings the whole bivalent to an equilibrium position on the spindle with the chiasmata on the 'equator' and the centromeres equidistant on opposite sides. Attachment of both centromeres of a bivalent may be initially to the same pole, but this is usually soon corrected. The orientation of one bivalent is in no way affected by that of its neighbouring bivalents. There is almost always a random assortment of maternal and paternal centromeres on each side of the equator, which in heterozygous genotypes accounts for the recombination of alleles at different loci on non-homologous chromosomes. The frequency with which all paternal centromeres come to lie on the same side of the equator, and all maternal ones on the other, will thus be 1 in 2^{n-1} where $n =$ the number of bivalents. For *Trillium erectum* ($2n = 2x = 10$), the frequency will be 1 in 16. As in mitosis, movement to the equator is known as *congression* and a bivalent with localized centromeres shows *co-orientation* as a result of the *syntelic* attachment of each of the two centromeres to opposite poles.

In the lily, at this stage all the bivalents group closely together for a short period as the spindle forms, before separating out across the equator of the spindle as the centromeres become attached to the poles by spindle fibres. In grasshoppers and locusts, centromeres can be recognized as small constrictions. Some chiasmata now appear as end-to-end associations due to terminalization. The X univalent may be slightly less contracted than the bivalents.

4 (*Metaphase I*) A period follows when the bivalents are aligned on the spindle equator, the nuclear envelope and usually the nucleolus have gone, and coiling is at a maximum and often clearly visible. The major coil in the two chromatids of each chromosome is paranemic so chromatids can later separate without complications. The centromeres are now drawn towards the nearest pole causing elongation of the centromeric loop and even conspicuous stretching of the chromosome arms between the centromere and the nearest chiasmata. It is the sister chromatid attraction distal to interstitial chiasmata (Fig. 2.17e,f), or the end-to-end attachment at fully terminalized chiasmata (Fig. 3.1b), which prevents the separation of homologues. It is not know how sister chromatids are held together, but it has been suggested that the end-to-end association of terminalized chiasmata represents as yet unreplicated telomeres.

This is the stage frequently studied in investigations of meiosis because earlier stages may for a variety of reasons be difficult to study and because chiasma distribution and bivalent co-orientation can be simultaneously studied and thus anaphase disjunction to some extent predicted. A disadvantage of this stage is that chiasmata may be difficult to distinguish when there are several in a very contracted bivalent. It is also necessary to determine whether terminalization has already occurred before making conclusions about the distribution of the genetical exchanges. The presence of any terminal end-to-end associations shows that some terminalization must have occurred. The position and number of chiasmata is as important as centromere position and chromosome length in determining bivalent morphology which therefore varies considerably within as well as between species (Fig. 2.16). In *Tradescantia* species the chiasmata are formed distally and frequently fully terminalize (Figs. 3.1b and 4.1a,e). Consequently, bivalents with one chiasma are rod-like with the chromosomes straight and end-to-end. Bivalents with a terminalized chiasma in each of the more or less equal arms therefore form an open ring with chiasmata on the equator and centromeres on either side. Where a bivalent forms a single proximal chiasma, as in *Trillium kamtschaticum*, a cross-shaped configuration is formed (Fig. 2.17a,c,d,f). If a single chiasma is proximal or median in each arm, the distal portions of the arms lie free, usually separated at an angle to each other, often either side of the equator (Fig. 2.17a,c,e). When there are two or more chiasmata in an arm, as in *Trillium grandiflorum*, the parts of the bivalent proximal and distal to all the chiasmata behave in the same way as corresponding regions in arms with a single chiasma, with centromeres separated as far as the

nearest chiasma will allow (Figs. 2.16 and 2.17b). In the interstitial regions between chiasmata, loops occur alternately at right angles to each other and the bivalent arm lies along the spindle equatorial plane. Each arm behaves independently and a chromosome could have, for example, a median and a proximal chiasma and a very stretched proximal segment in one arm and one distal chiasma with a large unstretched region next to the centromere in the other arm.

In the lily, the loops between chiasmata are often small, but the centromeres are usually extended towards the poles and clearly visible. A few chiasmata may be terminalized. The major coil is not clear. In the grasshopper, most chiasmata are median, distal or terminal due to terminalization and the mean chiasma frequency may be lower than at earlier stages for the same reason. The X univalent is noticeably under-contracted, and unable to co-orientate on the spindle equator. After oscillating from one side to the other, it eventually lies between the equator and one pole (Fig. 2.14e).

5 (*Anaphase I*) A sudden lapse of attraction of chromatids distal to chiasmata, or separation of chromosome ends when the chiasmata have fully terminalized, allows whole chromosomes to separate and be drawn by their undivided centromeres towards the nearest spindle pole. The lapse of chromatid attraction which accompanies the separation of homologues is revealed by the widely separated chromatid arms as the chromosomes move on the spindle (Figs. 2.14f, 2.18b and 4.16b,f). Chromosomes at this stage have four distinct arms if the centromere is median or submedian, or two distinct arms in telocentric and acrocentric chromosomes (Fig. 1.4). Disjunction is a synchronous event throughout the cell as in mitosis, and results in two groups of chromosomes at opposite spindle poles. Each group has one chromosome from each bivalent, and has therefore half the zygotic chromosome number but, as all the chromosomes are replicated, the DNA content is the same as at mitotic anaphase in the sporophyte. The two chromatids of each chromosome look similar but are not genetically identical as a result of exchanges at chiasma formation with one or both of the chromatids of the homologue, now at the other pole. The centromeres and proximal segments at each pole will usually be a random mixture of those inherited from the male parent and those from the female, as a result of random assortment of centromeres on the equator. In, for example, *Drosophila melanogaster* ($n = 4$) there can be 16 different combinations of material and paternal centromeres and for man ($n = 23$) over 8×10^6 combinations are possible.

In the lily, the major coil, which is not clear at earlier stages, can be seen in each arm of the separating chromosomes (Fig. 2.18b). In grasshoppers, the X chromosome passes undivided to one pole so that the two daughter nuclei differ in their chromosome complement (Fig. 2.14f). As the chromosomes approach the pole, the X univalent becomes more contracted.

6 (*Telophase I, Interphase, Prophase II*) Events between the completion of chromosome separation and the onset of the second division of meiosis differ between species, but in no case is there a replication of DNA between divisions, which makes this period almost unique among division cycles. In some, such as *Trillium* species and *Odonata* (dragonflies), the chromosomes enter the second division almost immediately with little change in coiling; in *Trillium*, the major coil remains, and does not give rise to a relic coil until pollen grain mitosis. In other cases the nuclei enter a brief interphase, with a reconstituted nuclear envelope reformed round the group of chromosomes, but no cytokinesis occurs. This is found in, for example, lily embryo sac mother cells and pollen mother cells of many dicotyledons including *Nicotiana*. The last alternative, characteristic of pollen of lily and *Tradescantia* and many other monocotyledons and

sperm mother cells of orthopterans, is that cytokinesis or cleavage occurs after the first meiotic division to produce two distinct cells, called *dyads*, each with a single interphase nucleus. Where such an interphase occurs, the chromosomes enter the second division like mitotic chromosomes except that the arms are widely separated, not relationally coiled, and each arm shows a loose relic coil. The relic coil is what is left of the major coil of first division following a short interphase. The standard coil of second division probably develops from the minor coil of the first division (Section 2.2.2).

In the lily, a clear wall forms between the interphase nuclei within the PMC, forming two dyad cells, but in the EMC no wall forms between the nuclei. Cleavage occurs in grasshopper sperm mother cells and one daughter nucleus has a dense chromocentre, the overcontracted X chromosome, which is still overcontracted as second division begins.

7 (*Metaphase II*) Following distintegration of the nuclear envelope, and contraction of the chromosomes if interphase nuclei reformed between divisions, each daughter group from meiosis I forms up on a separate spindle, often in a distinct dyad cell. The chromosomes behave in the same way mechanically as mitotic chromosomes, with autoorientation of amphitelic centromeres. The orientation of one chromosome in relation to another is indistinguishable under the microscope, but has genetic significance because the two chromatids of each chromosome are different as a result of earlier chiasmata, and the final genotypes of the four meiotic products depends as much on the independent orientation of 'half-bivalents' at second division as on the arrangement of bivalents at first division.

The orientation of second division spindles varies. In some, particularly embryo sacs and fungal asci, the tetrad is linear, with all 3 spindles parallel to each other and in line. Pollen tetrads are usually tetrahedral, isobilateral (where the second divisions spindles are parallel to each other but perpendicular to the first division spindle), or decussate (where second divisions are perpendicular to each other and to the first division).

In the dyad cells of the lily, the two spindles are perpendicular to the first division spindle and frequently perpendicular to each other (Fig. 2.18c). Twelve chromosomes can be seen on each equator, of which two each have four widely spaced long arms and ten have only two conspicuous arms. Polar views show that the chromosomes are spaced out with most of the centromeres arranged round the periphery of the spindle. The relic coil and the separated chromatids makes this metaphase 'untidy' and unsuitable for karyotype studies. In grasshoppers, the relic coil is not obvious, and the second division complements are clearly seen in polar view of squashed cells. One cell has an extra medium-sized acrocentric chromosome, the X chromosome, in addition to the gametic set of autosomes (Fig. 2.14g,h).

8 (*Anaphase II*) The centromeres of the aligned chromosomes then divide to allow the daughter chromosomes to separate to opposite ends of the spindle. The centromeres have remained undivided throughout the first division. Centromere division, as in mitosis, is synchronous within a cell, but two sister dyad cells may be a few hours out of phase. In grasshoppers, the X chromosome divides along with the others so that two of the four meiotic products contain an X chromosome and thus an interphase chromocentre (Fig. 2.14i,j).

9 (*Telophase II, Tetrads*) The four groups of daughter chromosomes, now both haploid in number and unreplicated, are then enclosed by nuclear envelopes, nucleoli reform and chromosomes enter the dispersed interphase condition. Meiosis achieves the segregation of allelic differences and the four nuclei produced by meiosis are inevitably genetically different from each other and from the

parent genotype if the parent is heterozygous for more than a few loci. A single chiasma in a bivalent heterozygous for two unlinked genes is enough to produce four genetically different meiotic products, and few plants or animals have less than four bivalents and many have several chiasmata per bivalent.

As meiosis is completed, the nuclei are separated by cell membranes and, in plants, cell walls. In those pollen mother cells where cytokinesis does not occur after meiosis I, cell walls are laid down, usually from the periphery inwards, simultaneously between all four nuclei. When separate cells are formed after first division, cytokinesis occurs independently in each dyad cell usually by centrifugal growth of a cell plate. The products of meiotic division in all plants, except a few relatively complex algae such as *Codium*, are spores of one sort or another. In *Codium*, and nearly all animals, the meiotic products develop directly into gametes, either eggs or sperm, and there is no mitosis in the haploid generation. After 'female' meiosis of most higher plants, and of animals where the very unequal divisions produce small polar bodies, only one of the four cells from a single meiocyte normally develops further. After 'male' meiosis of most higher plants and animals, all four cells produce sperm or gametophytes but only after separating. In most lower plants too, all meiotic spores are capable of development after separation. There are consequently few organisms in which the products of one meiocyte can be identified and their chromosome complements examined. This is however possible after bisporic or tetrasporic embryo sac development (Fig. 2.8a) when all the products of one or both second meiotic divisions remain unseparated by cytokinesis and can later be observed in mitosis within the same developing embryo sac or endosperm (Section 2.4.4, p. 44). In *Trillium*, where H-segments (Section 2.2.3d) provide morphological markers on the chromosomes, the reciprocal products of one second meiotic division can be analysed in endosperms

(a)

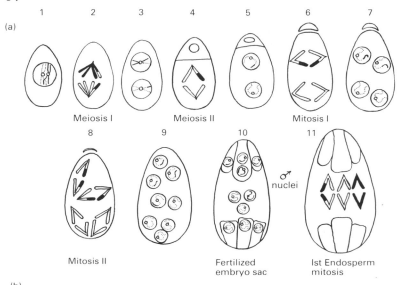

1   2   3   4   5   6   7

Meiosis I   Meiosis II   Mitosis I

8   9   10   11

♂ nuclei

Mitosis II   Fertilized embryo sac   Ist Endosperm mitosis

(b)

Number of proximal chiasmata at ♀ meiosis	None	One:		Two:
		in long arm	in short arm	one in each arm
Morphology of bivalent B	(diagram)	(diagram)	(diagram)	(diagram)
Complement of endosperm with respect to chromosome B after controlled cross:	(diagram) or (diagram)	* (diagram) or * (diagram)	* (diagram) or * (diagram)	* * (diagram) or (diagram)

♀ (diagram) × ♂ (diagram)

* New H-patterns

Fig. 2.19   The inheritance of H-segments in *Trillium*. **a**, Diagrammatic summary of bisporic embryo sac development demonstrating how the endosperm karyotype reveals the reciprocal products of one second meiotic division. **b**, The relationship between the endosperm karyotype and chiasma distribution in embryo sac mother cell meiosis after controlled crosses between a plant of *T. grandiflorum* heterozygous for two H-segments in different arms of chromosome B (see Fig. 2.16) as female parent and one homozygous for a different H-segment as male parent. Polymorphism for similar patterns is found in *T. erectum* (Fig. 2.5c). Heterozygous H-segments show first division segregation (i.e. they segregate at first meiotic division and therefore occur in both or neither of the maternal chromosomes of the endosperm complement) when there is no proximal chiasma between the segment and the centromere. The segments show second division segregation (i.e. they segregate at second meiotic division and therefore occur in one of the maternal chromosomes of the endosperm complement) when there is a single chiasma between the segment and the centromere. When a bivalent is heterozygous for two or more H-segments, second division segregation can produce new H-patterns (asterisk). It is not usually possible to compare in the same year chiasma distribution at female meiosis with the endosperm karyotype of the same plant because most individuals produce only one flower. However, the frequency of second division segregation for proximal H-segments is close to that expected from the chiasma frequency and distribution recorded at male and female meiosis of other individuals of the same species.

formed after controlled crosses and the segregation of H-segments compared to chiasma distribution (Fig. 2.19).

For ease of reference, the numbered sections in the preceding account of meiosis are related to the named arbitrary phases but, in using these terms, the continuity of the events must not be forgotten.

The events outlined include the major features of meiosis in all fertile diploids but in other organisms gene or chromosome mutations may modify the sequence. It is the discovery of mutants for meiotic irregularities including failure of pairing and chiasma formation, changed chiasma localization, co-orientation and disjunction, and persistent nucleoli which has demonstrated that these aspects of chromosome behaviour are under genetic control. At the same time, the study of meiotic behaviour in chromosome mutants forms the basis of cytogenetics, as described in the next section.

2.5.2 Materials and methods

Meiosis (Section 2.5.1) **Choice of material**

DEMONSTRATION OF MEIOTIC STAGES:
Males of *Chorthippus*, *Omocestus*, *Myrmeleotettix*, *Locusta*, *Schistocerca* and other genera of the grasshopper family Acrididae (Orthoptera) (especially for chiasmata, allocyclic X univalent and 'bouquet' arrangement).

Pollen mother cells of *Lilium* species (Fig. 2.4, 2.18) (especially for the sequence of stages and for material available in considerable quantity), *Hyacinthus*, *Endymion* and most genera of Liliaceae, *Allium* species (leave temporary preparation for 24 hours to harden before squashing to prevent rupture of fragile PMC), *Crocus balansae* (low chromosome number).

Tradescantia species are not good for the important stages of prophase I but at later stages show most features including particularly clear coiling. *T. virginiana* is one of the easiest plants in which to find meiosis.

The flowering season can be extended by cutting off the flowering shoots at the second node or by dividing the clump. By bringing plants into the greenhouse at an appropriate date and extending the day length by up to 4 hours with artificial light, meiosis can be obtained in winter or spring although pairing and chiasma formation is sometimes disturbed.

Diploid *Paeonia* species (e.g. *P. delavayi*, *P. emodi*, *P. lutea*, *P. potanii* and *P. suffruticosa*) provide a large number of anthers at various stages of meiosis in the young bud before the petals develop any colour and one bud is sufficient for a considerable number of people.

Meiosis occurs in a bud still contained within an underground bulb or corm in many spring flowering monocotyledons, and is strongly seasonal and cannot usually be forced out of season. Many monocotyledons yield good preparations of meiosis in embryo sacs as well as in pollen mother cells. Meiosis in embryo sacs may be earlier (e.g. *Hordeum vulgare*) or later (*Lilium* spp., *Trillium* spp.) than, or more or less simultaneous with (*Secale cereale*, *Triticum aestivum*) male meiosis.

CHIASMA TERMINALIZATION:
Chorthippus (grasshopper), *Locusta* (locust). Chiasma frequency and distribution is clear from early diplotene to metaphase I as frequency falls and proportion of terminal chiasmata increases.

CHIASMA FREQUENCY AND LOCALIZATION AT 'MALE' MEIOSIS:
Disperse: High frequency – American *Trillium* species (Figs. 2.16 and 2.17b) and *Lilium* species (Fig. 2.18a) with up to 9 chiasmata per bivalent. Intermediate frequency – *Allium senescens*, *A. cepa*,† *Chorthippus* (grasshopper), *Locusta* (locust). Low frequency – *Paeonia*, *Scilla* and *Endymion* species with 1–2 chiasmata per bivalent.

Proximal: *Allium fistulosum*,† *A. porrum*,

† Hybrids of *A. cepa* and *A. fistulosum* show a range of chiasma distribution.

Tulbaghia violacea (Fig. 2.17c) Japanese *Trillium* species (Fig. 2.17a).

Distal: *Tradescantia paludosa*, *Secale cereale*.*

Distal, followed by more or less complete terminalization: *Tradescantia bracteata* (Fig. 3.1b), *Tradescantia virginiana* (Fig. 4.1a,e,f), *Rhoeo discolor* (Fig. 3.10c), *Paeonia* species. *Periplaneta americana* (cockroach).

CHIASMA INTERFERENCE:
Interaction between chiasma frequencies in different arms can be demonstrated by the appropriate analysis of data from *Schistocerca* (locust), *Paeonia* or *Trillium*.

ACHIASMATE MEIOSIS:
Males of *Drosophila* (fruitfly) species and *Tipula caesius* (crane fly). Pollen mother cells of *Fritillaria japonica*, *F. amabilis* and related species.

CHIASMA FREQUENCY AND LOCALIZATION IN MALE AND FEMALE:
Chiasmata more frequent and less localized in EMC than PMC: *Lilium martagon*, *Tulbaghia violacea*, *Allium ursinum*, *Endymion non-scriptus*.

Chiasma frequency and distribution similar in EMC and PMC: *Secale cereale*, *Hordeum vulgare*.

In certain apomicts, including *Hieracium aurantiacum* and *Poa pratensis*, male meiosis can be normal while female meiosis is suppressed and in others, including *Taraxacum* and *Alchemilla vulgaris*, male meiosis is highly irregular but some bivalents are formed in the 'sub-sexual' embryo sacs.

PERSISTENT NUCLEOLI:
Grasses of the Panicoideae.

CELL WALL FORMATION:
Cell wall formation absent after first meiotic division: PMC of *Nicotiana*.

Cell wall formation absent after second meiotic division: Bisporic EMC of *Allium*, *Trillium* (Fig. 2.19a).

* Selected inbred lines of *S. cereale* differ in chiasma frequency and distribution.

Cell wall formation absent after both meiotic divisions: Tetrasporic EMC of *Lilium*.

Techniques

The techniques described below can be used with little or no modification with the appropriate material of any suitable species.

MEIOSIS IN *TRADESCANTIA* PMC:
The smear and squash techniques required are the same as for PGM (Section 2.4.4) but younger buds are selected, at the stage when the anthers begin to change from translucent off-white to yellow. In many plants, meiosis occurs when the anthers begin to develop their final colour, not necessarily yellow. *Tradescantia* pollen mother cell nuclei stain well and more rapidly than at PGM because the wall is thinner and more permeable. With practice, buds at meiosis can be selected fairly accurately on the basis of bud size, and in a regular inflorescence on the basis of position. As meiosis tends to be synchronous within a bud, not all inflorescences will include any particular required stage. It is possible to accumulate metaphase stages with colchicine or low-temperature treatment, but there is a danger that pairing and chiasma formation will also be affected. As with all meiotic preparations, little pressure is needed when squashing. If there is a tendency for PMC to burst, they should be left overnight in orcein before applying pressure.

MEIOSIS IN LILY PMC:
Lily anthers at meiosis are large and each contains enough material for several preparations, so selected anthers are useful for teaching or making sets of demonstration slides. As in *Tradescantia* and *Allium*, meiotic buds are easily accessible above ground, but in the lily they are restricted to a short summer season.

For a given variety, bud size is a very accurate indication of the meiotic stage. Thus for *Lilium auratum* in mid-season (late August):

3.3 cm long buds contain

               leptotene – zygotene.

3.6 cm long buds contain

               zygotene – diplotene.

3.8 cm long buds contain

            diplotene – metaphase I.

4.2 cm long buds contain

              interphase – tetrads.

For preparations of these stages, cut off the end of an anther and squeeze out, like toothpaste, about $\frac{1}{4}$ of the contents onto a clean slide. Tap out in orcein in the usual way. With a coverslip on, warm at about 60°C, over water if possible, to accelerate staining, which is slower than in *Tradescantia*, and to improve the contrast between the nucleus and cytoplasm. Leave for an hour or overnight if necessary to stain before squashing gently.

MEIOSIS IN LILY EMC:
The technique is identical to that for developing embryo sacs (Section 2.4.4) using slightly younger ovules. Meiosis in the EMC does not begin until after meiosis in the PMC has finished.

MEIOSIS IN LOCUST AND GRASSHOPPER SPERM MOTHER CELLS (SMC):
Male adult locusts are killed 2–3 weeks before sexual maturity, when the lobules at the free end of each follicle contain premeiotic mitoses and meioses occur towards the attached end. In older insects, meiosis will be found at the free end, mature sperm at the other. In grasshoppers, last instar nymphs are preferable.

Dissect out the lobed testes with associated fat bodies, yellow in locust, from the dorsal side of the abdomen. In a drop of physiological saline, 0.75% NaCl, dissect out 2 or 3 follicles and place them in a drop of orcein on a clean slide. Tease out the follicles with needles before lowering a coverslip. Tap *gently* on the coverslip if necessary to disperse the cells. Leave to stain adequately before squashing.

TEMPERATURE-INDUCED INHIBITION OF PAIRING AND CHIASMA FORMATION:
Score the distribution of chiasmata and the frequency of univalents and chiasmata at metaphase I at daily intervals during recovery in normal culture conditions after 48 hours high temperature treatment. The effect will vary with time after treatment according to the stage of meiosis affected. *Schistocerca gregaria* (locust) at 30°C after treatment at 40°C shows effects for 10 days after treatment. *Trillium grandiflorum* at 8°C after treatment at 36°C shows effects for up to 3 weeks after treatment.

Wire models

Each person should be supplied with eight 15 cm lengths of 22.S.W.G. wire, eight similar lengths of 1 mm PVC electric sleeving (four each of two different colours), four 1 cm lengths of 3 mm bore rubber tubing, transparent sellotape and a clear photograph of a diplotene bivalent, as in Fig. 2.14d. Using half the material, a diplotene model can be made in which the wire, *uncut* and crossing over intact at chiasmata, provides the physical continuity of each chromatid, while the plastic sleeve indicates the paternal or maternal origin of the genes and by cutting and exchanging different coloured segments shows the result of chiasmata. The rubber cylinders represent undivided centromeres holding together sister chromatids and the sellotape provides sister chromatid attraction either side of chiasmata. With the remaining material, a second model can be made to show the same bivalent at metaphase after chiasma terminalization and further separation of centromeres.

2.6 Further reading

BOSTOCK, C. J. and SUMNER, A. T. (1977). *The Eukaryotic Chromosome*. North Holland Publishing Company, Amsterdam, New York and Oxford.

* DU PRAW, E. J. (1970). *DNA and chromosomes*. Molecular and Cellular Biology Series. Holt, Rinehart & Wilson, New York.

* GARBER, E. D. (1972). *Cytogenetics – an Introduction*. McGraw-Hill, New York, (Chapters 1–3).

HESLOP-HARRISON, J. (1972). *Sexuality of Angiosperms*. Plant Physiology VIC. Ed. F. C. Steward. Academic Press, London and New York.

JOHN, B. (1976). *Population cytogenetics*. Studies in Biology no. 70. Edward Arnold, London.

JOHN, B. and LEWIS, K. R. (1965). *The Meiotic System*. Protoplasmatologia VI. Fi. Springer-Verlag, Berlin and New York.

JOHN, B. and LEWIS, K. R. (1968). *The Chromosomal Complement*. Protoplasmatologia VI A. Springer-Verlag, N. Y.

* JOHN, B. and LEWIS, K. R. (1972). *Somatic Cell Division* Oxford Biology Readers 26. Oxford University Press, Oxford.

* JOHN, B. and LEWIS, K. R. (1973). *The Meiotic Mechanism*. Oxford Biology Readers 65. Oxford University Press, Oxford.

* JOHN, B. and LEWIS, K. R. (1975). *Chromosome Hierarchy*. Clarendon Press, Oxford.

* KEMP, R. (1970). *Cell Division and Heredity*. Studies in Biology no. 21. Edward Arnold, London.

* LEWIS, K. R. and JOHN, B. (1964). *The Matter of Mendelian Heredity*. J. A. Churchill Ltd., Edinburgh.

LEWIS, K. R. and JOHN, B. (1970). *The Organisation of Heredity*. Contemporary Biology Series, Edward Arnold, London.

* MCDERMOTT, A. (1975). *Cytogenetics of Man and Other Animals*. Chapman and Hall, London.

* MCLEISH, J. and SNOAD, B. (1972). *Looking at Chromosomes*. 2nd Edition. Macmillan, London.

REES, H. and JONES, R. N. (1977). *Chromosome Genetics*. Edward Arnold, London.

SYBENGA, J. (1975). *Meiotic configurations*. Springer-Verlag. Berlin and New York.

* WHITE, M. J. D. (1973). *The Chromosomes*. 6th Edition. Chapman & Hall, London.

YEOMAN, M. M. (Ed.) (1976). *Cell Division in Higher Plants*. Academic Press, London and New York.

* Introductory texts.

3 Introducing cytogenetics – a matter of material

3.1 Introduction

In addition to its role in releasing a programmed sequence of genetic information during development, the chromosome has a central role in inheritance as the vehicle carrying nuclear genes from one generation to the next and as a means of maintaining particular combinations of functionally interacting loci. The study of the karyotype (Section 3.2) and chromosome behaviour in relation to the pattern of inheritance of chromosomal genes through reproduction is known as cytogenetics. The relevant chromosome behaviour includes any mitotic events which affect the karyotype of the germ line as well as the meiotic events of chromosome pairing, chiasma formation and disjunction. The pattern of inheritance concerns the transmission to subsequent generations of mutant alleles and it determines the extent to which alternative alleles of the same gene and alleles of different genes can recombine within a group of interfertile individuals to present to the selective forces of the environment each mutant phenotype in a variety of genetic backgrounds.

Cytogenetics thus has a central role in phylogenetic studies of plants and animals and in investigations of the biology of natural populations of a wild species, but it also has important practical applications. There is an urgent need to understand how to further improve and exploit long-cultivated crop plants, how to manipulate plants newly brought into cultivation and how to develop new techniques for creating novel genotypes using cell and tissue culture techniques which by-pass the limitations imposed by the normal sexual life cycle. In animals, cyto-genetic studies in several groups of invertebrates continue to be important in the control of certain pests and parasites. Relatively recent developments of technique have led to the current expansion of studies into the chromosomal basis of successful crossing and selection in a wide range of vertebrates of economic importance to man and have produced new evidence on the relationship of man to other primates. At the same time, the study of the human chromosome complement in relation to congenital diseases and malformations has led to the most rapidly growing area of applied cytogenetics.

Much of our knowledge of the role of the chromosome complement in inheritance, adaptation and evolution has come from investigations of the effect of visible changes in the chromosomes on recombination and fertility. The level of analysis possible varies with the material. Species with, for example, large or polytene chromosomes, clear pachytene chromomeres or H-segments (Section 2.2.3) will reveal structural changes in the chromosomes not detectable in other species. The effects of cryptic chromosome changes are often difficult to distinguish from those of gene mutations and frequently become the concern of the geneticist rather than the cytologist.

The level of recombination achieved through the two unique events of sexual reproduction, meiosis and fertilization, is not wholly dependent on chromosomal characteristics but is in part dependent on the level of heterozygosity established in the zygote at fertilization (Table 3.1). This is in turn determined by the amount of genetic diversity in the population and the extent of gene flow between members of the population.

Table 3.1   The factors determining the level of variation which can be produced by recombination during sexual reproduction in higher plants.

Factors regulating the level of heterozygosity established each generation by FERTILIZATION	Potential variation		Factors regulating the generation of variation from heterozygosity by MEIOSIS	Potential variation	
	increased	decreased		increased	decreased
Breeding population size	Large	Small	Chromosome number (x)	High	Low
Pollination mechanism	Cross[1]	Self	Chiasma frequency	High	Low
Pollen dispersal	Wide	Restricted[2]	Chiasma localization	Absent	Present
Incompatibility mechanisms[3]	Present	Absent	Chromosome symmetry	Symmetrical	Asymmetrical
Species isolation	Incomplete	Complete			
Seed dispersal	Wide	Restricted	Karyotype symmetry	Symmetrical	Asymmetrical
Seed longevity	Long[4]	Short	Polyploidy	Absent	Present
Life span	Long[4,5]	Short[5]	Structural heterozygosity	Absent	Present

1 i.e. Outcrossing between flowers of different individuals, in contrast to selfing within one flower or between flowers of same individual. Extent of outcrossing is affected by the number and position and structure of flowers, timing of anther and ovule maturity, and foraging behaviour of vector. Cross-pollination between genetically identical members of a clone is equivalent to self-pollination.

2 Including restriction of total range and/or restriction to certain plants within the range due to flower-constant behaviour of vector (e.g. honey bee) in contrast to random pollination by wind or promiscuous insects.

3 Including the selective retardation of self-pollen growing in competition with cross-pollen as well as those mechanisms which totally suppress self-pollen even in the absence of cross-pollen.

4 Recombination between members of different generations increased, but at expense of recombination between members of same generation when monocarpic.

5 Plants with a long life span will have a greater potential for recombination per generation but fewer generations per unit time than short lived plants.

The amount of genetic diversity is related to the effective size of the breeding population as governed by such features as the number of fertile female or hermaphrodite individuals, the extent of clonal propagation of genetically identical individuals, longevity and age at sexual maturity as they affect the chance of crossing between the products of different sexual generations and the rate of replacement of one generation by another, and the distance covered by motile or dispersal phases of the life cycle. Gene flow between individuals is determined by the factors affecting the chances of successful cross-fertilization. These include, for example, the mating behaviour of higher animals and the variety of structural and physiological mechanisms in higher plants which regulate the access of self pollen to the embryo sacs. In many plants, both cross- and self-fertilization occur but one or other may predominate.

The level of genotypic variation achieved through sexual reproduction also depends on the extent to which the heterozygosity introduced into the zygote at fertilization can be translated into new allelic combinations in the succeeding generation of gametes through the events of meiosis (Section 2.5). It is in this context that inherited chromosome characteristics are important (Table 3.1). In a predominantly heterozygous diploid, it is the number of non-homologous chromosomes over which a single complete gene complement is distributed which, through random assortment of centromeres, normally determines the maximum level of recombination between loci on different chromosomes (Section 2.5.1). In the absence of crossing over an increase in basic number from $x = 2$ to $x = 3$ increases the maximum number of genotypes in the gametes from 4 (i.e. 2^2) to 8 (i.e. 2^3). At the same time, it is the number and distribution of chiasmata within each bivalent which determines the level and pattern of recombination between genes on the same chromosome (Section 2.5.1). Introduction of a single chiasma per bivalent increases the number of gamete genotypes where $x = 3$ from 8 (i.e. 2^3) to 64 (i.e. 4^3). The major contribution of these two cytological features to the potential for recombination at meiosis is recognized in the Recombination Index (RI), equal to the sum of the number of bivalents and the mean chiasma frequency. However, it must be remembered that, alone, this figure provides an unreliable forecast of the level of variability in the next generation. For example, structural heterozygosity is commonly associated with a reduced level of recombination because of its effect at meiosis, while inbreeding generates uniformity even when the numbers of bivalents and chiasmata are high.

Thus, although some restriction on recombination is universal because genes are not free individuals within the species pool, the greatest potential for variation is found in out-breeding diploids forming structurally homozygous bivalents with many, dispersed chiasmata. Near maximum variability may be advantageous for immediate survival where the environment is very unstable or where rigorous selection dictates that at best only a few of the progeny will survive anyway. However, in some situations, such as certain stable environments and open, uniform, habitats such as dunes, flood plains and burnt areas where there is initially little competition for pioneering species, success depends on the ability to reproduce rapidly while at the same time conserving, at least for a while, favoured gene combinations, even at the expense of future adaptability. Only by clonal asexual reproduction can recombination be totally suppressed and the genotype be maintained unchanged, and

some organisms maintain sexual and asexual reproduction side by side to obtain the benefits of both conservation and variation. Nevertheless, considerable restriction of recombination is possible within sexual reproduction and this can be achieved by changes in one or more components of the meiotic and breeding systems, such as the establishment of inbreeding, low chromosome numbers, few and localized chiasmata and heterozygosity for chromosome rearrangements. These changes arise spontaneously, are inheritable and thus subject to selection.

Few, if any, species combine all the mechanisms which suppress recombination. In most situations, conditions will favour individuals with an intermediate level of recombination which achieves a compromise between the conservation necessary for maximum exploitation of the present habitat and the variation necessary for future survival. Because many of the relevant changes are irreversible, successive past alterations in the level of recombination will have left in each organism an accumulation of chromosomal and reproductive features, some individually favouring free recombination and others suppressing it, which interact and oppose each other to establish a relatively stable level near the optimum for current conditions. Legacies from past adaptations will also impose limitations, or in some cases create new possibilities, for future developments so that different organisms adapting to the same type of environment may achieve the desired level of recombination in different ways. Thus, all weedy plants show some feature which enables them to rapidly replicate new and successful genotypes to exploit to the maximum the disturbed ground they have colonized. There are, however, three types of weed; perennials which perpetuate the genotype by asexual reproduction, annuals which conserve the genotype by inbreeding and other, outbreeding, annuals which reduce recombination by means of low chromosome

numbers, chromosome asymmetry and reduced chiasma frequencies. In the out-
breeding annuals such variation as occurs
will be at a constant low level while in the
predominantly inbreeding species, the occasional cross-pollination will result in
sporadic and more abrupt variation followed
by periods of constancy.

Inheritable changes affecting the chromosomes fall into two categories; those affecting
aspects of chromosome behaviour such as
pairing, chiasma formation, centromere
orientation and disjunction which arise as a
result of gene mutations altering cellular
activities, and those affecting chromosome
number or structure which arise as a result of
chromosome mutations produced by errors
of replication or division. In the former, the
gene mutation may be present in every cell,
but the expression of the gene may only occur
in certain cells, not necessarily in the germ
line, at particular stages of development. The
effect on the chromosomes may be modified
or even reversed later in the life cycle by the
activity of other genes. After the second kind
of change, chromosome mutation, all the
derivative cells are affected by an event which
is abrupt, spontaneous, and not directly
reversible. Only at the population level, by
removing the selective advantage of individuals with the altered karyotype and once
more favouring the original form, can a trend
be reversed. Chromosome mutation is not
under genetic control, although there may be
an inherited propensity for error, nor is it
directed by external pressures, although the
possibilities may be limited by previous
changes and the products will be subsequently subject to selection.

Within a comparison of the dividing
chromosome complements of a group of
related organisms is contained information
on the past history, present relationships and
likely future developments of the species
concerned, but to understand the full
significance of the observations on one
individual requires an intensive study of the
chromosomes and their behaviour and an
extensive study of the biology of the species
and its relatives (Section 4.5.2). A full
discussion of karyotype evolution is beyond
the scope of this book but as an introduction
to cytogenetics it is a relatively simple matter,
using only the techniques described in
Chapters 1 and 2, even in the absence of a full
understanding of the biology of the organism, to demonstrate the main features of
chromosome complements by the appropriate choice of material. Chapter 3 is thus
concerned primarily with providing names of
suitable species under a number of headings,
each relating to an aspect of the complement
and with a short introduction to indicate the
scope of the topic. After introducing in
Section 3.2 the terminology relating to
karyotypes, it is convenient to present the
material in two major sub-sections. In
Section 3.3 are included the variable features
which produce the diversity of karyotypes
and the main inferences which can be drawn
from them about past chromosome mutations. In Section 3.4, the origin, immediate
effects and evolutionary significance of the
various types of chromosome mutation are
considered individually. It is the immediate
effects on vigour, fertility and recombination
which determine whether a mutation will
become successfully established in a new
cytotype or be rapidly eliminated.

3.2 The karyotype

The *karyotype* is the phenotype of the
complement, the sum of all the detectable
structural features of the chromosome including number, size and morphology as seen
at mitotic metaphase and the arrangement of
homologous segments as deduced from
meiotic pairing (Sections 2.2 and 3.3). The
karyotype is usually recorded, after an
appropriate pre-treatment to make the
individual chromosomes clearer (Section
1.4), in the form of a diagrammatic summary,
or *idiogram*, together with a written des-

cription (Section 1.6). The idiogram may show all the chromosomes, or only the *basic chromosome set or complement* where this is exactly repeated two or more times (Fig. 1.3). The basic chromosome set can be defined as a viable complement of non-homologous and indispensable chromosomes which are each represented once. The basic complement contains one complete set of the genes necessary for full development. Within a species, population or even individual, there may be two or more different and distinguishable basic sets as a result of chromosome rearrangements and there may be more than two basic sets in the zygotic complement as a result of spindle failures. Irregular disjunction may produce incomplete basic sets.

The number of chromosomes in a basic set is known as the *basic chromosome number*, '*x*'. This must be distinguished from the terms referring to the phases of the life cycle. Thus the *gametic number*, '*n*', which in most plants refers also to the gametophyte generation is typically, as a result of meiosis, equal to half the *zygotic number* '*2n*' produced by

fertilization, referred to in plants also as the *sporophytic number*. The gametic number of organisms with no polyploid ancestry is equal to the basic number. In angiosperms, a unique tissue, the endosperm, also formed by fusion of male and female nuclei, has a characteristic number of chromosome sets, which can however differ between species as a result of modifications of embryo sac development. Most endosperms begin development with three gametic complements, i.e. the *endospermic number* is $3n$, but $2n$, $5n$ and other endosperms are known. Thus for *Tradescantia bracteata*, $2n = 2x = 12$, $n = x = 6$ (Fig. 3.1) and the endosperm is $3n = 3x = 18$, while in the related *Tradescantia virginiana*, $2n = 4x = 24$ and $n = 2x = 12$ (Figs 2.1a and 4.1e–h). Only in certain apomictic situations, particularly recurrent gametophytic agamospermy, is this pattern disturbed, but in these, this system of symbols becomes unworkable. For example, where an embryo is produced abnormally by parthenogenetic development of an unfertilized egg, it inherits the gametic complement (hence

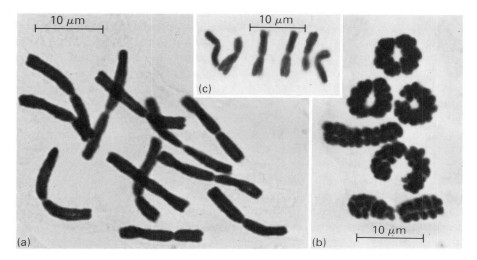

Fig. 3.1 The gametic and sporophytic metaphase complements of *Tradescantia bracteata* ($n = x = 6$). **a**, Root tip mitosis after colchicine pre-treatment, showing near median centromeres in each chromosome. **b**, Pollen meiosis, showing four 'ring' bivalents with a terminalized chiasma in each arm and two 'rod' bivalents with a terminalized chiasma in only one arm of each. **c**, Pollen grain mitosis, showing a single genome.

haploid animals and angiosperms) and when unreduced nuclei are produced by failure of meiotic disjunction, the gametes and gametophytes inherit the zygotic complement. In both situations the usual symbols would produce the formula $n = 2n$. There are unfortunately no generally accepted symbols, such as Z, G and E, to represent the zygotic, gametic and endospermic numbers defined according to cell type and independently of the details of meiosis and embryo sac development, but they would sometimes be useful. For example, describing the endosperm of *Tulbaghia violacea* as $E = 3n = 3x = 18$ compared with $E = 3n = 6x = 36$ for *Tradescantia virginiana* and $E = 5n = 5x = 60$ for *Lilium* conveys a lot of information in a compact form. Similarly the formula $G = S = 2n = 3x = 123$ for *Dryopteris pseudo-mas* informs us that this fern, which is a sexually sterile hybrid, is triploid in origin and maintains the original sporophytic complement through both sporophyte and gametophyte phases of an apomictic life cycle by modification of meiosis and omission of fertilization (it is diplosporous and apogamous).

Complements of one intact basic set of chromosomes are *haploid* or *monoploid*; those with two are *diploid*. All other complements are *heteroploid*. Under this term are included three very different types of numerical variation. *Euploid* changes result in *polyploidy* (Section 3.4.2i) where the numbers form a series of exact multiples of basic numbers initially due to doubling the complement by failure of disjunction at division. The basic sets in a polyploid need not all be the same in structure or even in number. *Aneuploid* (Section 3.4.2h) changes are those resulting in chromosome numbers which fall between the members of the euploid series because of the presence of one or more chromosomes of a basic set in addition to one or more complete basic sets. (Some authors, e.g. Stebbins, use the term in a broader sense to include dysploidy, defined below.) The distinction between aneuploid and euploid conditions is, however, not clear in those complements which have gained or lost not whole chromosomes but segments of a chromosome and thus show some features of both conditions. A good case can be made for distinguishing these as *segmental aneuploids* (Section 3.4.2f and g). *Dysploid* (Section 3.4.2e) changes occur when the basic chromosome number increases or decreases in steps of one as a result of rearrangement of chromosome segments and loss or incorporation of centromeres without any significant change in the genotype. *Agmatoploid* changes occur when polycentric chromosomes (Section 2.2.3a) break to give stable fragments and thus an increase in chromosome number with no accompanying change in genotype, as has occurred frequently in *Carex* spp.

3.3 Karyotype diversity and analysis

The karyotype (Section 3.2) is a phenotypic character which, having allowed for any changes with development (Section 2.4) is an indicator of relationships. Where detectable karyotypic changes have occurred during recent evolution, cryptic species may be revealed by karyotype analysis (Section 4.5.2). Where chromosomal changes have been less rapid than the evolutionary divergence of other phenotypic characters, the karyotype may reveal previously unsuspected relationships between species. Where the karyotype has long been very stable, examination will not assist in discovering species relationships, but may reveal more distant origins through similarities between genera or sub-families. For such investigations, several individuals of each species should be compared for as many karyotype characters as possible, but it is nevertheless possible to draw some tentative conclusions even from examination of a single individual.

Chromosome number is the most readily available, but least informative, feature of a karyotype and is the minimal description which can be made of a complement. The biological significance of the often considerable differences in *chromosome size* between complements is still something of a mystery, but the major repercussion on karyotype investigations is that where chromosomes are small analysis is limited to chromosome number and meiotic pairing. *Chromosome morphology*, which is revealed by more detailed examination, is more informative and may indicate a variety of previously unsuspected conditions as well as go far to confirm situations suggested by chromosome number. *Meiotic behaviour* is in some respects the most informative characteristic as it usually provides an assay of genetic homology within the complement which cannot be assessed any other way, but it is also the most laborious to obtain even when material at the right stage is available.

3.3.1 Chromosome number

If a single individual only is examined, chromosome number alone is not very informative. A very low number indicates previous dysploid changes, and a high number suggests polyploidy. An uneven zygotic number indicates hybridity, structural heterozygosity including specialized sex chromosome mechanisms, aneuploidy indicating meiotic abnormalities, or supernumerary chromosomes. If chromosome counts from other plants are available, variation within or between species may give a clearer indication of the underlying situation. Multiples of the same number indicate polyploidy (Section 3.4.2i); multiples or combinations of two or more numbers indicate dysploidy (Section 3.4.2e); a range of numbers which are not multiples of one or a few basic numbers indicates aneuploidy (Section 3.4.2h), supernumerary B chromosomes (Section 3.4.2g) or poly-

centric chromosomes (Section 2.2.3a); and two numbers, differing by one, indicate aneuploidy, dysploidy, B chromosomes or specialised sex determining chromosomes (Section 3.4.3).

3.3.2 Chromosome size

There are two distinct aspects of chromosome size. One concerns the variation in chromosome length independent of width as found within a complement. This is considered under chromosome morphology (Section 3.3.3). The other concerns the variation in chromosome length with a parallel but not necessarily proportional variation in width which results in the marked differences in average chromosome volume between complements. Such differences arise within an individual during development but no change in DNA content is involved (Section 2.4.1). Differences in volume between individuals of a species have been shown in at least one instance (*Lolium perenne*) to be due to the effect of a single recessive mutant gene, but it is not known if the DNA content is affected. Differences in chromosome size of up to 10-fold between species of one genus are accompanied by parallel differences in DNA content. In hybrids between species which differ in chromosome size, the relative sizes of the two complements may not be the same as when they occur separately in the two parent species, indicating that comparisons can be complicated by changes in metabolic activity. However, unpaired segments at meiosis in such hybrids suggest that tandem duplication of certain segments is at least partly responsible for the differences in size. Differences in nuclear DNA content of 300-fold within the angiosperms and of 3000-fold within the plant kingdom are also thought to be largely due to varying amounts of repetitious DNA. Comparison of the minimum levels of nuclear DNA between the major plant groups shows an increase accompanying the evolution of greater complexity.

Nuclear doubling by polyploidy and by differential replication of certain segments will have different consequences. Polyploidy will duplicate every locus and probably reduce cell cycle times but chromosome pairing and segregation will be modified. Increased chromosome volume will leave some loci at the unreplicated level and probably increase cell cycle time but retain unchanged pairing relationships at meiosis.

Among angiosperms, the smallest chromosomes, and the associated low nuclear DNA content and short cell cycle (Section 2.5), are found in annuals, particularly ephemerals and those flowering in winter. In some families a correlation has been noted between chromosome size and geographical distribution, those species with large chromosomes occurring in colder regions with seasonal climates and those with small chromosomes growing in warm, more uniform conditions. The smallest metaphase chromosomes, about 0.5 μm long, are almost iso-diametric and lack clear morphological features. The longest chromosomes are about 30 μm long but increase in length is not accompanied by a proportional increase in width, so the largest chromosomes are up to twenty times as long as they are wide. Chromosome width rarely exceeds 3 μm. Thus, while chromosome size does not directly yield much information to the cytogeneticist, it is indirectly important in that only if the chromosome length exceeds 2 μm is a study of morphology possible.

3.3.3 Chromosome morphology

For all but the smallest chromosomes, the morphology of a mitotic complement can be defined in terms of at least three features, chromosome lengths, centromere positions and the number and position of active nucleolar organizers (Fig. 3.2 and Section 2.2.3). Other features, such as heterochromatic regions and chromomeres or polytene

bands can be exploited when available. Some complements have genomes which are symmetrical, both in relation to the complement as a whole, in that all the chromosomes are very similar in length, and in relation to each chromosome individually where there is a localized centromere, in that the two arms are of similar length. Other complements are asymmetrical with variation in size between chromosomes within a genome or between the two arms of each chromosome, or both. The most extreme forms of asymmetry are bimodal complements, as in birds, butterflies and the angiosperm *Aloe*, among others, where the large chromosomes are up to fifty times as long as the small ones, and complements of telocentric chromosomes, as in the locust *Schistocerca gregaria*. It has been suggested that in plants the more symmetrical complements are found in the species with the least structural rearrangement of the chromosomes during karyotype evolution while the asymmetrical complements of other species are derived forms in which symmetry has been lost as a consequence of such rearrangement. Such a trend from symmetry to asymmetry may well characterize the recent history of certain plant groups but this should not lead to the assumption that the most primitive ancestral eukaryotic genomes were symmetrical and that all evolutionary change has been towards asymmetry. In several animal groups, including mammals, and even some plants, symmetry has been maintained or enhanced as the karyotype has evolved by structural rearrangement. Perhaps decreasing and increasing asymmetry can follow each other in succession during evolution.

Although measurements of chromosome length are subject to various errors, major differences between complements in respect of chromosome size and symmetry can be conveniently summarized in terms of total length, average arm ratio (total length of long arms : short arms) and chromosome length ratio (length of longest : shortest). Ratios close to unity indicate symmetry, while ratios

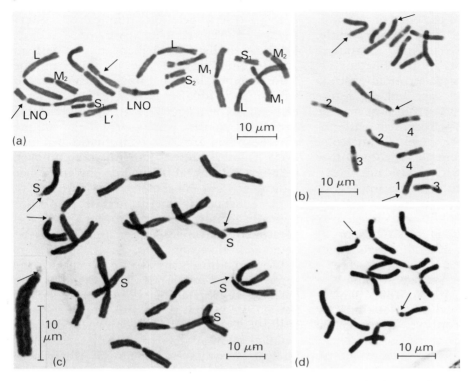

Fig. 3.2 Examples of plant root tip chromosome complements at mitotic metaphase
after colchicine pretreatment. Arrows indicate the positions of nucleolar organizers.
a, *Hyacinthus orientalis* cv. 'Tubergen's Scarlet' (= 'Mme du Barry') ($2n = 2x = 16$).
The diploid hyacinth complement consists of four pairs of long chromosomes (L), one
of which has a sub-terminal nucleolar organizer (LNO), two pairs of medium length
chromosomes (M_1 and M_2) and two pairs of short chromosomes (S_1 and S_2).
'Tubergen's Scarlet', a sport of 'Distinction', and its double flowered derivative
'Scarlet Perfection' are heterozygous for a large terminal deletion in one of the long
chromosomes. **b**, *Bellevalia romana* ($2n = 2x = 8$). Each genome in the two adjacent
cells shown consists of a long chromosome with a median centromere and a nucleolar
satellite (1), a long acrocentric (2) and two smaller acrocentrics (3 and 4). **c**,
Nothoscordum inodorum (*N. fragans*) ($2n = 4x = 19$). The root tip complement consists
of thirteen large chromosomes with near median centromeres (L) and six shorter
chromosomes with almost terminal centromeres (S). Four of the S chromosomes have
nucleolar satellites on the very small short arms (see also inset.) This apomictically
reproduced plant is thought to be a tetraploid of hybrid origin with one genome of four
L chromosomes and three genomes of three L and two S chromosomes. **d**, *Tulbaghia
verdoornia* ($2n = 2x = 12$). This plant is heterozygous for a distal heterochromatic
satellite on the nucleolar organizer on the short arm of the small acrocentric
chromosome.

above 1 indicate the degree of asymmetry.
Smaller differences within genomes, masked
by the overall value, may be revealed by
detailed comparison of individual chromosomes identified by differences in length, arm
ratio or nucleolar organizer position.

Nucleolar organizers usually occur relatively close to centromeres. This may be for
mechanical or functional reasons. A nucleolus forming at telophase on the end of one
of the longest arms of the complement would
be at the periphery of the nucleus as the

envelope reforms round the ends of chromosomes furthest from the spindle pole. Nucleoli forming close to the centromere would be more central in the nucleus. It further appears that a near terminal position is frequently preferred, particularly where this is compatible with proximity to the centromeres, as on an acrocentric chromosome. It is these near-terminal nucleolar organizers on acrocentric chromosomes which, for reasons which are not clear, provide the most frequent examples of structural heterozygosity in chromosomes. The distal *satellite*, in addition to frequently being heterochromatic, is often absent or smaller in one member of a homologous pair (Fig. 3.2d). Where the satellite is very small it may fold back against the chromosome arm in most cells and the position of the organizer can only be confirmed by looking for attached nucleoli at prophase. Every viable genome has at least one nucleolar organizer site and a few have five or more all on different chromosomes. Thus every normal zygote has at least two such sites, even if they may be difficult to see. There are no genomes described where every chromosome has an organizer, although in *Trillium grandiflorum* four out of five chromosomes form nucleoli.

As a diagnostic character, chromosome morphology in conjunction with chromosome number can be of considerable value, even when the observations are based on a single zygotic complement. The presence of more than two chromosomes of a distinctive type is a further indication of aneuploidy or polyploidy. Where several distinctive chromosomes are each represented three or more times, polyploidy can be confidently diagnosed, but polyploidy might remain undetected in an amphidiploid in the absence of further information. Where several distinctive chromosomes are represented only once, haploidy or hybridity is suggested. A zygotic complement of an hermaphrodite with an even chromosome number and two unique chromosomes lacking morphologically similar partners, indicates heterozygosity for a deletion, duplication, interchange or pericentric inversion (Section 3.4.2). A similar complement, or one with an uneven number and one or three unique chromosomes, in an organism with male and female individuals, indicates the heterogametic sex of a species with distinguishable sex chromosomes, particularly if the unique chromosomes are heterochromatic. An uneven zygotic number including an uneven number of noticeably smaller chromosomes indicates B chromosomes. Even numbers of large euchromatic supernumeraries, morphologically similar sex chromosomes and paracentric inversions are unlikely to be detected in this way.

Where comparisons can be made with the karyotypes of other related individuals, the pattern of variability of numbers and associated morphology will further assist analysis. Even where the number is constant, detailed comparisons of chromosome morphology may reveal structural differences between genomes. It should not however be assumed that similar karyotypes necessarily mean identical structure; the similarity may mask a number of major rearrangements which leave chromosome morphology little changed.

Further resolution of the ambiguities remaining after careful analysis and comparison of the mitotic chromosome morphology requires investigation of meiotic behaviour.

3.3.4 Meiotic pairing and disjunction

The basic pattern of events at meiosis with regular bivalent formation and disjunction has been described in Section 2.5. However, examination of metaphase I of meiosis in a variety of organisms reveals bivalents varying in morphology due to differences in chromosome size and symmetry and in chiasma frequency and distribution (Fig. 2.16) as well as a range of other pairing relationships from only unpaired univalents to a single multivalent ring incorporating every chromosome in the complement. With a few exceptions, multivalent formation means that at least one chromosome has regions homologous with regions on two or more other chromosomes, that changes of partner occurred during pairing and that some chromosomes were involved in more than one chiasma. Univalent formation on the other hand is attributable to three factors acting separately or together; physical factors within the environment, the genotype within the individual and the number and distribution of homologous segments within the complement. Environmental disturbance, such as extremes of temperature during meiotic prophase can inhibit pairing or chiasma formation (Fig. 2.17d). It is known that various aspects of chromosome behaviour, including homologous pairing, chiasma formation and distribution, co-orientation and disjunction, are controlled by genes on the chromosomes themselves and mutations at these loci can result in partial or total inhibition of these events in some individuals. If, after culture under natural conditions and examination of the complement in a range of genotypic backgrounds, univalents still consistently occur then the most likely explanation is lack of homology. However, recognition of homology according to metaphase I associations suffers from a serious disadvantage. There is as yet no independent method of assessing *homology*, the similarity in composition and organization of nucleoprotein which results from a recent common origin, except through the little understood process of recognition and intimate association, the basis of the zygotene pairing, which precedes chiasma formation. Consequently, where gene controlled restriction of pairing or chiasma formation has become an integral part of an organism's meiotic mechanism, it may be very difficult to recognize all the homologous relationships present. Thus in some polyploids of hybrid origin pairing is limited to chromosomes of identical genomes and does not occur between corresponding chromosomes (*homoeologues*) of different but related genomes even though they have some homologous segments in common. The classic example of this is hexaploid bread wheat, where pairing between homoeologues of the three genomes present can take place but is normally suppressed in favour of exclusive bivalent-forming pairing between homologues because of the action of the dominant allele of a single gene which arose in a tetraploid ancestor. Other examples of situations where metaphase associations fail to reveal the full extent of homology include: i) autopolyploids where an inherited low chiasma frequency restricts the maintenance of the maximum possible number of multivalents even though full pairing may have taken place at prophase, ii) congested polyploid nuclei where mechanical interference at prophase prevents the maximum possible pairing involving changes of partner between homologues and iii) multivalent-forming interchange heterozygotes such as *Rhoeo* (Fig. 3.10c), where distally localized chiasmata reveal the distribution in the complement of the interchanged terminal regions of chromosome arms but not the relationships between the interstitial segments containing the near-median centromeres. Similarly, small B chromosomes rarely reveal their homologies by full multivalent formation. In addition, successful formation of metaphase associations may mask structural differences between the homologues, particularly if chiasmata are few or localized, unless they are large enough to produce visibly asymmetrical (heteromorphic) bivalents.

Despite these limitations, meiotic studies almost invariably add significantly to the information from investigation of the mitotic complement because the events of meiosis largely determine the genetic constitution and viability of gametes, and thus the future if any of the genotype, while at the same time reflecting in a unique way the structural

Table 3.2 Preliminary diagnosis of chromosome complements from meiotic pairing behaviour and mitotic karyotype (see Section 3.3.5d).

Meiotic pairing ($2n$)	Mitotic karyotype analysis (2n) *Possible morphological differences between corresponding chromosomes of different genomes	Diagnosis
ALL BIVALENTS All symmetrical	$2x$	Standard diploid; hybrid of close relatives with indistinguishable karyotypes
	$2x + 2B, 4B$, etc.	Diploid with even number of homologous supernumerary chromosomes
	$2x - 2, 4x - 2$	Nullisomic diploid or amphidiploid
	$4x, 6x$, etc.★	Amphidiploid polyploid, e.g. AABB, or A′A′A″A″ with preferential pairing
	$4x, 6x$, etc.	Autopolyploid with few pairing initiation points or chiasmata and selection for bivalent formation
One asymmetrical	$2x$★	Structural heterozygote – duplication, deletion, translocation, centric shift or pericentric inversion
	$2x$★ dioecious	XY or ZW Sex chromosomes
Most or all asymmetrical	$2x$★	Diploid hybrid of closely related parents e.g. A′A″
BIVALENTS WITH UNIVALENTS	x	Haploid with duplicated segments on non-homologous chromosomes
	$2x$★	Diploid hybrid e.g. A′A″; unpaired XY sex chromosomes
	$2x$★ dioecious, ♂ and ♀ complements differ by 1	XO sex chromosomes
	$2x + 1B, 2B, 3B$, etc.	Diploid with unpaired supernumerary chromosomes
	$2x, 3x, 4x$, etc.	Chiasmata or pairing inhibited by environment or genotype
	$2x, 3x, 4x$, etc.★	Allopolyploid, e.g. A′A′A′; ABB; etc.; polyhaploid, e.g. A′A′, A′A′A′
ALL UNIVALENTS	x	Haploid
	$2x, 3x$, etc.★	Polyhaploid or diploid hybrid, e.g. AB, ABC
	$2x, 3x, 4x$, etc.	Chiasmata or pairing inhibited by environment or genotype
BIVALENTS WITH ONE OR TWO MULTIVALENTS	$2x, 4x$★ = even no.	Diploid or amphi-diploid interchange heterozygote
	= odd no.	'Robertsonian translocation' heterozygote
	$2x$★ dioecious, ♂ and ♀ complements differ by 1	Complex sex chromosomes mechanism, e.g. XY_1Y_2
	$2x + 1, 2$	Aneuploid diploid
	$3x, 4x$, etc.	Autopolyploid with restricted pairing or chiasma formation, e.g. AAA, etc.
	$3x, 4x$, etc.★	Segmental allopolyploid with restricted pairing or chiasma formation, e.g. A′A′A″A″, A′A″A″

BIVALENTS WITH MORE THAN TWO MULTIVALENTS	$2x\star$	Multiple interchange heterozygote
	$3x - 1, 2, 3,$ etc., $4x - 2, 3, 4,$ etc.	Aneuploid polyploid
	$3x, 4x,$ etc.	Autopolyploid with restricted pairing or chiasma formation, e.g. AAA, etc.
	$3x, 4x,$ etc.$\star$	Allopolyploid: $A'A'A''A''$, etc. with restricted pairing or chiasma formation; AABB interchange heterozygote
MULTIVALENTS AND UNIVALENTS	$3x, 4x,$ etc.$\star$	Polyploid with restricted pairing or chiasma formation
	$3x + 1B, 2B,$ etc.; $4x + 1B, 2B,$ etc.	Polyploid with unpaired supernumeraries
ALL MULTIVALENT(S)	$2x\star$	Multiple interchange heterozygote
	$3x + 1, 4x + 1,$ etc.	Aneuploid polyploid
	$3x, 4x,$ etc.	Autopolyploid AAAA; allopolyploid, e.g. $A'A'A''A''$ or AAA BBB

relationships between the chromosomes which indicate their origins and history. Most investigations of meiosis include an analysis of metaphase I configurations because these provide a minimum estimate of previous pairing, reflecting homology, and at the same time indicate the probable events at disjunction, determining fertility. Analysis of pairing relationships at meiotic metaphase I in conjunction with analysis of the mitotic karyotype based on chromosome number and morphology permits the preliminary diagnosis of a wide variety of chromosomal conditions (Table 3.2).

In addition to metaphase I, three other phases of meiosis, pachytene, diplotene and anaphase yield additional information. Pachytene studies, though laborious, provide the most detailed information on zygotene pairing and can reveal otherwise undetectable heterozygosity for deletions, duplications and inversions of small segments as well as the positions of homologous segments in multivalent associations. Interstitial duplications and deletions produce laterally extended loops of the unpaired segment (Section 3.4.2f). Similar segments on the ends of chromosomes result in a terminal unpaired region. Interstitial regions where segments of both chromosome have failed to pair indicate a lack of homology or an inhibition of the pairing process. Inversion heterozygosity induces the formation of characteristic loops in the paired chromosomes (Section 3.4.2c). However, pachytene studies alone cannot accurately predict later events because pairing is no guarantee of subsequent chiasma formation.

Examination of early diplotene will show where chiasmata form and thus, because chiasmata can only form in previously paired regions, indicate some though probably not all of the homologous regions when the more detailed information from pachytene is not available. At the same time comparison with chiasma distribution at later stages will demonstrate whether interpretation at metaphase must allow for previous chiasma terminalization which could displace chiasmata into regions which are not homologous.

Observations on anaphase I and II provide data on the chromosome constitution of the four meiotic products. When bridges and fragments are found, they also provide the most striking indication of chromatid breakage and U-type non-sister reunion or, if fragments of the same size are seen in several cells, of the previous formation of a chiasma in the pachytene loop of a paracentric inversion heterozygote (Section 3.4.2c).

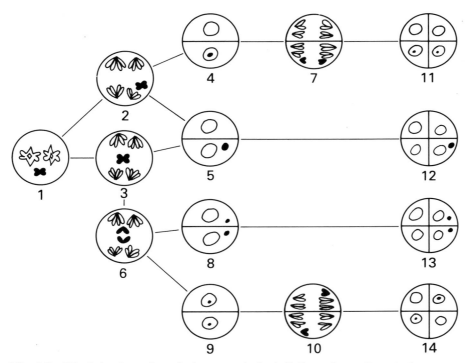

Fig. 3.3 The behaviour of a univalent at meiosis. 1, Failure of syntelic univalent congression at metaphase I (to 2 or 3). 2, Late movement of univalent towards one pole (to 4 or 5). 3, Late congression of univalent after becoming amphitelic at spindle equator (to 5 or 6). 4, Inclusion of univalent in one daughter nucleus (to 7). 5, Univalent left in cytoplasm at telophase I as a micronucleus still visible in tetrad (to 12). 6, Precocious division of univalent at anaphase I (to 8 or 9). Alternatively, misdivision of centromeres to form telocentrics may occur (see Section 3.4.2b). 7, Division of univalent at anaphase II. Daughter chromosomes included in telophase nuclei (to 11). 8, Failure of daughter chromosomes to enter daughter nuclei at telophase I to form two micronuclei, still visible in tetrad (to 13). 9, Inclusion of daughter chromosomes in nuclei at telophase I (to 10). 10, Disjunction of daughter chromosomes at anaphase II to one telophase nucleus in each dyad (to 14).

Observations at these stages also demonstrate the relationship between metaphase co-orientation and anaphase disjunction. Univalents, with the exception of single sex chromosomes as in male grasshoppers and B chromosomes showing directed non-disjunction, are prone to irregular behaviour at anaphase I (Fig. 3.3). Multivalents sometimes show regular disjunction with equal numbers of chromosomes moving to each spindle pole (Fig. 3.4). However, this is clearly not possible in trivalents and higher associations of an uneven number of chromosomes, and, in the quadrivalents of interchange heterozygotes, only the separation of pairs of alternate chromosomes in the quadrivalent give genetically balanced products and disjunction of adjacent chromosomes produces numerically balanced but usually inviable gametic complements. Moreover, even in autopolyploids with four, six or eight identical genomes, regular co-orientation of equal numbers of centromeres on each side of the spindle equator becomes less likely for mechanical reasons as the number of chromosomes and the number of chiasmata in each multivalent increases. Other modifications and irregularities of meiotic anaphase frequently occur in conjunction with recurrent apomixis.

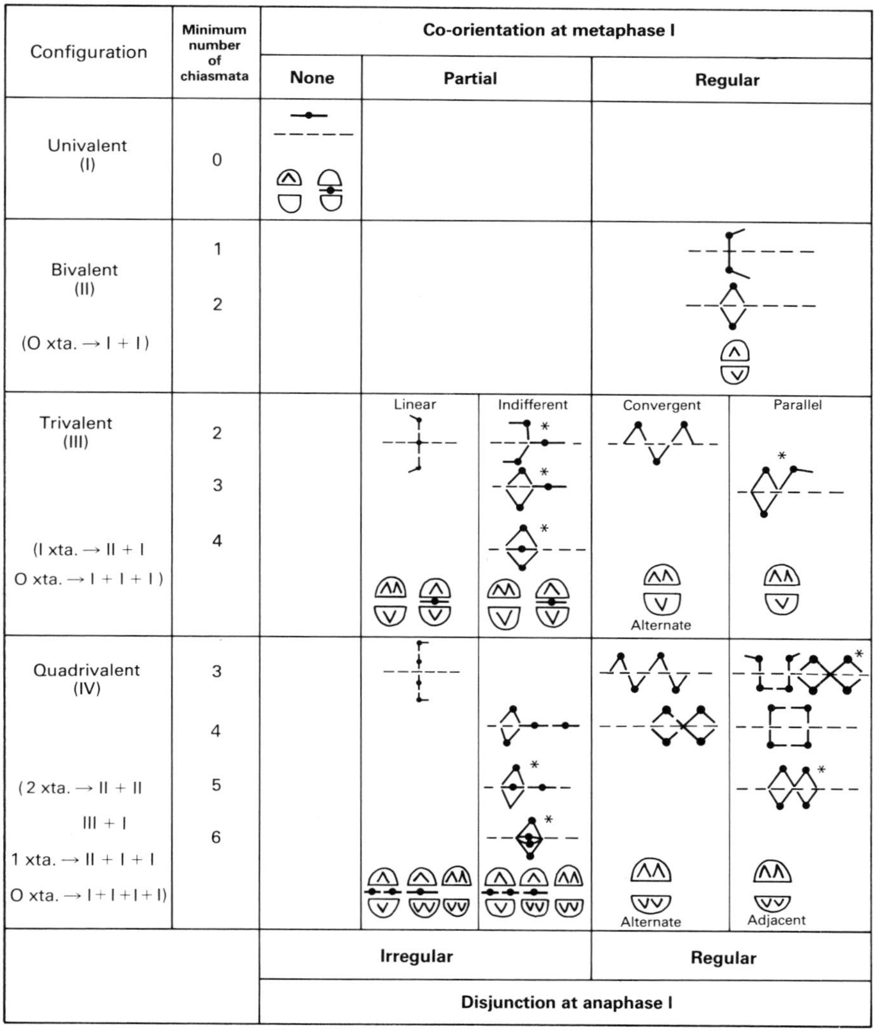

Configuration	Minimum number of chiasmata	Co-orientation at metaphase I			
		None	Partial		Regular
Univalent (I)	0				
Bivalent (II) (O xta. → I + I)	1 / 2				
Trivalent (III) (I xta. → II + I, O xta. → I + I + I)	2 / 3 / 4		Linear / Indifferent	Convergent (Alternate)	Parallel
Quadrivalent (IV) (2 xta. → II + II, III + I, 1 xta. → II + I + I, O xta. → I + I + I + I)	3 / 4 / 5 / 6			Alternate	Adjacent
		Irregular		Regular	
		Disjunction at anaphase I			

Fig. 3.4 Co-orientation and disjunction of univalents, bivalents and multivalents with fully terminalized chiasmata. The bottom diagram in each rectangle represents disjunction of the configuration(s) immediately above it. Multivalents marked ★ require at least two chiasmata in one or more arms. Multivalents with more chiasmata, dispersed chiasmata or more chromosomes have an increased likelihood of irregular disjunction. xta = chiasmata.

3.3.5 Materials

Every complement has features of interest and there are almost limitless variations of karyotype and meiotic behaviour. The following highly selective lists represent examples chosen for their availability and ease of maintenance, preparation and interpretation in order to illustrate this diversity and to provide examples of a variety of conditions capable of diagnosis by karyotype and meiotic analysis. All the methods required are described in Chapters 1 and 2.

Some of the species listed can be obtained

from wild populations in Britain and a few from commercial suppliers of biological material such as Philip Harris Biological Ltd., Oldmixon, Weston-super-Mare, Somerset. Other plants can be obtained as seed from Botanical Gardens or seedsmen such as Thompson and Morgan (Ipswich) Ltd., or as clonally propagated plants from nurserymen such as P. de Jager and Sons Ltd. of Marden, Kent, Perry's of Enfield and Hillier and Sons of Winchester.

a) Chromosome number (Section 3.3.1)

1 Low: *Haplopappus gracilis* $(x = 2, 2n = 4)$; *Crepis capillaris*, *Crocus balansae*, *Crocus candidus*, *Ornithogalum virens* $(x = 3, 2n = 6)$; *Crepis pulchra* (Fig. 1.3), *Bellevalia romana* (Fig. 3.2b), *Drosophila melanogaster* (Fruit fly) $(x = 4, 2n = 8)$.

2 High: *Iris versicolor* $(2n = 72)$; *Helianthus tuberosus* $(2n = 102)$. (Highest angiosperm numbers: Dicotyledon – *Morus nigra*, $2n = 308$; Monocotyledon – *Poa litorosa*, $2n = 265$. Highest plant number: *Ophioglossum reticulatum*, (fern) $2n = $ c.1260.)

See **d)** below and Section 3.4 for examples where chromosome number reveals polyploidy, aneuploidy, diploidy, B chromosomes and structural heterozygosity.

b) Chromosome size (Section 3.3.2)

1 Large: *Trillium* spp. $(2x = 10)$; *Hyacinthus orientalis* $(2x = 16)$ (Fig. 3.2a); *Bellevalia romana* $(2x = 8)$ (Fig. 3.2b); *Lilium* spp. $(2x = 24)$; *Nothoscordum inodorum* $(= N.\ fragrans)$ $(4x = 19)$ (Fig. 3.2c); *Tradescantia* spp. $(2x = 12, 4x = 24)$ (Fig. 3.1a); *Tulbaghia* species $(2x = 12)$ (Fig. 3.2d).

2 Small: *Antirrhinum majus* $(2x = 16)$ (Fig. 2.12c); *Arabidopsis thaliana* $(2x = 10)$; *Cucurbita pepo* $(2x = 40)$; *Lactuca sativa* $(2x = 18)$; *Sedum acre* $(2x = 16)$.

c) Chromosome morphology (Section 3.3.3)

1 Symmetrical karyotypes and chromosomes: *Campanula persicifolia* $(2x = 16)$; *Helianthus* spp. $(2n = 34,102)$; *Rhoeo discolor* $(2x = 12)$; *Tradescantia* spp. $(2n = 12,24)$ (Fig. 3.1a); *Secale cereale* $(2x = 14)$.

2 Karyotype asymmetry:

BIMODAL COMPLEMENT – SIZE: *Aloe* spp., *Gasteria* spp. $(2x = 14)$; *Ornithogalum pyrenaicum* $(2x = 16)$; *O. umbellatum* $(2x = 18)$; *Agave* spp., *Hosta* spp., *Yucca* spp. $(2x = 60)$.

BIMODAL COMPLEMENT – SIZE AND MORPHOLOGY: *Lilium* spp. $(2x = 24)$, *Lycoris aurea* $(2x = 12,13,14)$; *Nothoscordum inodorum* $(= N.\ fragrans)$ $(4x = 19)$ (Fig. 3.2c); *Vicia faba* $(2x = 12)$.

THREE OR MORE DISTINCT CHROMOSOME TYPES: *Allium* spp. $(2x = 14,16,18)$; *Bellevalia romana* $(2x = 8)$ (Fig. 3.2b); *Hyacinthus orientalis* $(2x = 16)$ (3.2c); *Tulbaghia* spp. $(2x = 12)$ (Fig. 3.2d).

b) 3 Contrast in size between related species:

Large	Small
Allium cepa $(2x = 16)$	*Allium fuscum* $(2x = 16)$
Ranunculus cortusifolius $(2x = 16)$	*Ranunculus pedatus* $(2x = 16)$
Lathyrus hirsutus $(2x = 14)$	*Lathyrus angulatus* $(2x = 14)$
Vicia faba $(2x = 12)$	*Vicia sativa* $(2x = 12)$
Lolium temulentum $(2x = 14)$	*Lolium perenne* $(2x = 14)$
Crepis capillaris $(2x = 6)$	{ *Crepis zacintha* { *Crepis fuliginosa* $(2x = 6)$

ALL CHROMOSOMES DISTINGUISHABLE: *Crepis capillaris* $(2x = 6)$; *Endymion nonscriptus* $(2x = 16)$ (Fig. 1.1); *Haplopappus gracilis* $(2x = 4)$; *Ipheon uniflorum* $(2x = 12)$; *Kniphofia uvaria* $(2x = 12)$; *Ornithogalum virens* $(2x = 6)$; *Puschkinia libanotica* $(2x = 10)$ (Fig. 4.2c); *Ranunculus ficaria* $(2x = 16)$ (Fig. 4.3b); *Trillium* spp. $(2x = 10)$ (Fig. 2.5c); *Drosophila melanogaster* (fruit fly) $(2x = 8)$.

3 Chromosome asymmetry:

ALL ACROCENTRICS: *Crocus balansae* $(2x = 6)$, *Kniphofia* spp. $(2x = 12)$.

SOME TELOCENTRICS: *Zebrina pendula, Z. purpurii* $(2x = 24)$; *Z. flocculosa* $(2x = 22)$.

ALL TELOCENTRICS: *Tradescantia micrantha* $(2x = 14)$; *Schistocerca gregaria, Locusta migratoria* (locusts) $(2x = 23,24)$.

4 Number of nucleolar organizers:

ONE PER GENOME: *Allium cepa* $(2x = 16)$, *Bellevalia romana* $(2x = 8)$ (Fig. 3.2b); *Crocus balansae* $(2x = 6)$; *Hyacinthus orientalis* $(2x = 16)$ (Fig. 3.2a); *Ranunculus ficaria* $(2x = 16)$ (Fig. 4.3b).

TWO PER GENOME: *Festuca ovina* $(2x = 14)$; *Lilium auratum* $(2x = 24)$.

THREE PER GENOME: *Trillium kamtschaticum* $(2x = 10)$.

FOUR PER GENOME: *Trillium grandiflorum* $(2x = 10)$.

FIVE PER GENOME: *Lilium regale* $(2x = 24)$.

5 Position of nucleolar organizers:

INTERSTITIAL, CONTINUOUS WITH CENTROMERES: *Caloscordum neriniflorum* $(2x = 16)$; *Nothoscordum inutile* $(2x = 16)$.

INTERSTITIAL, IN ONE OF THE LONGER ARMS OF THE GENOME: *Lilium auratum* $(2x = 24)$; *Vicia faba* $(2x = 12)$; *Hyacinthus orientalis* $(2x = 16)$ (Fig. 3.2a). In cultivars 'Rosalie' $(2x+1 = 17)$, 'Eclipse' $(3x = 24)$, 'Ben Nevis', 'L'Innocence' $(3x+3 = 27)$ and 'Carnegie' $(4x-3 = 29)$ with 3 or more nucleolar organizers, one or two are less conspicuous than the rest.

INTERSTITIAL, IN THE SHORT ARM OF AN ACROCENTRIC: *Crocus balansae* $(2x = 6)$; *Lilium auratum* $(2x = 24)$.

TERMINAL OR NEAR-TERMINAL ON A LONG ARM: *Bellevalia romana* $(2x = 8)$ (Fig. 3.2b); *Tradescantia paludosa* $(2x = 12)$; *Trillium grandiflorum* $(2x = 10)$.

TERMINAL OR NEAR TERMINAL ON THE SHORT ARM OF AN ACROCENTRIC: *Allium cepa*★ $(2x = 16)$; *Endymion nonscriptus* $(2x = 16)$ (Fig. 1.1); *Ipheon uniflorum* $(2x = 12)$; *Nothoscordum inodorum* $(= N.\ fragrans)$ $(4x = 19)$; *Ranunculus ficaria*★ $(2x = 16, 4x = 32)$ (Fig. 4.3b); *Trillium* spp. $(2x = 10)$; *Tulbaghia verdoornia*★ $(2x = 12)$ (Fig. 3.2d).

★Nucleolar satellite often allocyclic or structurally heterozygous.

See **d)** below and Section 3.4 for examples where chromosome morphology reveals polyploidy, aneuploidy, dysploidy, B chromosomes and structural heterozygosity.

d) Meiotic pairing (Section 3.3.4)

Material to illustrate the range of pairing relationships at metaphase I is listed below in the sequence shown in Table 3.2, p. 80–81. The same examples could equally well be used as 'unknowns' for exercises in karyotype analysis. In the species marked ★, the condition is also clearly indicated by the mitotic chromosome number. In those marked † the condition is also indicated by mitotic chromosome morphology.

1 All bivalents, symmetrical:

STANDARD DIPLOID: see Section 2.5 for suitable examples including localized chiasmata etc.

DIPLOID WITH TWO HOMOLOGOUS B CHROMOSOMES: *Puschkinia libanotica*★† $(2x = 10 + 2B)$ (selected individuals).

DIPLOID NULLISOMIC: *Punica granatum* var *nanum*★ $(2x - 2 = 16)$.

AMPHIDIPLOID ALLOPOLYPLOID WITH PREFERENTIAL PAIRING: *Triticum aestivum*★† ($6x = 42 = $ AABBDD); *Triticum dicoccum*★† ($4x = 28 = $ AABB); *Triticale* (wheat/rye hybrid)★† (e.g. $8x = 56 = $ AABBDDRR).

AUTOPOLYPLOID WITH LOW CHIASMA FREQUENCY OR FEW PAIRING INITIATION POINTS: *Tulipa chrysantha*★ ($4x = 48$); *Paris quadrifolia*★ ($4x = 20$). Probably also *Lolium perenne* 'Reveille'★† ($4x = 28$) and *L. multiflora* 'Serenade'★† ($4x = 28$).

2 All bivalents, one asymmetrical (heteromorphic) bivalent:

DIPLOID STRUCTURAL HETEROZYGOTE:

Deletion: *Hyacinthus orientalis* cultivar 'Tubergen's Scarlet' (Fig. 3.2a) (= 'Mme. du Barry', 'Scarlet O'Hara') and its double flowered sport 'Scarlet Perfection'† ($2x = 16$).

Supernumerary segments: *Chorthippus brunneus*,† *C. parallelus*† (grasshoppers) ($2x = 17, 18$).

DIOECIOUS DIPLOID WITH SEX CHROMOSOMES: *Silene alba* (= *Melandrium album*)♂† ($2x = 22 + $ XY); *S. dioica* (= *M. rubrum*)♂† ($2x = 22 + $ XY); *Rumex angiocarpus*♂† ($2x = 12 + $ XY); *R. acetosa*♂† ($2x = 12 + XY_1Y_2$); *Humulus lupulus*♂† ($2x = 18 + $ XY); *Drosophila melanogaster*♂† (fruit fly) ($2x = 6 + $ XY).

3 All bivalents, most or all asymmetrical:

Diploid hybrids between related species differing in several structural rearrangements; univalents and interchange multivalents also present in some cells; *Lilium* cultivar 'Black Beauty' ($2x = 24$); *Lilium* cultivar 'Marhan'† ($2x = 24$) (= *L. martagon* × *L. hansoni*); *Tulipa* hybrids ($2x = 24$); *Lolium temulentum* × *L. perenne*† ($2x = 14$); *Paeonia delavayi* × *lutea* hybrids ($2x = 20$); *Crepis rubra* × *C. foetida*† ($2x = 10$); *Silene alba* × *S. dioica*† ($2x = 24$).

4 Bivalents with univalent(s):

HAPLOID WITH DUPLICATED SEGMENTS: not generally available but reported in haploid *Antirrhinum majus* ($x = 8$).

DIPLOID HYBRID BETWEEN RELATED SPECIES: *Narcissus* cultivar 'Geranium' ($2x = 17$) (= *N. poeticus*, $2x = 14$, × *N. tazetta*, $2x = 22$); *N.* × *biflorus* (= *N. poeticus*, $2x = 14$, × *N. pseudo-narcissus*, $2x = 14$). See also **3** above.

DIOECIOUS DIPLOID WITH UNPAIRED SEX CHROMOSOME(S): *Chorthippus* spp.★†♂ (Grasshopper) ($2x = 16 + $ X); *Schistocerca gregaria*, *Locusta migratoria*★†♂ (locusts) ($2x = 22 + $ X)

DIPLOID WITH ONE B CHROMOSOME: *Puschkinia libanotica*★† ($2x = 10 + $ 1B) (selected individuals).

ENVIRONMENTAL SUPPRESSION OF PAIRING: low temperature induces partial or complete failure of pairing and chiasma formation in *Tradescantia virginiana* ($4x = 24$). Chiasma localization or failure is induced by 48 hours at 35–40°C in several plants and animals including *Hyacinthus orientalis* cv. 'Roman hyacinth' ($2x = 16$); *Endymion non-scriptus* ($2x = 16$); *Trillium* spp. ($2x = 10$); *Schistocerca gregaria*♂ (locust) ($2x = 23$).

GENOTYPIC SUPPRESSION OF PAIRING: partially or totally asynaptic mutants have been found sporadically in many species but are sterile and not widely available.

ALLOPOLYPLOID WITH RESTRICTED PAIRING: *Rosa canina* ($5x = 35 = $ AABCD); *Tulbaghia* hybrid ($3x = 18 = $ AAV) (= *Tulbaghia violacea*, $2x = 12 = $ VV, × *T. alliacea*, $4x = 24 = $ AAAA). See also under **7** below.

POLYHAPLOID: several vigorous and fertile polyhaploids of *Solanum tuberosum* have been obtained and maintained experimentally but are not generally available.

5 All univalents:

HAPLOID: haploids and polyhaploids have been induced in several species including *Nicotiana tabacum*, *Lycopersicum esculen-*

tum and *Hordeum vulgare* by a variety of techniques including temperature shocks, disturbance of pollination or fertilization and pollen culture, but they are sterile and lack vigour and are not easily obtained or maintained. Exceptions are clonally propagated *Pelargonium zonale* cultivar 'Kleine Liebling' (= 'Little Sweetheart')★ ($x = 9$) and *Thuya gigantea* var. *gracilis*★ ($x = 11$). The males of certain insects including the honey bee are normally haploid. The free living gametophytes of many algae, mosses and ferns are also haploid.

DIPLOID HYBRID: at least some cells of many hybrids show complete failure of pairing. See **3** and **4** above.

ENVIRONMENTAL AND GENOTYPIC SUPPRESSION OF PAIRING: see **4** above.

6 Bivalents with one or two multivalents:

DIPLOID INTERCHANGE HETEROZYGOTE: *Allium sativum* (many-flowered form with violet bulb coat and 'cloves' in two groups)† ($2x = 16$); *Hyacinthus orientalis* cultivar 'Fireball'† ($2x = 16$); *Campanula persicifolia* ($2x = 16$); *Oenothera hookeri* ($2x = 14$); *Paeonia californica* ($2x = 10$); *Periplaneta americana* ($2x = 33,34$). Sporadically in some *Allium* spp. and in certain species of *Commelinaceae*. Also in certain species hybrids including *Allium cepa* × *A. fistulosum* ($2x = 16$) and *T. verdoornia* × *T. violacea* ($2x = 12$).

DIPLOID OR AMPHIDIPLOID HETEROZYGOUS FOR CENTROMERE FUSION/FISSION OR ASSOCIATION/DISSOCIATION ('ROBERTSONIAN TRANSLOCATION'): see Section 3.4.2e. *Nothoscordum inodorum* (= *N. fragrans*)★† ($4x = 19$); *Lycoris aurea*★† ($2x = (12)13(14)$); *Polygonatum* hybrid★† ($2x = 19$) (= *P. multiflorum*, $2x = 18$, × *P. odoratum*, $2x = 20$); Probably also in *Iris reticulata* cultivar 'Joyce'★† ($2x = 19$) (= *I. histrioides*, $2x = 18$, × *I. reticulata*, $2x = 20$).

DIOECIOUS DIPLOID WITH SEX CHROMOSOMES: *Humulus japonicus*♂★† ($2x = 14 +$ XY_1Y_2); *Rumex hastatulus*♂★† ($2x = 6 + XY_1Y_2$); *R. acetosa*♂★† ($2x = 12 + XY_1Y_2$); *Forficula auricularia*♂★† (earwig) ($2x = 22 + X_1X_2Y$) (other forms exist).

ANEUPLOID DIPLOID: *Hyacinthus orientalis* cultivar 'Rosalie'★† ($2x + 1 = 17$).

POLYPLOIDS WITH LOW CHIASMA FREQUENCY: see under **7** below.

7 Bivalents with more than two multivalents:

DIPLOID MULTIPLE INTERCHANGE HETEROZYGOTE: some individuals of *Periplaneta americana* (cockroach) ($2x = 33,34$).

ANEUPLOID POLYPLOID: *Hyacinthus orientalis* cultivars, including 'City of Haarlem', 'Eros'★† ($3x - 1 = 23$); 'Van Speyk'★† ($3x - 3 = 21$).

POLYPLOID WITH FEW CHIASMA OR PAIRING INITIATION POINTS: pairing in the following species is less than the theoretical maximum in some or most cells even in optimal conditions; univalents may also be present, particularly in $3x$ and $5x$; in some cells, particularly in allotriploids, multivalents may be absent; see also under **4, 6** and **8**; *Endymion non-scriptus*★† ($3x = 24$); *E. hispanicus*★† ($3x = 24$); *Lilium tigrinum*★† ($3x = 36$); *Tulipa gesneriana*★†, *T. praecox*★† ($3x = 36$); *Allium carinatum*★† ($3x = 24$); *Tradescantia virginiana* × *T. brevicaulis* hybrid★† ($3x = 18$) (Section 4.4.1, Fig. 4.1a); *Hyacinthus orientalis* cvv. 'Amethyst', 'Anne Marie', 'Bismark', 'Cyclops', 'Eclipse', 'Jan Bos'★† ($3x = 24$), cv. 'Blue Giant'★† ($4x = 32$); *Allium schoenoprasum*★ ($4x = 32$); *Tradescantia virginiana* ($4x = 24$) (Fig. 4.1e); *Tulipa clusiana*★ ($5x = 60$).

POLYPLOID INTERCHANGE HETEROZYGOTE: some individuals of *Anthoxanthum odoratum* ($4x = 20$); *Dactylis glomerata* ($4x = 28$).

8 Multivalents and univalents:

POLYPLOIDS WITH LOW CHIASMA FREQUENCY: see under **7** above.

POLYPLOIDS WITH B CHROMOSOMES: *Tradescantia virginiana*⋆† ($4x = 24 + 1$ to 5B) (Fig. 3.11) (usually also some bivalents, see under **7** above).

9 All multivalent(s):

DIPLOID MULTIPLE INTERCHANGE HETERO-ZYGOTE (whole complement involved in one or two large multivalents): *Oenothera biennis*, *O. muricata*, *O. strigosa* ($2x = 14$); *Hypericum punctatum* ($2x = 16$); *Rhoeo discolor* ($= R. spathacea$) ($2x = 12$) (Fig. 3.10c); *Paeonia californica* ($2x = 10$).

POLYPLOID WITH FULL PAIRING: rarely occurs in every cell of a polyploid (see under **7** above); occurs relatively frequently in *Endymion non-scriptus*⋆† ($3x = 24$); *E. hispanicus*⋆† ($3x = 24$) and some autotetraploids of *Secale cereale* ($4x = 28$) and *Lolium perenne* ($4x = 28$); occurs in occasional cells of *Tradescantia virginiana* ($4x = 24$) (Fig. 4.1f).

e) Meiotic disjunction (Section 3.3.4)

1 Inversion bridges and fragments at anaphase I and II: Some cells of *Festuca pratensis* ($2x = 14$); *Tradescantia virginiana* ($4x = 24$); *Trillium grandiflorum* ($2x = 10$) (Fig. 3.10a); *Paeonia suffruticosa* ($2x = 10$); and hybrids of *Lilium* species ($2x = 24$), *Tulipa* species ($2x = 24$), *Paeonia* species ($2x = 10$) and *Tulbaghia verdoornia* × *T. violacea* ($2x = 12$). Breakage and 'U' type reunion of non-sister chromatids can produce similar results.

2 Non-disjunction and loss at anaphase I: common in univalents and multivalents of hybrids and polyploids; e.g. *Tradescantia virginiana* × *T. brevicaulis* ($3x = 18$) (Fig. 4.1b and c, Section 4.6.1); *Hyacinthus orientalis* cultivars 'Amethyst', 'Anne Marie', 'Bismark', 'Cyclops', 'Eclipse', 'Jan Bos' ($3x = 24$).

3 Suppression of anaphase I: found as a regular feature of apomixis in e.g. *Taraxacum* and *Alchemilla* and also in some recent hybrids e.g. *Narcissus* cultivar 'Geranium' ($2x = 17$) ($= N.$ *poeticus*, $2x = 14$, × *N. tazetta*, $2x = 20$) where bivalents are maintained until anaphase II.

3.4 Chromosome mutation and karyotype evolution

One of several remarkable features of the process whereby the chromosome complement is replicated and distributed each time a cell divides is its precision. Nevertheless, it is far from infallible and karyotype evolution depends on chromosome mutations, the occasional spontaneous errors of chromosome replication and separation which lead to numerical or structural changes, independent of development and in an essentially stable system. A wide range of mutation types occur but most are inherently unstable or deleterious at least under the conditions prevailing at the time. Those which survive a succession of critical stages at which rigorous elimination occurs and ultimately become established as successful new karyotypes represent only a small and highly selected sample of those first formed. It is these selected chromosome mutations which are of particular evolutionary significance and are widely studied and described. It must be remembered however that the full range of mutations is only to be found in the individual cells in which they first occur, while the important and often neglected early stages of the selection process immediately following mutation in mitotic cells can only be examined in the resulting chimaera. In this section, the major mutation types will be introduced together with lists of material in which they can be found. More detailed accounts of their behaviour at meiosis and their adaptive significance can be found in most books on cytogenetics (Section 3.5).

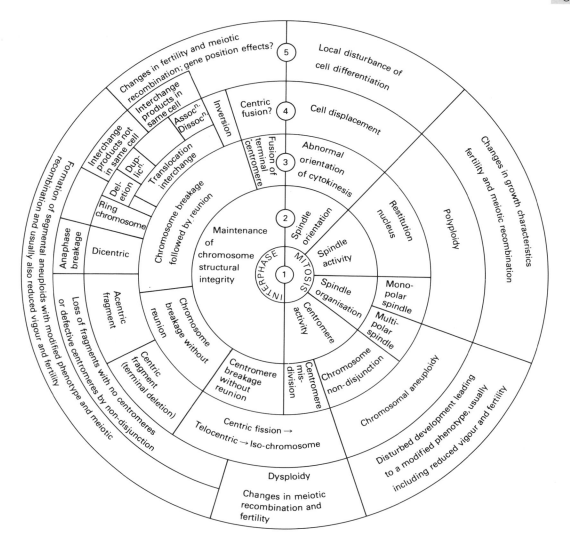

Fig. 3.5 The origins and consequences of chromosome mutations during the cell cycle. By following any radius out through the concentric rings, the cause and effect of a particular type of mutation can be correlated. The rings represent: 1 Phase of the cell cycle during which mutation occurs. 2 Division activity initially modified by mutation. 3 Initial effect. 4 Initial product. 5 Consequence after later divisions and ultimate effect on development and fertility. At meiosis asynapsis and multivalent formation can be an additional cause of irregular disjunction and restitution.

3.4.1 The origin and establishment of chromosome mutations

Most spontaneous chromosome mutations can be attributed to division errors of two main types: the failure of normal centromere and spindle activities during the active division stages, and the failure to maintain the structural integrity of the chromosomes during interphase, perhaps due to aberra-

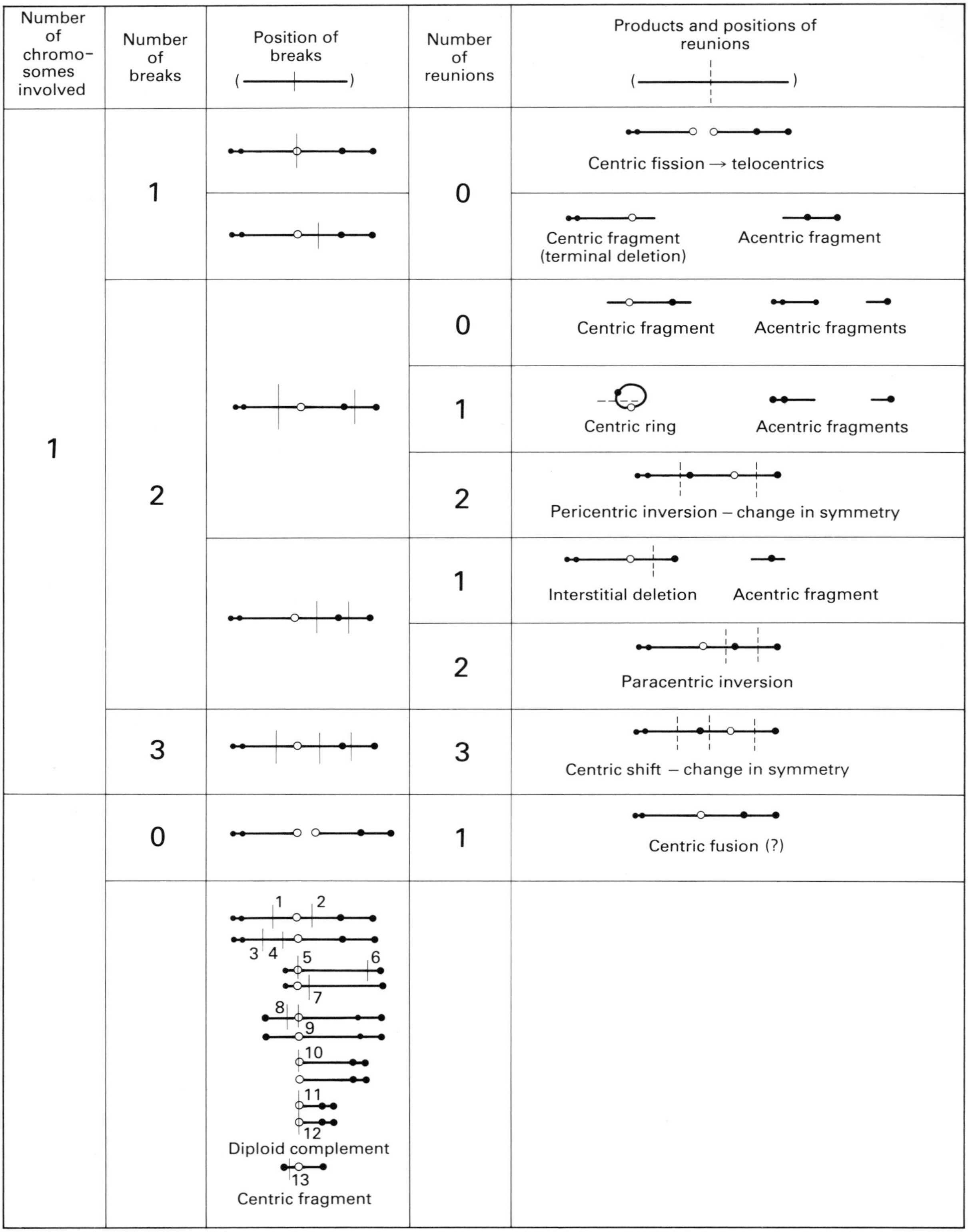

Number of chromosomes involved	Number of breaks	Position of breaks (——+——)	Number of reunions	Products and positions of reunions (——+——)
1	1		0	Centric fission → telocentrics
				Centric fragment (terminal deletion) Acentric fragment
	2		0	Centric fragment Acentric fragments
			1	Centric ring Acentric fragments
			2	Pericentric inversion – change in symmetry
			1	Interstitial deletion Acentric fragment
			2	Paracentric inversion
	3		3	Centric shift – change in symmetry
	0		1	Centric fusion (?)
		Diploid complement Centric fragment		

Fig. 3.6 Structural rearrangements of chromosomes following breakage and reunion. In the chromosome diagrams, the open circles represent centromeres and the solid circles represent morphological markers. The

2	2	7 + 8	1	Terminal translocation / Centric & Acentric fragments
		1 + 3	2	**Homologous** — Duplication / Interstitial deletion
		2 + 4		Pseudo-isochromosomes _or_ Dicentric / Acentric
		11 + 12		Pseudo-iso-chromosome
		6 + 7		Dicentric / Acentric
		7 + 8, 5 + 9		**Non-homologous** — Chromosome association (with loss of centric fragment) → increased symmetry
		10 + 11		Chromosome association (pseudo − centric fusion)
		2 + 13		Chromosome dissociation → reduced symmetry, increased chromosome number
		2 + 7		Symmetry unchanged
		2 + 6		Reduced symmetry _or_ Dicentric / Acentric
	3	1 + 3 + 4	3	Homologous: Duplication / Interstitial deletion
		3 + 4 + 6		Non-homologous: Interstitial deletion / Insertion

Reciprocal terminal translocation = interchange (for number 2)

Interstitial translocation (for number 3)

numbers in column 3 refer to the positions of chromosome breaks as indicated in the hypothetical chromosome complement at foot of p. 90.

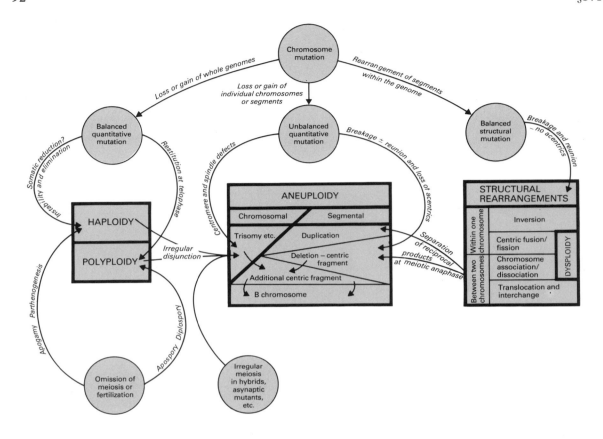

Fig. 3.7   The major types of mitotically stable chromosome mutations and their interrelationships.

tions of replication or repair processes (Fig. 3.5). The former results in cell displacement, which may affect subsequent differentiation, centromere mis-division, producing telocentric chromosomes, and euploid and aneuploid changes in the number of chromosomes. Interphase errors induce structural changes as a result of so-called 'breaks' which may be followed by the reunion of recently broken ends. The type of ensuing rearrangement depends on the number and position of the breaks and any subsequent reunions (Fig. 3.6, 3.8). In some species, including *Vicia faba* and man, breaks resulting in rearrangements are not randomly distributed but concentrated near nucleolar organizers or allocyclic segments, perhaps due to mechanical interference with reunion by the inter-

phase nucleoli or chromocentres. Some of the products of breakage are eliminated at the next mitosis. As centromeres cannot be created *de novo*, fragments with defective centromeres, or no centromere at all (acentrics), are lost. Dicentrics are broken.

Mitotically stable products of chromosome mutation can be considered under three headings according to their effect on the gene complement (Fig. 3.7). Where segments are merely rearranged but not initially lost, as for example in interchanges and inversions, the genotype is unchanged although there may be minor changes in gene activity. Where whole genomes are gained or lost, as in polyploid or haploid nuclei, there are quantitative changes but the balance of the genotype is maintained, all genes being represented equally, and the phenotypic effect, of polyploidy at least, is relatively slight. After both types of change, the nuclei remain euploid. Where the gain or loss affects individual chromosomes, as in chromosomal aneuploids, or individual segments, as in the segmentally aneuploid deletions and duplications, the genotype is unbalanced, usually with marked effects on cell and plant development.

Some mitotically stable conditions are unstable at meiosis. Separation to different nuclei of the reciprocal products of translocation will produce genetically unbalanced nuclei with uncompensated deletions and duplications. Chiasma formation between an inverted segment and the unchanged homologue has a similar effect. Irregular disjunction in haploids and polyploids will give rise to unbalanced chromosomal aneuploids. Irregular disjunction in aneuploids can create new aneuploid conditions or even restore euploidy. Non-disjunction of small centric fragments following interchange may produce dysploid changes, where the number of chromosomes in the genome is altered with no significant change in the genotype, or create the progenitors of supernumerary B chromosomes. Those mutations which are more stable at meiosis will nevertheless modify chromosome pairing and disjunction in a way which will affect gene segregation and recombination and it is frequently these effects which are of adaptive significance. The main types of mitotically stable euploid and aneuploid mutations, and some of their derivatives, are shown diagrammatically in Fig. 3.8 and considered further in Section 3.4.2.

It is not easy to determine the frequency with which chromosome mutations arise. Surveys of young individuals in a number of plant and animal species and man suggest that 0.1 to 1.0% have mutant karyotypes. While not all of these will reach maturity, these samples do nevertheless already represent a selected population of the more successful mutants capable of near normal embryogenesis. It is likely that the frequency of chromosomal abnormalities is higher at the zygote stage. In man, examination of young foetuses reveals that up to 10% of zygotes are abnormal but most abort spontaneously. It is probable that many zygotic abnormalities arise through errors during the complex events of the preceding meiosis although some of these will have already succumbed during the intervening gametogenesis and fertilization, including gametophyte development where applicable.

The simpler process of mitosis appears to be more stable but there are of course many mitotic divisions in the life cycle of a higher plant or animal. Surveys of root tip cells indicate that mutant karyotypes produced by mitotic errors rarely occur with a frequency greater than 0.05%, but this corresponds to a total of 50 000 separate mutations in a small herbaceous plant of 10^8 cells and that may be an underestimate because the endosperm and perhaps other ephemeral tissues can have a higher mutation rate. Thus unless the germ line mitoses of the shoot apex are free from such errors, which seems unlikely, chromosome mutation at mitosis can make a significant contribution to karyotype change.

There are occasional circumstances in which the level of mitotic mutation is dramatically higher. Repeated chromosome fragmentation is not uncommon in diseased and parasitised plants and tissue cultures. Repeated non-disjunction results in *aneusomaty* or *karyotype instability* where a variety of aneuploid complements occur within one tissue. In extreme cases, the effects are cumulative and almost every dividing cell has a different complement. Aneusomaty also occurs in infected plants and tissue cultures where physiological disturbance is to be expected. In intact healthy plants, karyotype instability is not found in regular diploids but is closely correlated with newly induced or high levels of polyploidy, with recent hybridization or with both. Aneusomaty may be more common than has been appreciated in hybrids which fail to reach maturity and

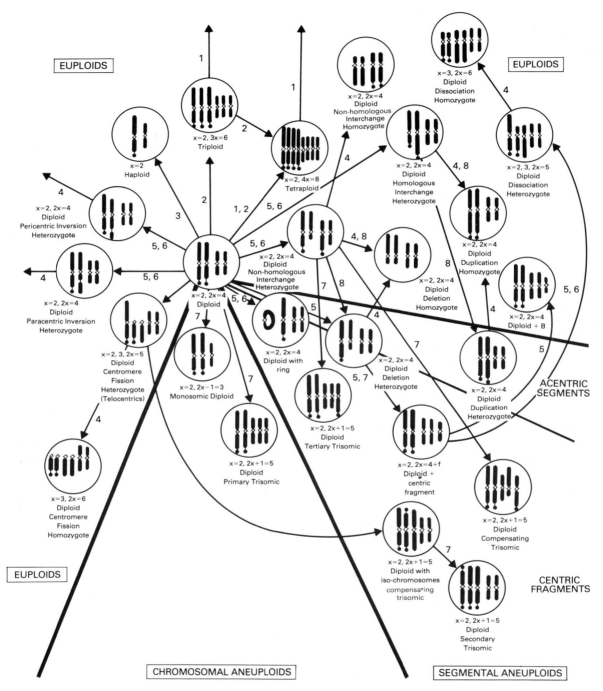

Fig. 3.8 Euploid and aneuploid derivatives of a structurally homozygous diploid karyotype. Key to derivations:
1, Somatic doubling. 2, Fertilization of unreduced gametes. 3, Parthenogenesis, somatic instability.
4, Homozygosity by inbreeding. 5, Chromosome breakage. 6, Chromosome reunion. 7, Non-disjunction.
8, Separation at meiotic anaphase of the reciprocal products of translocation.

abort during embryo and endosperm development. Karyotype instability may therefore be a significant factor in species isolation. Associated with aneusomaty is the likely cause; lagging chromosomes, degenerating micronuclei and multipolar spindles at mitosis and meiosis resulting from irregularities of spindle organization and centromere activity. In a few plants, the resulting complements show peak frequencies corresponding to euploid numbers, perhaps due to more rapid division and greater stability, or to preferential formation, of balanced nuclei with intact genomes. The so-called *chromosome elimination* described in hybrids between wheat or barley and *Hordeum bulbosum* and in some *Nicotiana* hybrids is an extreme example of the latter process. In the cereal hybrids, all the *H. bulbosum* chromosomes are selectively and progressively lost during embryogenesis leaving the other parental complement intact in a haploid or polyhaploid seedling. Now being exploited in plant breeding, this phenomenon may account for many past examples of what appeared to be parthogenetic or androgenic embryos after hybrid pollination. Occurring naturally, the loss of whole genomes by accumulated mitotic errors could provide a mechanism for reversing polyploidy during karyotype evolution but only if both stability and vigour are restored in the product.

A new karyotype has no evolutionary potential, and is of limited interest, unless it can exist as the sole complement characterizing a whole individual. Mutations arising at meiosis and surviving until fertilization occur immediately throughout the subsequent gametophyte and, at least in the heterozygous condition, the sporophyte which follows. Whether mutations arising in mitotic cells reach this stage depends on their position in the organism and on their ability to survive rigorous selection during development.

Regardless of its effect on the cell, only those mutations which occur in cells of the germ line (Fig. 2.8) can contribute to the next generation. In angiosperms, mutations arising in roots and leaves and secondary shoot meristems are usually undetected and rarely transmitted sexually although they may be maintained vegetatively for a period. The mitotic products of the more successful mutant meristem cells form an identifiable cell lineage, the distribution of which reflects the organization of normal development. Investigation of these cytochimaeras, individuals with two or more cytologically distinct cell lines, reveals that a mutation in a root tip can produce a complete sector of mutant cells extending back from the growing apex. However, the stem apex maintains two or three developmentally distinct layers and the mutation is normally restricted to the layer in which it arose. The mutant cell lineage may in time extend round the entire circumference of that layer, so that the initial mericlinal chimaera forms a relatively stable periclinal chimaera, but only if the orientation of cell division is disturbed, as after wounding, will the mutation enter other layers. Each layer ultimately gives rise to particular tissues of the mature stem and its derivatives, and the meiocytes and thus the gametes are derived only from the subepidermal layer. Thus the chimaerical condition cannot be transmitted through sexual reproduction and a mutant karyotype, however vigorous, can only enter the next generation if it occurs in the second layer of the apex. Mutants arising early in development will form larger sectors and thus more meiocytes than those arising later. Mutants, of whatever type, arising in the outer or central layers of the apex are as unlikely to become established as those occurring in leaves or roots.

Equally important for the evolutionary potential of a mutation as the position of the cell in which it first occurs is the ability to survive a succession of critical tests of its viability. Many products of mutation will be eliminated before they enter a zygote, particularly critical phases being cell growth during the succeeding interphase, the first mitotic division, tissue and organ development, meiosis and gametogenesis. Quantitative changes in the genotype such as polyploidy, haploidy and aneuploidy may affect cell growth and slow or even prevent preparation for division. Some products of structural rearrangement, such as acentrics, side-arm bridges and dicentrics, are lost at the first mitosis and produce further unbalanced genotypes in the products. Some abnormal cells will be eliminated during growth in competition with their normal neighbouring cells. This has been demonstrated after X-ray induced chromosome mutation. Those which survive may induce slow or abnormal growth of tissues and organs. Of those mutant karyotypes which enter the meiocytes, many, including haploids, aneuploids, and some polyploids, are not regularly transmitted at meiosis because of irregular disjunction, in some cases despite previous vegetative vigour. Those mutations which pass successfully through meiosis will be subjected to further rigorous selection in the gametophytes and gametes when the mutation is fully exposed in the vulnerable haploid or polyhaploid complement. Only the survivors which enter the zygote through one or both gametes to give rise to mutant individuals are subjected to the final test, competition with established cytotypes in a polymorphic population. The minority that succeed, frequently because of an adaptive advantage of altered patterns of gene recombination resulting from modified chromosome pairing behaviour, provide the basis for karyotype evolution (Section 3.4.3).

3.4.2 Chromosome mutations

In this section, the more common types of mutation are introduced as a basis for examining the material listed in Section 3.4.4. For further information on their behaviour, effect and adaptive significance, consult the references listed in Section 3.5

3.4.2a Side-arm bridges, dicentrics, ring chromosomes and acentrics

These mutations are considered together because they are all unstable at mitotic or meiotic division, or both, and are not among those which can have a long term evolutionary significance.

The cause and structure of side-arm bridges, which appear to involve breakage and reunion of subchromatid units, is not certain and a number of models have been suggested. Sometimes concentrated in long arms of the complement and near nucleolar organizers, they have been reported in hybrids and aneuploids and after temperature shock, irradiation and chemical treatment. The bridges may be broken at anaphase, or, if sufficiently strong, induce chromosome breakage or nuclear restitution.

Dicentrics, accompanied by acentrics, are not uncommon after irradiation and occur spontaneously in occasional individuals, usually at pollen grain mitosis, in association with previous meiotic inversion bridges or U-type non-sister chromatic reunions, or in the early divisions of seedling roots. Unless the centromeres are so close as to act as one, or one dominates the other, dicentrics are eliminated at mitosis by breakage of chromosome bridges. Very rarely, a dicentric breakage-fusion-breakage cycle is repeated when terminal fusion of sister chromatids results in a single strand dicentric which breaks at anaphase. After interphase replication, the freshly broken ends of the sister chromatids once more fuse and the cycle is repeated.

Centric and acentric ring chromosomes also occur spontaneously and after irradiation. Centric rings are stable at mitosis but may suffer the disadvantages of other types of deletion. They are usually eliminated at meiosis because of the anaphase bridges formed after pairing with the structurally normal homologue. An acentric cannot generate a new centromere and is excluded from the spindle at the first mitosis after

Stage of meiosis	Metaphase I	Anaphase I	Telophase I /prophase II (no interphase replication)	Anaphase II	Telophase II, early interphase	Late interphase (after replication)
Normal centromere division						
Centromere misdivision at meiosis II (mitosis similar)						* Iso-
Centromere misdivision at meiosis I						Telo-

Fig. 3.9 The formation of isochromosomes and telocentrics by centromere misdivision. The formation by misdivision at mitosis or meiosis II of telocentrics able to replicate in step with the normal chromosomes requires separation of chromatids at the same time. Isochromosomes can be formed directly by misdivision at meiosis I only if sister chromatids reunite at the centromere during interphase I, in the absence of replication, and remain attached throughout meiosis II.
* Sister chromatid reunion at the centromere.

formation, produces micronuclei and degenerates. One of the remaining complements is, as a result, deficient for that segment.

3.4.2b Telocentrics and Isochromosomes

Although other mechanisms can be envisaged, the most likely origin of a telocentric with a truly terminal centromere is by transverse mis-division at the centromere of a univalent with delayed congression and disjunction at meiosis I. Both products might then divide normally at meiosis II and replicate and divide alongside other chromosomes during subsequent mitosis (Fig. 3.9). Telocentrics are not always stable and irregular disjunction at mitosis or meiosis due to defective centromeres can result in aneuploid conditions. The more stable ones can be incorporated in a diploid derivative of the original complement, or become an addition to the euploid complement as a potential supernumerary B chromosome.

Other telocentrics are stabilized as isochromosomes, probably formed during the interphase following formation of a telocentric by centromere mis-division at mitosis (Fig. 3.9). Sister chromatid fusion of the broken ends within the centromere accompanied by normal replication of both chromatid arms will produce an *isochromosome* with two identical, replicated, arms which may be capable of normal division at the next mitosis. Although frequently transmitted regularly by mitosis, isochromosomes almost inevitably induce a segmentally aneuploid state (Fig. 3.8) with its attendant effects on development, and internal pairing and non-disjunction at meiosis may prevent their sexual transmission to offspring. Consequently isochromosomes are rarely found except as B chromosomes.

3.4.2c Inversions and centric shifts

Inversion, which usually occurs first in the heterozygous state, results in no direct loss of genetic material and little or no initial effect on phenotype, but fertility is likely to be reduced if chiasmata form in the affected segment at meiosis.

Complete pairing in a paracentric inversion heterozygote produces an *inversion loop* at pachytene (Fig. 3.10d). A similar loop is produced by somatic pairing in dipteran polytene chromosomes. If a single chiasma is formed in the loop, a dicentric and acentric fragment are formed which become conspicuous at late anaphase I as a *bridge and fragment* (Figs. 3.10a,d). In the absence of chiasma localization the frequency of bridge formation in an inversion reflects the length of the segment while the size of the fragment reflects the position of the segment, not that of the chiasma. For a particular inversion, the fragment is of a constant size corresponding to twice the distance from the middle of the inversion to the end of the arm. Additional chiasmata in the same arm may eliminate the bridge or give rise to additional bridges at anaphase I or II depending on whether they were within the inversion and which chromatids were involved. The acentrics are lost and the dicentrics broken at meiosis or the next mitosis, and deficient and usually inviable gametic complements result. Chiasmata within the affected segment of a pericentric inversion heterozygote have essentially the same result, although no bridges and fragments are formed. There is therefore effectively no recombination by crossing over between the gene loci of the inverted segment in the heterozygote. Thus the potential adaptive value lies either in bringing closer together on the same chromosome two groups of genes situated close to the breaks, so that recombination between them is reduced even in the homozygote, or

in retaining intact a particular combination of alleles within the segment in the heterozygote, particularly if the reduction in fertility can be overcome. In addition, pericentric inversions, like centric shifts, may have a more general effect through a change, frequently a decrease, in chromosome symmetry. The overall level of recombination tends to be lower in asymmetric chromosomes with one long arm because the chiasma frequency per unit length is often less. Centric shifts may also resemble certain inversions in that should a chiasma form in the transposed acentric segment of a heterozygote a bridge and fragment could form (Fig. 3.10e). However, the dicentric in the case of a centric shift contains all the loci of the original chromosome and breakage and non-disjunction at anaphase could give rise to a dysploid increase in chromosome number.

3.4.2d Translocations and interchanges

Although, like inversions, mitotically stable, initially euploid and usually with little or no phenotypic effect, translocations frequently affect meiosis and fertility. The reciprocal products of homologous translocations always, and of non-homologous translocations sometimes, separate at meiotic anaphase to produce segmentally aneuploid daughter nuclei, with uncompensated duplications and deletions, which are frequently inviable. Thus a bivalent-forming heterozygote for a small non-homologous translocation will give rise to 50% gamete lethality after random assortment of the chromosomes. An interchange of larger segments will result in quadrivalent formation in the heterozygote (Figs. 3.10b,f) and again sterility except when both the interchange products or both the unaltered chromosomes pass to the same pole. This is most likely where terminal segments of similar size are exchanged within a complement of symmetrical chromosomes with chiasmata distally localized within the exchanged segments, so that an open ring quadrivalent with evenly spaced

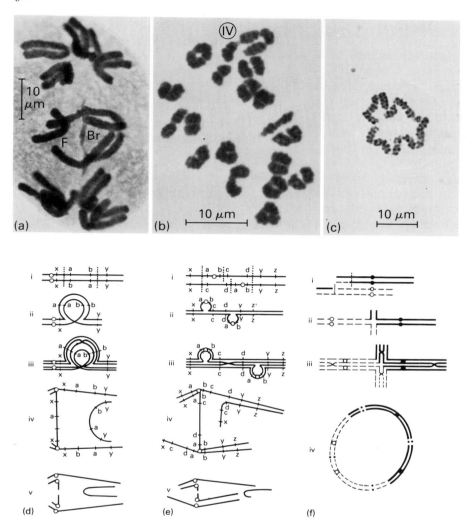

Fig. 3.10 Meiosis in structural heterozygotes. **a**, A bridge (Br) and fragment (F) in the short arm of chromosome A (see Fig. 2.16) at anaphase I of pollen meiosis of *Trillium grandiflorum* ($2x = 10$). This is the expected result of a chiasma in the affected segment of a plant heterozygous for a paracentric inversion near to the centromere of that arm. Both homologues of chromosome A are held by the bridge at the equator of the spindle while the homologues of the other four pairs of chromosomes separate to opposite poles. (Aceto-carmine preparation.) **b**, A ring quadrivalent (IV) at pollen meiosis in an interchange heterozygote of *Dichorisandra thyrsiflora* ($2n = 38$). Most individuals of this species form 19 bivalents but in the interchange heterozygote up to 55% of pollen mother cells form a ring quadrivalent, 22% form a chain quadrivalent and 2% a trivalent and a univalent. Anaphase is invariably numerically balanced ($n = 19$, Fig. 2.11) and over 80% of the pollen grains germinate in culture. The tolerance in the pollen of the genetic imbalance resulting from the frequent adjacent disjunction of interchange quadrivalents with parallel co-orientation (see Fig. 3.4) may be due to a polyploid origin. **c**, A ring of all twelve chromosomes at pollen meiosis in *Rhoeo discolor* ($= R. spathacea$) ($2n = 12$), a permanent structural heterozygote with 6 interchanges. The ring undergoes regular convergent co-orientation and alternate disjunction. **d**, Pairing and bridge and fragment formation in paracentric inversion heterozygote. i) mitotic karyotype, ii) zygotene pairing loop, iii) pachytene chiasma formation, iv) anaphase dicentric bridge and acentric fragment and v) rupture of bridge results in two deficient chromosomes. **e**, Pairing and bridge and fragment formation in a centric shift heterozygote. Stages as for **a**. Rupture of the bridge results in two acrocentrics, together genetically equivalent to one original chromosome. **f**, Pairing and ring quadrivalent formation in a terminal interchange heterozygote. i) mitotic karyotype, ii) zygotene quadrivalent, iii) distal chiasma formation at pachytene and iv) diakinesis ring quadrivalent with terminalized chiasmata (indicated by black dots).

centromeres is formed at metaphase. In this ring, the two interchange products alternate with the unchanged chromosomes, so fer- tility is improved by selection in favour of the convergent metaphase co-orientation and alternate anaphase disjunction which is necessary to produce balanced gametic complements.

Non-homologous translocations may have an advantage as homozygotes when favourable allelic combinations of functionally linked loci on different chromosomes are brought close together on the same chromosome so that recombination between them is reduced. Alternatively, by concentrating most of the genes on to a few long chromosomes in an asymmetrical complement, the overall level of recombination can be reduced by unequal interchange although the distance from the spindle pole to the cell plate at cytokinesis will impose limits on this trend. Interchanges can in addition have an adaptive significance in the heterozygous condition because of their influence on recombination in the affected chromosomes. When the interchanged segments are small, there is no chiasma formation within them because bivalent formation is unaltered, and effectively no recombination between them because separation of the reciprocal products leads to sterility, but recombination still occurs in the non-translocated segments due to crossing over. An interchange of large terminal segments, in conjunction with distally localized chiasmata, results in the reverse pattern of linkage. Crossing over in the quadrivalent then occurs in the translocated segments but, as few chiasmata are formed elsewhere and only the products of alternate disjunction of the quadrivalent are viable, recombination is virtually eliminated within as well as between the other regions of the two chromosome pairs involved. Each viable combination of non-homologous chromosomes from the quadrivalent thus forms a single large linkage group. This can be exploited further, where the heterozygote is sufficiently fertile, to stabilize the genotype and protect heterozygosity in spite of inbreeding. Additional superimposed interchanges can build up larger multivalent rings and extend the linkage groups to other chromosomes until ultimately all the chromosomes in the complement are incorporated in a single ring containing just two major linkage groups as in some forms of *Rhoeo spathacea* (= *R. discolor*) (Fig. 3.10c), *Oenothera lamarkiana* ($2x = 14$) and *Paeonia californica* ($2x = 10$).

3.4.2e Chromosome association/dissociation and centric fusion/fission

These terms, variously applied in the literature, here refer to two somewhat different mechanisms, sometimes collectively known as *Robertsonian translocations*, which achieve essentially the same dysploid changes in the complement. *Chromosome association* involves an unequal non-homologous interchange between two acrocentric chromosomes. This results in one large chromosome, with a near median centromere and containing all the necessary genetic information of the two original chromosomes, and one small centric fragment chromosome which can be lost with no harmful phenotypic effects and a consequent reduction in the basic number and an increase in karyotype symmetry. *Dissociation* is the reverse process, following crossing over in a centric shift heterozygote (Fig. 3.10e) or an unequal interchange which incorporates the centromere of an additional centric fragment into the basic complement, by which the basic number and asymmetry is increased. Centric fission is the formation of two stable telocentrics by mis-division of an interstitial centromere, while centric fusion is the reverse process by fusion of two terminal, non-homologous centromeres. It has not been established that fusion of intact centromeres occurs and centric fusion may only be possible after previous breakage within the two centromeres. It is not always obvious without additional, non-cytological, information whether the evolutionary trend of a series of dysploid changes is towards an increase or a decrease in basic number. Dysploid decrease may be accompanied by other rearrangements resulting in a loss of symmetry as the plant and its karyotype becomes more specialized, as in *Crepis*, but in other species, including *Lycoris*, dysploid reduction is associated with a reversal of a previous trend towards chromosome asymmetry.

Like other translocations, dysploid changes, which alter the chromosome number and symmetry without significantly changing the genotype, have little effect on somatic development but they affect recombination by altering the number and size of linkage groups, whether in the homozygous or heterozygous condition. An increase of one in the basic chromosome number doubles the possible number of different recombinant genotypes due to random assortment. However, the heterozygotes are frequently less fertile due to irregular disjunction of the hetero-trivalent formed at meiosis and are usually only temporary phases in the establishment of a new karyotype.

3.4.2f Deletions and duplications

Deletions arise in conjunction with acentrics when breakage is not accompanied by reunion and with complementary duplications after translocation. Duplications within the same chromosome occur after homologous translocation. As long as all the products of breakage remain to compensate each other within the same nucleus, there is little effect on the cell, but acentrics will be lost at the next mitosis, to produce deficient nuclei (Fig. 3.2a), while meiotic separation of reciprocal products of translocation (see (d) above) will produce deficient nuclei with uncompensated deletions and nuclei with duplications within the same chromosome or elsewhere in the same complement (= insertions). Nuclei with uncompensated duplications or deletions are segmental aneuploids for acentric segments.

Uncompensated deletions, even those too small to be recognized cytologically except by chromomere analysis, are frequently lethal in the homozygous and hemizygous condition.

In heterozygotes, exposed recessives may have marked phenotypic effects but for small segments this may be compensated by the lack of recombination in the unpaired remaining segment of the asymmetrical bivalent which can preserve a favourable combination of closely grouped alleles, as in an inversion heterozygote. Deletions may also be involved in the erosion of the differential segments of sex chromosomes during the evolution of sex determining mechanisms of dioecious species.

Duplications are more easily tolerated than deletions even when they contain genes with a recognizable effect and may even confer an advantage by preserving heterozygosity despite inbreeding or by providing a source of new genes by mutations. In this they are perhaps similar to B chromosomes (Section 3.4.2g) but without the same numerical flexibility. The significance is less clear when the duplicated segments increase the amount of repetitive-sequence DNA which has little phenotypic effect, as in the case of the supernumerary segments of *Chorthippus*. In *Chorthippus*, the segments are associated with changes in chiasma frequency, a property shared by many if not all B chromosomes, and presumably duplications of whatever kind prolong the cell division cycle but whether these are the significant effects is not known.

3.4.2g Centric fragments and supernumerary B chromosomes

The presence of a newly formed centric fragment creates a segmental aneuploid condition. When it replaces a normal member of the genome, it is synonymous with a deletion of an acentric segment but when it is present in addition to a complete genome it can be considered as a centric duplication or a deletion polysomic and here the distinction between chromosomal and segmental aneuploidy is an artificial one. As with all aneuploid conditions, it will have an effect on phenotype and fertility in accord

Table 3.3 The phenotypic effects of some B chromosomes. *Grasshopper.

Feature affected	Species	Phenotypic effect on individuals
DISTRIBUTION	*Centaurea scabiosa*	Greater success in dry habitats
	Festuca pratensis	Greater success on clay soils
	Lolium perenne	Greater success in crowded populations
	Ranunculus ficaria 2x	Exclusion from north of range
	Myrmeleotettix maculatus	Restriction to warmer habitats
VIGOUR	*Centaurea scabiosa*	Vigour increased by 1–3B, decreased by >5B
	Trillium grandiflorum	Vigour decreased by >3B
	Zea mays	Vigour decreased by >10B
MITOSIS AND MEIOSIS	*Puschkinia libanotica* *Secale creale*	Mitotic cycle lengthened
	Puschkinia libanotica *Trillium grandiflorum* *Myrmeleotettix maculatus*★	Average chiasma frequency of standard chromosomes increased
	Ranunculus ficaria 2x *Lolium perenne*	Average chiasma frequency of standard chromosomes decreased
	Lolium perenne × *L. temulentum*	Homoeologous pairing in hybrids suppressed; multivalent formation in tetraploid decreased
POLLEN, FRUIT AND SEED DEVELOPMENT	*Tulipa* sp.	Additional divisions of pollen vegetative nucleus induced, subsequent sterility
	Plantago coronopus	Male sterility induced by >1B
	Haplopappus gracilis	Pericarp pigment increased
	Allium porrum	Seed germination accelerated
	Secale creale	Seed germination delayed

with its gene content and, like chromosomal aneuploidy, may affect meiotic pairing associations and disjunction. Unpaired fragments will frequently form micronuclei at meiosis. As a consequence most will be eliminated.

The supernumerary, accessory, or B, chromosomes found in addition to the standard genomes in about 200 diploid and polyploid species are more permanent centric fragments (Section 4.4.2, Fig. 4.2c). In these the deleterious effects have been reduced, and the loss by non-disjunction, particularly of telocentrics, has been eliminated by the acquisition during evolution of certain unique characteristics. Supernumeraries occur in variable numbers in some individuals of some populations. They are almost always smaller, often very much smaller, than any of the standard chromo-

somes and telocentrics and isochromosomes are unusually frequent amongst supernumeraries. B chromosomes are not infrequently lost by random non-disjunction at mitosis or meiosis and in some species they are excluded from certain tissues, including adventitious roots, by controlled non-disjunction at predetermined stages of development (§2.4.3). In about half of the species studied, B chromosomes form chromocentres at interphase (Fig. 4.2). Phenotypic effects are usually inconspicuous, although not necessarily trivial (Table 3.3). For example, an effect on the length of the cell cycle and on chiasma frequency and distribution has been revealed in most of the plants in which the necessary investigation has been made, and these effects could be important.

Although established B chromosomes can pair with each other when two or more similar ones are present (Fig. 3.11) and even form multivalents when, as in rye and *Puschkinia*, they are large enough to include two chiasmata, they never pair with any of the members of the basic genome even though they are presumably originally derived from one of them. This differential pairing behaviour is a critical and diagnostic feature of B chromosomes.

There is some evidence that supernumeraries are not maintained indefinitely in asexual clones but in some sexually reproducing animals and plants, loss of supernumeraries at division or by elimination of those individuals with large numbers of B chromosomes is compensated by complex boosting mechanisms incorporating directed non-disjunction at meiosis or mitosis prior to gametogenesis (Section 2.4.3). Most species with boosting mechanisms at mitosis, whereby both daughter B chromosomes go to the same pole, have heterochromatic (Section 2.2.2) supernumeraries while in most species without mitotic boosting mechanisms they are euchromatic at all stages. The evolution of these boosting mechanisms provides support for the theory that B chromosomes can under some circumstances have an effect and confer a selective advantage. The relevant effect on the phenotype may be a specific one relating to particular loci on the chromosome, or a more general one affecting growth rate or recombination level caused by the increase in nuclear DNA. If the former, the important feature of these chromosomes may be that they are duplications which, like other duplications, allow heterozygosity to be maintained despite inbreeding but, unlike inserted acentric duplicate segments, are flexible in that in each generation selection can favour individuals with more, less or no duplications.

It is likely that B chromosome systems are continually evolving from spontaneous centric fragments, rather than constituting a distinct and uniform category. Intermediate conditions exist, as in *Clarkia* where what appear to be B chromosomes pair with the

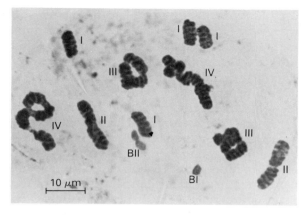

Fig. 3.11 Meiotic configurations in a PMC of an aneuploid plant of *Tradescantia virginiana* ($2n = 4x - 2 + 3B = 22 + 3B$). In addition to univalents (I), bivalents (II), trivalents (III) and quadrivalents (IV) of the standard chromosomes, two of the supernumeraries have formed a bivalent (BII).

standard chromosomes and in *Narcissus bulbocodium* where there is a variable number of heterochromatic chromosomes which are indistinguishable from the smaller euchromatic chromosomes of the genome apart from their allocycly, which is apparently controlled by a single gene.

Evolution of B chromosomes from a few of the centric fragments which arise spontaneously appears to involve, not necessarily in the order given, (i) genetic isolation by control of pairing, (ii) reduction of the deleterious consequences of aneuploidy by deletion, allocycly and controlled elimination from certain somatic tissues and (iii) development of boosting mechanisms to compensate for random loss. Thus small size, allocycly and controlled non-disjunction are probably advanced characters which shift the balance between deleterious and advantageous effects of B chromosomes in favour of the latter.

3.4.2h Chromosomal aneuploidy

Chromosomal aneuploids arise in all ploidy levels by irregular disjunction, particularly of meiotic univalents and multivalents. Once formed, they are usually stable at mitosis but they are genetically unbalanced and usually there are conspicuous effects on development. The severity of these effects depends upon a number of factors. Gain is more easily tolerated than loss and polyploids (Fig. 3.11) are more tolerant of both than diploids or haploids. Aneuploidy for one chromosome is in general less disturbing than when several are involved and a small chromosome has less effect than a large one. The consequences also depend on the particular chromosome concerned because of the specific effect of the genes it carries, as a result of which each aneuploid karyotype has a characteristic abnormal phenotype. Finally, tolerance to aneuploidy varies with the species, some, such as *Hyacinthus orientalis*, being particularly insensitive.

In those aneuploids capable of full development, univalents and multivalents and the associated irregular disjunction occur at meiosis, as a result of which the original aneuploid condition is not passed on to all gametes and some new aneuploid condition may be generated. Those aneuploid gametes which are formed may be at a disadvantage in competition with any balanced gametes produced at the same time and, if so, the majority of any viable progeny will be chromosomally normal. Thus fertility may not be severely reduced in these individuals, but the transmission rate of the original aneuploid condition is often low.

Because of weak and abnormal growth and instability at meiosis, aneuploids rarely persist under natural conditions and are of little evolutionary significance. They have however, been exploited extensively in experimental breeding of certain crops, for example, in producing alien addition and substitution lines, in gene location and chromosome identification.

Most aneuploids are of the so-called primary type in which the affected chromosomes are identical with members of the standard complement. The number of representatives of an affected chromosome, at any level of ploidy, is indicated by the terms nullisomic, monosomic, disomic etc. (Table 3.4). Where, more rarely, two or more chromosomes are affected, the adjectives double, triple etc. can be added. Thus a diploid with two extra chromosomes ($2n = 2x + 2$) could be a double trisomic, where the extra chromosomes are not homologous, or a single tetrasomic where they are identical. It is usual to refer an aneuploid condition to the nearest euploid level, so that when $x = 5$, $2n = 12 = 2x + 2$ and not $3x - 3$.

The most common class of primary aneuploid is the single trisomic diploid, with one extra chromosome. Where the extra chromosome is an isochromosome for one arm of the genome, the aneuploid is distinguished as a secondary trisomic. Where aneuploidy has resulted from non-disjunction of the quadrivalent in an interchange heterozygote, tertiary and compensatory trisomics are produced (Fig. 3.8). These conditions can all be distinguished from primary trisomics by their diagnostic configurations after achiev-

Table 3.4   Terminology of aneuploid conditions relating to one chromosome (C) of a basic set of three non-homologous chromosomes (ABC).

Level of aneuploidy	Number of homologous genomes			
	1 Haploid†	2 Diploid*	3 Auto-triploid	4 Auto-tetraploid
0 Nullisomic	AB $x-1$	AABB $2x-2$	AAABBB $3x-3$	AAAABBBB $4x-4$
1 Monosomic	—	AABBC $2x-1$	AAABBBC $3x-2$	AAAABBBBC $4x-3$
2 Disomic	ABCC $x+1$	—	AAABBBCC $3x-1$	AAAABBBBCC $4x-2$
3 Trisomic	ABCCC $x+2$	AABBCCC $2x+1$	—	AAAABBBBCCC $4x-1$
4 Tetrasomic	ABCCCC $x+3$	AABBCCCC $2x+2$	AAABBBCCCC $3x+1$	—

†Including polyhaploids with homoeologous genomes.   *Including amphidiploid allopolyploids with homoeologous genomes.

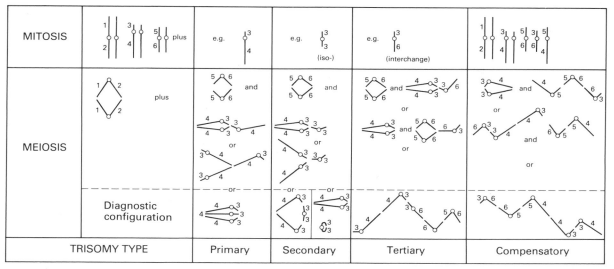

Fig. 3.12 Meiotic configurations in different types of trisomics. Combinations including univalents due to pairing failure have been omitted.

ing maximum pairing at meiosis (Fig. 3.12). Like centric fragments, secondary, tertiary and compensatory trisomics can equally well be considered as centric segmental aneuploids.

3.4.2i Haploidy and polyploidy

Spontaneous haploids arise infrequently by the development of unfertilized eggs, particularly after pollination with ineffective pollen. There is usually a marked effect on the phenotype, presumably due to exposure of recessives, and they are of low fertility following irregular disjunction of univalents at meiosis I (Figs 3.3, 3.9). The few commercially available haploid cultivars are maintained by vegetative propagation. The chance of producing a balanced haploid product by random movement of univalents to the same pole is 1 in $2^n/2$ where n equals the number of univalents, although suppression of anaphase I may give further viable restitution products.

Polyploids are classified according to a terminology which is simple in principle but not always easy to apply precisely. The level of polyploidy is indicated by a prefix, so that

x = monoploid or haploid, $2x$ = diploid, $3x$ = triploid, $4x$ = tetraploid etc., but the value for x is not always easy to determine, particularly in long established polyploids where the diploid relatives no longer exist. A further distinction can be made, and indicated in the terminology by an additional prefix, between those in which all the genomes are identical or at least structurally indistinguishable, autopolyploids, and those of hybrid origin where there are two or more different genomes, allopolyploids. However, the only test for chromosome homology is meiotic pairing which does not always accurately reflect genomic relationships (Section 3.3.4). It is likely that most polyploids are segmental allopolyploids with different degrees of similarity between genomes. Even in some which are first formed as autopolyploids by somatic doubling of a structurally homozygous diploid, the genomes have become differentiated from each other by chromosome mutation. At the same time, most if not all those in which dissimilar genomes never pair with each other probably retain some segments which are common to all the chromosomes sets present.

Polyploids first arise in a diploid species as triploids if one gamete is unreduced following mitotic or meiotic restitution, or as tetraploids if both gametes are affected as is likely in self-fertile hermaphrodites after somatic doubling earlier in development. However, unless the unreduced gametes come from different plants the new tetraploid will be still homozygous for each genome, which will restrict variation in the progeny.

The direct effects of polyploidy can only be determined if a diploid is compared with its isogenic (e.g. colchicine induced) polyploids. The effects usually include increased nuclear, cell and plant size at least up to the octoploid level; a slower development and life cycle; altered incompatability reactions permitting successful crosses between plants which are intersterile at the diploid level; and significant changes in segregation ratios and fertility.

The changes in fertility are explained by the behaviour of chromosomes at meiosis. Most triploids are sterile or nearly sterile, whatever the genome relationships, and whether or not the third genome forms univalents or trivalents, because random distribution of the chromosome to the spindle poles will rarely produce balanced haploid or diploid products capable of further normal development (Section 4.4.1). In tetraploids, it is possible at least in theory to produce numerically balanced nuclei by meiosis, and to explain why only some are fertile and others are sterile requires a closer look at their meiosis.

When all the genomes are identical or nearly so, as in a tetraploid derived from a bivalent-forming diploid, each set of four homologues can form a quadrivalent at meiotic prophase, despite the fact that pairing can only involve two chromosomes at any one point, if changes of partner occur along the chromosome. These multiple associations are then maintained during metaphase I if chiasmata form in the paired segments. When each chromosome arm has two or more pairing initiation points and chiasmata are frequent and dispersed, all possible multivalent associations are formed regularly but the configurations are complex and co-orientation and disjunction frequently irregular, leading to unbalanced products and sterility. If pairing initiation points and chiasmata are fewer, and particularly if they are distally localized, the quadrivalents are more open and disjunction can be more regular but maximum multivalent formation may not be achieved and maintained in all cells (Fig. 3.4 and 4.1e–h). If the chiasma frequency in the diploid parent is very low, approaching the minimum of one per bivalent necessary for regular meiosis, few multivalents will be maintained, even after full pairing, in the tetraploid derivative because to produce a metaphase quadrivalent at least two of the four homologues must form two chiasmata each. Similarly, if pairing initiation points are limited to one per chromosome then, regardless of the number of chiasmata subsequently produced, no multivalents can form because there is no opportunity for the required changes of partner. Failure to achieve the pairing or chiasma frequency required for quadrivalent formation usually results in a predominance of bivalents but some trivalents and univalents with irregular disjunction are also likely (Section 4.4.1). Autotetraploids therefore have low fertility unless pairing or chiasma formation is restricted in such a way that only simple quadrivalents or bivalents with regular disjunction are formed.

Allotetraploids with a single genome incapable of pairing with the rest, such as might result from tetraploid hybridization, are also sterile because of the irregular disjunction of univalents. However, allotetraploids with two dissimilar genomes each represented twice are frequently highly fertile. The failure of pairing between homoeologues which restricts bivalent formation in a diploid hybrid enhances bivalent formation in the derived tetraploid. Indeed, in the presence of an exact homologue in the tetraploid, pairing between homoeologues may be less than in the diploid and even totally suppressed, a phenomenon known as preferential pairing. Thus while the diploid may form some bivalents together with univalents with irregular disjunction leading to sterility, the tetraploid will form few or no multivalents, only bivalents with regular disjunction leading to fertility. Such a polyploid is described as an amphidiploid. Preferential pairing is under genetic control and improvement of fertility by selection for bivalent formation as a result of increased suppression of homoeologous pairing has been of critical importance in the evolution of the polyploid crops wheat and oats and no doubt in many other polyploid plants as well. At the same time it masks the partial homology that remains between the genomes.

As a general rule therefore, doubling the complement of a fertile diploid with regular bivalent formation produces a sterile tetraploid, while doubling a sterile diploid hybrid with limited pairing produces a fertile vigorous tetraploid, although exceptions and intermediates also exist. Thus, the considerable evolutionary significance of polyploidy, at least in plants, lies not so much in its direct effect on vigour but in its immediate restoration of fertility to new hybrid combinations and the subsequent release of variation. As a result, while most autopolyploids survive, if at all, only as uniform vegetatively propagated clones, sexual amphidiploids provide the starting point for a fresh burst of evolution leading to the formation of new species and even genera.

3.4.3 Karyotype evolution

Chromosome mutations arise repeatedly and presumably in all species, creating a potential for karyotype change to accompany or even direct the evolution of new species. Many mutations are eliminated before they enter a zygote (Section 3.4.1). Some of the remaining cytotypes fail in competition with other individuals in polymorphic populations. The few stable mutant karyotypes which will survive to characterize a new species must be associated with vigour, fertility, isolation and a competitive advantage over their progenitors, at least under some conditions. As previously described (Section 3.4.2), most mutations affect vigour or fertility or both. Many established mutations also create their own genetic isolation through the reduced fertility of the hybrid with the parental cytotype. However, it is the competitive advantage conferred by a change in the level or pattern of variability released during sexual reproduction, as a result of the effect of the mutation on recombination at meiosis, which is frequently most significant in determining the long term success of the new genome. All departures from the maximum recombination potential of a structurally homozygous, bivalent-forming diploid with many dispersed chiasmata, a high basic chromosome number and a symmetrical karyotype are specialized conditions likely to be accompanied by specialization of structure or physiology as well as reduction of variability.

Thus, in a situation of continuous change, a survey of intraspecific polymorphism will reveal the more recently derived karyotypes, including those with no advantage but not yet eliminated, such as aneuploidy; those with temporary advantage, such as certain polyploids, B chromosomes and structural heterozygotes; and those which represent early stages in the establishment of potential and cryptic species. Interspecific polymorphism will reveal the successful permanent changes of the more distant past, including chiasma localization, allopolyploidy, dysploidy and altered karyotype and chromosome symmetry resulting from structural rearrangements, although the consecutive stages may not all be represented.

In the evolution of a group of species, one type of karyotype change may predominate, while in others all occur in turn. Some species, particularly those with short life cycles, show rapid karyotype changes as conditions alter or the species extends its range; others, like long-lived woody plants have more stable karyotypes and isolation and regulation of recombination depends on other features of the life cycle. However, in some genera, including *Tulbaghia*, *Lilium* and *Paeonia* the karyotype stability is more apparent than real because, although selection has favoured the maintenance of a similar pattern of chromosome and karyotype asymmetry in all species, meiosis in hybrids reveals that considerable structural rearrangements have accompanied speciation.

Sex determining chromosome mechanisms, found in most animals, the 5% of angiosperms which have dioecious sporophytes and the lower plants with dioecious gametophytes, provide a special example of karyotype evolution. In most higher organisms, the male is the heterogametic sex and the basic evolutionary sequence appears to be the development of cytologically recognizable $♀XX/♂XY$ systems by differentiation and erosion by deletion and translocation of the Y chromosome. The X may be larger, smaller or similar to the autosomes. Subsequent disappearance of the Y creates an XX/XO system as found in some orthopterans. Finally, translocation between sex chromosomes and autosomes can create a variety of more complex systems, XX/XY giving rise to XY/XX_1Y_2, $X_1X_1X_2X_2/X_1X_2Y$ or $X_1X_1X_2X_2/X_1X_2Y_1Y_2$ systems and XX/XO producing the so-called neo XX/XY and neo $X_1X_1X_2X_2/X_1X_2Y$ systems. In most birds and lepidopterans and perhaps one or two plants, the female is heterogametic in $♂ZW/♂ZZ$ or ZO/ZZ systems. In dioecious lower plants, the XY sporophyte gives rise to $♀X$ and $♂Y$ gametophytes.

3.4.4 Materials

It is not easy to demonstrate the full range of spontaneous chromosome mutations. Occasional examples turn up unpredictably in most extensive chromosome investigations, but there is no rapid way of screening the large number of individuals necessary to assemble a comprehensive collection of the different types, and even then it would not be possible to maintain all of them in culture and the collection would soon become a self-selected non-random sample of the more stable mutations.

One partial solution to this problem is to induce mutations by the appropriate physical or chemical treatment (Section 4.2.4). A wide range of structural aberrations can be produced by chemical treatment or irradiation of dividing cells and by aging of dormant seeds. Polyploid cells can be produced by colchicine treatment. A wide range of aneuploid conditions can be found among the products of meiosis in certain polyploids, particularly triploids (Section 4.4.2). Where the treatment produces somatic mosaics, it is possible to demonstrate the selective elimination of unstable complements by the appropriate cytological investigations during subsequent growth and reproduction. However, to demonstrate the distribution of cell lineages formed by dividing mutant cells requires additional techniques for sectioning the material.

A simpler approach requiring no additional techniques is to select as wide a range as possible of established and readily available mutations which retain the essential features of newly altered karyotypes. Such a sample excludes all those structural mutations which are eliminated during mitosis and, unless they can be maintained asexually, all those mutant karyotypes which break down during meiosis or cause major disturbances of development. Moreover, the early stages in the establishment of mutations during somatic growth are no longer represented, although the essential features of the structure, development and inheritance of mosaics and chimaeras can be demonstrated using mutations with more conspicuous phenotypic effects, such as those preventing chloroplast development. Following this approach, plants and animals which provide examples of the main types of chromosomal mutation are listed below. Material under **a)** and **b)** has been rigorously selected from a long list for its easy availability from the wild or from commercial sources (Section 3.3.5), for its suitability for chromosome preparations and for the high frequency of individuals with the required chromosome condition. In some, a mitotically stable condition is maintained clonally and may be of relatively recent origin and never subjected to natural selection while in others the complement is transmitted sexually and may be successfully established in the wild. Further examples can be found at a lower frequency in the plants and animals selected to illustrate polymorphism of cytotype within and between species and listed under **c)**. Many other examples are reported in the literature but most are less widely obtainable or less easily maintained.

a) The origin and establishment of chromosome mutations (Section 3.4.1)

1 Induced mutations: Gamma-irradiated seed of *Vicia faba*, barley (*Hordeum vulgare*) and other species can be obtained, with photomicrograph transparencies and teaching notes, from Gammaseed, 2 Royal Oak Drive, Bishops Wood, Staffordshire, ST19 9AN. Preparations of germinating roots of these seeds reveal chromosome aberrations at colchine-treated metaphase and untreated anaphase of mitosis (see also Section 4.2.4).

2 Stable chimaeras for chloroplast mutation to demonstrate chimaerical structure:
PERICLINAL: *Pelargonium zonale* (= ×*hortorum*) cv. 'Flower of Spring' (GWG), cv. 'Freak of Nature' (GWW).
MERICLINAL: Variegated *Tradescantia fluminensis* (G/W sector in sub-epidermal layers).

3 Karyotype instability causing aneusomaty: *Hymenocallis calathina* ($x = 23$; $2n = 23–92$; 23–82 reported within one plant); *Claytonia virginica* ($x = 7$; $2n = 14–58$; 14–36 reported within one plant); *Chrysanthemum* cv. 'Golden Favourite' ($x = 9$; $2n = 53–57$) and 'Orange Sweetheart' ($x = 9$; $2n = 51–59$).

b) Chromosome mutations (Section 3.4.2)

1 Side arm bridges: H-segments of mitotic anaphase in *Trillium grandiflorum* ($2x = 10$) after 96 hours at 2°C.

2 Telocentrics and Isochromosomes:
TELOCENTRICS: *Zebrina pendula* ($2x = 24$); *Schistocerca gregaria* (locust) ($2x = 23/24$)
TELOCENTRIC SUPERNUMERARIES: *Allium cernum* ($2x = 14 + 0–20B$); *Festuca ovina* ($2x = 14, 21, 42, 49, 56, 70 + B$); *Tradescantia virginiana* ($4x = 24 + 0–5B$); *Trillium grandiflorum* ($2x = 10 + 0–9B$).
ISOCHROMOSOMES: *Nicandra physaloides* ($2x = 18 + 1–2$ isos.). Seedlings with two isochromosomes germinate first but may lose an isochromosome during development.
ISOCHROMOSOME SUPERNUMERARIES: *Allium cernum* ($2x = 14 + 0–20B$); *Festuca pratensis* ($2x = 14 + 0–16B$).

3 Paracentric inversion heterozygosity: *Tradescantia virginiana* ($4x = 24$); *Trillium grandiflorum* ($2x = 10$) (Fig. 3.10a). *Anopheles* (mosquito) spp., *Drosophila* (fruit fly) spp., *Simulium* (black fly) spp. (inversion heterzygosity is relatively common in all these dipteran genera and revealed by pairing and banding of polytene chromosomes. The absence of chiasmata in ♂ *Drosophila* prevents bridge and fragment formation.)

4 Interchange heterozygosity: *Campanula persicifolia* ($2x = 16$); *Hyacinthus orientalis* cv. 'Fireball'

$(2x = 16)$; *Rhoeo spathacea* ($= R. discolor$) $(2x = 12)$ (Fig. 3.10c). *R. spathacea* var. *concolor* from Belize is a bivalent-forming structural homozygote; *Periplaneta americana* (cockroach) $(2x = 33/34)$.

5 Chromosome dissociation/association heterozygosity: *Nothoscordum inodorum* ($= N. fragrans$) $(4x = 19 = 13\wedge + 6 i = 3 (3 \wedge + 2 i + 1 (4 \wedge))$ (Fig. 3.2c); *Lycoris aurea* $(2x = 12 (10\wedge + 2i), 13(9\wedge+4i), 14(8\wedge+6i))$. *Polygonatum* hybrid $(2x = 19)$ (*P. multiflorum*, $2x = 18$, × *P. odoratum*, $2x = 20$).

6 Deletion and duplication heterozygosity:

DELETION: *Hyacinthus orientalis* cv. 'Grace Darling' $(2x = 16$, deletion in short arm of a medium chromosome); cv. 'Tubergen's Scarlet' (Fig. 3.2a) (= 'Scarlet O'Hara', 'Mme. Du Barry') and its double flowered sport, cv. 'Scarlet Perfection' $(2x = 16$, large deletion in a non-nucleolar long chromosome; arose as a sport of normal $2x$ complement of cv. 'Distinction'.); *Allium cepa* $(2x = 16$, deletion of satellite on terminal nucleolar organizer; not uncommon in other *Allium* species including *A. paradoxum*; see also Fig. 3.2d).

DUPLICATION OF SUPERNUMERARY SEGMENTS: *Chorthippus brunneus* $(2x = 17/18)$.

7 Supernumerary B chromosomes:
Allium cernum $(2x = 14 + 0–20B$; very small euchromatic telocentric B's); *Puschkinia libanotica* (Fig. 4.2c) $(2x = 10 + 0–7B$; large heterochromatic B chromosomes with terminal or sub-median centromeres frequently pairing with each other at meiosis); *Trillium grandiflorum* $(2x = 10 + 0–9B$; euchromatic B chromosomes of several types with terminal or sub-terminal centromeres).

8 Chromosomal aneuploidy:
NULLISOMIC DIPLOID, $2x - 2$: *Punica granatum* var. *nanum* $(x = 9)$

PRIMARY TRISOMIC DIPLOID, $2x - 1$: *Hyacinthus orientalis* cv. 'Rosalie' $(x = 8)$
PRIMARY DISOMIC TRIPLOID, $3x - 1$: *Hyacinthus orientalis* cv. 'Eros' $(x = 8)$
PRIMARY TETRASOMIC TRIPLOID, $3x + 1$: *Hyacinthus orientalis* cv. 'Ostara' $(x = 8)$
PRIMARY TRISOMIC TETRAPLOID, $4x - 1$: *Hyacinthus orientalis* cv. 'Dr. Streseman' (= 'Winston Churchill') $(x = 8)$.
Also gametophytic complements of triploids and some tetraploids (see below).

9 Haploid and Polyploidy:
HAPLOID: *Pelargonium zonale* cv. 'Kleine Liebling' $(x = 9$; diploid form also known); *Thuya gigantea* var. *gracilis* $(x = 11$; diploid chimaeras and sports also known).
AUTOTRIPLOID: *Hyacinthus orientalis* cvv. 'Amethyst', 'Anne Marie', 'Bismark', 'Cyclops' or 'Jan Bos' $(x = 8)$.
SEGMENTAL ALLOTRIPLOID: *Aconitum napellus* cv. 'Sparke's Variety' (= *A. napellus* × *A. variegatum*, $x = 9$); *Lilium* cv. 'Sonata' $(x = 12)$; *Tradescantia virginiana* × *T. brevicaulis* $(x = 6)$. (Fig. 4.1a–d, Section 4.4.1).
AUTOTETRAPLOID; *Campanula persicifolia* cv. 'Telham Beauty' $(x = 8)$; *Hyacinthus orientalis* cv. 'Blue Giant' $(x = 8)$; *Lolium multiflorum* cv. 'Serenade' $(x = 7)$; *L. perenne* cv. 'Reveille' $(x = 7)$.
SEGMENTAL ALLOTETRAPLOID: *Nothoscordum inodorum* ($= N. fragrans$) $(4x = 19$, Fig. 3.2c); *Tradescantia virginiana* $(4x = 24$, probably of hybrid origin despite occasional full quadrivalent formation, Fig. 4.1e–h). Bivalent-forming amphidiploids: *Primula kewensis* (*P. floribunda* × *P. verticillata*, $x = 9$); *Hordeum murinum* $(x = 7)$; *Triticum dicoccum* $(x = 7)$; *Paris quadrifolia* $(x = 5)$.
SEGMENTAL ALLOHEXAPLOID: bivalent-forming amphidiploids: *Triticum aestivum* $(x = 7)$; *Avena sativa* $(x = 7)$.

c) Karyotype evolution (Section 3.4.3)

1 Uniform genome morphology and

basic number, sometimes masking considerable structural rearrangement: *Pinus* spp. ($2x = 24$); *Bromus* spp. ($2x = 14$); *Lilium* spp. ($2x = 24$); *Oenothera* spp. ($2x = 14$); *Paeonia* spp. ($2x = 10$); *Trillium* spp. ($2x = 10$); *Tulbaghia* spp. ($2x = 12$).

2 Intraspecific polymorphism:

PARACENTRIC INVERSION: *Festuca pratensis* ($2x = 16$); *Paeonia suffruticosa* ($2x = 10$); *Paris quadrifolia* ($4x = 20$) (see also b)3).

PERICENTRIC INVERSION: *Crocus vernus* ($2x = 8$); *Paeonia californica* ($2x = 10$).

INTERCHANGES: *Allium fistulosum* ($2x = 16$), *A. sativum* ($2x = 16$), *A. triquetrum* ($2x = 18$); *Chrysanthemum carinatum* ($2x = 18$); *Dichorisandra thyrsiflora* ($2x = 38$) (Fig. 3.10b); *Festuca pratensis* ($2x = 14$); *Oenothera biennis*, *O. lamarckiana* ($2x = 14$); *Paeonia californica* ($2x = 10$); *Chorthippus brunneus* (grasshopper) ($2x = 17/18$) (see also b)4).

MULTIPLE STRUCTURAL POLYMORPHISM: *Anthoxanthum odoratum* ($x = 5$, $2n = 10$, 15, 20, various combinations of morphologically distinct chromosomes from different diploid ancestors); *Trillium grandiflorum*, *T. erectum* ($2x = 10$, heterozygosity within and polymorphism between individuals with respect to H-segments patterns (Section 2.2.3d; Fig. 2.5c)).

CHROMOSOME DISSOCIATION/ASSOCIATION, DYSPLOID CHANGES: *Alisma plantago-aquatica* ($x = 6,7$; $2n = 12,14$); *Campanula persicifolia* ($x = 8$, 9; $2n = 16,18$); *Crocus biflorus* ($x = 4,5,6$; $2n = 8,10,12,20,22$); *Crocus chrysanthus* ($x = 4,5$; $2n = 8,9,10$); *Crocus speciosus* ($x = 6,7,8,9$; $2n = 12,14,16,18$); *Vicia cracca* ($x = 6,7$; $2n = 12,14,28$) (see also b)5).

SUPERNUMERARY B CHROMOSOMES: *Agrostis canina* ($x = 7$; $2n = 28 + 0$–13B); *Allium porrum* ($x = 8$; $2n = 32 + $ B); *Anthoxanthum odoratum* ($x = 5$; $2n = 10 + 0$–4B); *Crepis capillaris* ($x = 3$; $2n = 6 + $ 0–4B); *Festuca pratensis* ($x = 7$; $2n = 14 + $ 0–16B); *Fritillaria imperialis* ($x = 12$; $2n = 24 + 0$–12B); *Haplopappus gracilis* ($x = 2$; $2n = 4 + $B); *Lilium japonicum* ($x = 12$; $2n = 24 + 0$–3B), *L. martagon* ($x = 12$, $2n = 24 + 0$–3B); *Narcissus bulbocodium* ($x = 7$, $2n = 14$–21 + 0–4B); *Ornithogalum umbellatum* ($x = 9$, $2n = 18 + 0$–6B); *Ranunculus acris* ($x = 7$; $2n = 14 + 0$–10B), *R. ficaria* ($x = 8$; $2n = 14 + 0$–10B, Section 4.5.3); *Secale cereale* ($x = 7$; $2n = 14 + 0$–10B); *Tradescantia paludosa* ($x = 6$; $2n = 12 + 0$–12B), *T. virginiana* ($x = 6$; $2n = 24 + 0$–5B); *Locusta migratoria* (locust) ($x = 11/12$; $2n = 23/24 + 0$–4B); *Myrmeleotettix maculatus* (grasshopper) ($x = 8/9$; $2n = 17/18 + 0$–3B) (see also b)7).

CHROMOSOMAL ANEUPLOIDY: *Caltha palustris* ($x = 8$; $2n = 28,32,48,53$–64); *Chrysanthemum indicum* 'Sweetheart' and 'Favourite' cultivars ($x = 9$; $2n = 45$–63): 'Bronze Sweetheart' ($2n = 54$); 'Apricot Sweetheart' ($2n = 55$); 'Golden Sweetheart' ($2n = 56$); 'Primrose Favourite' ($2n = 57$); *Hyacinthus orientalis* ($x = 8$; $2n = 16$–32) Table 3.5; *Narcissus bulbocodium* ($x = 7$; $2n = 14$–21); *Poa pratensis* ($x = 7$; $2n = 28$–124); *Scilla peruviana* ($x = 8$; $2n = 14$–17, 19–20, 22–23, 28) (see also b)8).

POLYPLOIDY: *Agrostis stolonifera* ($x = 7$; $2n = 2x$, $3x$, $4x$, $5x$, $6x$, $7x$, $8x$, $10x$); *Allium carinatum* ($= A. flavum$) ($x = 8$; $2n = 2x$, $3x$), *A. neapolitanum* ($x = 7$; $2n = 2x$, $3x$, $4x$, $5x$), *A. schoenoprasum* ($x = 8$, $2n = 2x$, $3x$, $4x$); *Caltha palustris* ($x = 8$; $2n = 3x$, $4x$, $7x$, $8x$, $9x$, $10x$); *Endymion hispanicus* ($x = 8$; $2n = 2x$, $3x$) *E. non-scriptus* ($x = 8$; $2n = 2x$, $3x$); *Festuca ovina* ($x = 7$; $2n = 2x$, $3x$, $4x$, $6x$, $7x$, $8x$, $10x$); *Lilium tigrinum* ($x = 12$; $2n = 2x$, $3x$); *Lycoris radiata* ($x = 11$; $2n = 2x$, $3x$), *L. squamigera* ($x = 9$; $2n = 2x$, $3x$); *Narcissus bulbocodium* ($x = 7$; $2n = 2x$, $3x$, $4x$, $5x$, $6x$); *Ornithogalum nutans* ($x = 7$; $2n = 2x$, $4x$, $6x$), *O. umbellatum* ($x = 8$; $2n = 2x$, $3x$, $4x$,

Table 3.5 Aneuploid cultivars of *Hyacinthus orientalis*.

Cultivar	2n	Chromosome constitution Long (nucleolar)	Long	Medium	Short
'La Victoire' 'Pink Pearl' 'Vanguard' }	$2x = 16$	2	6	4	4
'Rosalie'	$2x + 1 = 17$	3	6	4	4
'Cinderella'	$2x + 2 = 19$	3	8	4	4
'Rosea maxima'	$2x + 4 = 20$	10		5	5
'Van Speyk'	$3x - 3 = 21$	10		6	5
'L'Orde Parfait'	$3x - 2 = 22$	11		6	5
'City of Haarlem'	$3x - 1 = 23$	3	9	6	5
'Eros'		2	9	6	6
'Eclipse'	$3x?$	2(3?)	10(9?)	6	6
'Blue Orbit' 'Cote D'Azure' 'Ostara' }	$3x + 1 = 25$	3	9	7	6
'Blue Herald'	$3x + 2 = 26$	13		7	6
'Ben Nevis'		2	13	6	6
'L'Innocence'	$3x + 3 = 27$	4	11	6	6
'Lord Balfour'		3	11	7	6
'Queen of the Blues' }		3	12	6	6
'Blue Horizon'		3	12	7	6
'Nevada' }	$3x + 4 = 28$	3	12	7	6
'Sapphire'		3	12	5	8
'Carnegie'		2(3?)	13(12?)	6	8
'Iron Duke' }	$4x - 3 = 29$	3	12	7	7
'Perfection'		3	12	6	8
'China Pink'		3	12	7	8
'Gainsborough' }	$4x - 2 = 30$	3	12	8	7
'Myosotis'		4	11	8	7
'Dr Streseman' (= 'Winston Churchill')		4	12	8	7
	$4x - 1 = 31$				
'Perle Brilliante'		4	12	8	7

For 3x and 4x cultivars, see b)9 above.

$5x$, $6x$, $8x$); *Ranunculus ficaria* ($x = 8$; $2n = 2x, 3x, 4x, 5x, 6x$; Section 4.5.3, Fig. 4.3); *Tulipa clusiana* ($x = 12$; $2n = 2x, 4x, 5x$), *T. gesneriana*, *T. praecox*, *T. saxatilis* ($x = 12$; $2n = 2x, 3x$).

3 Interspecific polymorphism:

CHIASMA LOCALIZATION: *Trillium grandiflorum* ($2x = 10$, disperse) (Fig. 2.16), *T. kamtschaticum* ($2x = 10$, proximal, Fig. 2.17a); *Allium cepa* ($2x = 16$, disperse), *A. fistulosum* ($2x = 16$, proximal).

INTERCHANGE: *Oenothera hookeri* ($2x = 14$, heterozygous for few or no interchanges), *O. biennia*, *muricata*, *strigosa* ($2x = 14$, multiple interchanges involving all chromosomes).

MULTIPLE STRUCTURAL POLYMORPHISM: Species hybrids of *Allium* (e.g. *A. cepa* × *A. fistulosum* $2x = 14$); *Iris* (e.g. *I. reticulata* cv. 'Joyce', $2x = 19 = I.$ *reticulata* × *I. histrioides*); *Lilium* (e.g. cv. 'Black Beauty', 'Marhan' (= *L. martagon* × *L. hansonii*), $2x = 24$); *Paeonia* and *Tulipa* reveal (by mitotic karyotype, asymmetrical bivalents, multivalents or anaphase bridges) polymorphism for structural rearrangements, particularly translocations and inversions. Meiosis in the hybrid *Tulbaghia verdoornia* × *T. violacea* ($2x = 12$) reveals that the species differ by three major interchanges and four inversions (Section 4.5.1)

CHROMOSOME SYMMETRY:

Differences in symmetry with no change in basic number: *Aegilops aucherii*, *A. bicornis*, *A. speltoides* (symmetrical); *A. umbellulata*, *A. caudata* (asymmetrical) ($x = 7$).

Dysploid change in basic number with little change in symmetry: *Allium* spp. (see below).

Dysploid reduction in basic number accompanied by increasing asymmetry: *Crepis* spp. (see below).

CHROMOSOME DISSOCIATION/ASSOCIATION, DYSPLOID CHANGES:

Allium $x = 7,8,9$. *A. narcissiflorum*, *A. ursinum* ($x = 7$); *A. cepa*, *A. fistulosum*, *A. paradoxum* ($x = 8$); *A. karataviense*, *A. triquetrum* ($x = 9$).

Crepis $x = 3, 4, 5, 6, 7, 8$ (ancestral number, $x = 6$). *C. capillaris*[1], *C. fuliginosa*[2] ($x = 3$); *C. kotschyana*[3], *C. neglecta*[2], *C. setosa*, *C. tectorum*[1] ($x = 4$); *C. foetida*[3], *C. rubra* ($x = 5$); *C. kashmirica*, *C. mungieri* ($x = 6$). Species pairs 1,1, 2,2 and 3,3 form hybrids with a heterotrivalent at meiosis which reveals that the complement with the lower number was derived by chromosome association from one similar to that of the other species.

Crocus $x = 3, 4, 5, 6, 8, 10, 11, 12, 13, 14, 15$. *C. balansae*, *C. candidus* ($x = 3$); *C. aureus*, ($x = 4$); *C. ochroleucus* ($x = 5$); *C. susianus* ($x = 6$); *C. chrysanthus* cv. 'Cream Beauty', *C. tomasinianus* ($x = 8$); *C. chrysanthus* cv. 'Zwanenburg Bronze' ($x = 9$); *C. korolkowii* ($x = 10$); *C. sieberi* ($x = 11$); *C. minimus* ($x = 12$); *C. niveus*, *C. versicolor* ($x = 13$); *C. longiflorus* ($x = 14$); *C. tournefortii* ($x = 15$).

Lycoris $x = 6, 7, 8, 9, 11$ (ancestral number $x = 11$). *L. aurea* ($x = 6$, 7; $2x = 12$ ($10_\wedge + 2i$), $13(9_\wedge + 4i)$ or $14(8_\wedge + 6i)$); *L. straminea* ($x = 8$; $2x = 16(6_\wedge + 10i)$); *L. squamigera* ($x = 9$; $2x = 18(4_\wedge + 14i)$); *L. sanguinea* ($x = 11$; $2x = 22(22i)$).

Ranunculus $x = 7, 8$. *R. acris* ($x = 7$); *R. bulbosus*, *R. ficaria* ($x = 8$).

Scilla $x = 6, 7, 8, 9, 10, 11$ (ancestral number $x = 6$). *S. sibirica* ($x = 6$); *S. autumnalis* ($x = 7$); *S. italica* ($x = 8$); *S. bifolia* ($x = 9$); *S. hyacinthoides*, *S. verna* ($x = 11$).

POLYPLOIDY:

Bromus ($x = 7$). *B. arvensis* ($2x$); *B. mollis* ($4x$); *B. brevis* ($6x$); *B. maritimus* ($8x$); *B. riparius* ($10x$); *B. arizonicus* ($12x$).

Festuca ($x = 7$). *F. pratensis* ($2x$), *F. ciliata* ($4x$); *F. arundinacea* ($6x$); *F. californica* ($8x$); *F. maritima* ($10x$).

Paeonia ($x = 5$). *P. delavayi*, *P. emodii*, *P. laciflora*, *P. lutea*, *P. potanii*, *P. suffruticosa* ($2x$); *P. humilis*, *P. mollis*, *P. peregrina* ($4x$).

Ranunculus ($x = 8$). *R. bulbosus* ($2x$); *R. repens* ($4x$); *R. stricticaulis* ($5x$); *R. muricatus* ($6x$); *R. sulphureus* ($12x$); *R. linga* ($16x$).

Tradescantia ($x = 6$). *T. bracteata*, *T. brevicaulis*, *T. paludosa* ($2x$); *T. virginiana*, *T. subaspera* ($4x$).

Tulipa ($x = 12$). *T. kaufmanniana*, *T. orphanidea* ($2x$); *T. gesneriana*, *T. praecox*, *T. saxatilis* ($3x$); *T. turkestanica*, *T. whittallii* ($= T. orphanidea$?) ($4x$).

SEX CHROMOSOME MECHANISMS:

Humulus. *H. lupulus* ($2x = 20 = 18 + XX/XY$ or $16 + X_1X_1X_2X_2/X_1X_2Y_1Y_2$), *H. japonicus* ($2x = 16/17 = 14 + XX/XY_1Y_2$).

Rumex. *R. angiocarpus* ($2x = 14 = 12 + XX/XY$), *R. acetosella* ($2x = 42 = 40 + XX/XY$), *R. hastatulus* ($2x = 10 = 8 + XX/XY$ or $8/9 = 6 + XX/XY_1Y_2$).

Drosophila (fruit fly). *D. melanogaster* ($2x = 10 = 8 + XX/XY$), *D. annulimanna* ($2x = 9/10 = 8 + XX/XO$), *D. americana americana* ($2x = 8/9 = 6 + XX/XY_1Y_2$), *D. prosaltans* II ($2x = 10 = 6 + X_1X_1X_2X_2/X_1X_2Y_1Y_2$).

3.5 Further reading

AVERY, A. G., SATINA, S. and RIETSEMA, J. (1959). *Blakeslee: The Genus Datura*. Chronica Bot. Int. Biol. and Agric. Ser. No. 20. New York.

BRIGGS, D. and WALTERS, S. M. (1969). *Plant Variation and Evolution*. Wiedenfeld and Nicolson, London.

CLELAND, R. G. (1972). *Oenothera: Cytogenetics and Evolution*. Experimental Botany Monograph 5. Academic Press, London and New York.

DARLINGTON, C. D. (1958). *Evolution of Genetic Systems*. Oliver and Boyd, Edinburgh.

DARLINGTON, C. D. (1973). *Chromosome Botany and the Origin of Cultivated Plants*. Third edition. George Allen and Unwin Ltd., London.

GARBER, E. D. (1972). *Cytogenetics – an Introduction*. McGraw Hill, New York.

GRANT, V. (1975). *Genetics of Flowering Plants*. Columbia University Press, New York.

JOHN, B. (1976). *Population Cytogenetics*. Studies in Biology, no. 70. Edward Arnold, London.

JOHN, B. and LEWIS, K. R. (1965). *The Meiotic System*. Protoplasmatalogia VI Fi. Springer-Verlag, New York.

JOHN, B. and LEWIS, K. R. (1968). *The Chromosome Complement*. Protoplasmatalogia VI A. Springer-Verlag, New York.

JOHN, B. and LEWIS, K. R. (1975). *Chromosome Hierarchy*. Clarendon Press, Oxford.

KHUSH, G. S. (1973). *Cytogenetics of Aneuploids*. Academic Press, London and New York.

LEWIS, K. R. and JOHN B. (1973). *Chromosome Marker*. Second edition. J. and A. Churchill Ltd., London.

MCDERMOTT, A. (1975). *Cytogenetics of Man and Other Animals*. Outline Studies in Biology. Chapman and Hall, London

MOORE, D. M. (1976). *Plant Cytogenetics*. Outline Studies in Biology. Chapman and Hall, London.

NEILSON-JONES, W. (1969). *Plant Chimeras*. Second edition. Methuen, London.

REES, H. and JONES, R. N. (1977). *Chromosome Genetics*. Edward Arnold, London.

STEBBINS, G. L. (1971). *Chromosomal Evolution in Higher Plants*. Contemporary Biology Series. Edward Arnold, London.

SYBENGA, J. (1975). *Meiotic configurations*. Springer-Verlag. Berlin.

WHITE, M. J. D. (1954). *Animal cytology and evolution*. Second edition. C.U.P.

WHITE, M. J. D. (1973). *The Chromosomes*. Sixth edition. Chapman and Hall, London.

WILLIAMS, W. (1964). *Genetical Principles and Plant Breeding*. Blackwell, Oxford.

4 Investigating chromosomes – a matter of approach

4.1 Introduction

In the previous three chapters the aim has been to provide the information necessary to prepare, and interpret with understanding, demonstration slides of all the major features of chromosome structure and behaviour to be seen during division, development, reproduction and evolution. However, even the most diligent and comprehensive study of these demonstrations will not alone produce a cytogeneticist capable of independent research, although it would no doubt instill an unusual awareness of the techniques and possibilities for further investigation. To extend the existing knowledge of chromosomes requires the active investigation of new situations, not merely the passive observation of events already described. Thus, as the technical repertoire and interpretative versatility increases through making and examining demonstration preparations, it becomes necessary to change the approach to one of enquiry. Even to understand fully a demonstration slide it is necessary to explore the context in which the event took place. A cytological event considered in isolation is rather like the family album of a stranger; beyond the immediately obvious and often trivial characteristics of the people, places and activities, the photographs are almost meaningless without some understanding of the relationships and events leading up to the captured instant.

This change in approach has several facets. The chromosomes in a cell have to be considered not as representatives of a static, uniform situation with an established explanation but as one state in a dynamic process

and one variant in a variable condition, the interpretation of which is one speculation among several. The change in conceptual approach demands changes in practical approach – an illustrated description of a single cell is no longer sufficient. As the timing and frequency of an event may be as significant as the details of the event itself, quantitative data are essential, as are sampling methods and statistical techniques which will produce data reflecting accurately the variation between cells, individuals and species and the changes with time. Clearly therefore, to be effective every investigation requires a plan and an objective, both necessarily based on the current understanding of the situation. However, neither must be so rigidly formulated or adhered to that they prevent the recognition and investigation of new or unexpected events or, if necessary, the modification of the initial interpretation.

In a cytogeneticist's training, the transition from observation to investigation need not be abrupt. Some cytological conditions can be demonstrated within the context of a controlled or 'staged' investigation where the result is highly predictable. This can lead on to selected open-ended projects, which need not be elaborate, in which usable results are assured but answers to the particular questions posed are unknown. These introduce the principles of recognizing and defining a problem and designing the experimental approach to solving it before progressing to guided research into entirely new situations. These principles apply in general to all scientific investigation and will not be discussed further here, but to exercise them in the context of cytogenetics requires the appropriate choice of material and treatment. In this last section, a number of suitable open-ended projects are outlined to illustrate the possibilities. In each case a situation is introduced, but no detailed programme of further investigation is provided as this would defeat the purpose of stimulating original thought. There is of course an almost limitless number of other equally good projects which could be substituted, and where access to material, equipment or expert advice provides other opportunities, these should be exploited. No claim of special merit is made for the selection provided here beyond the facts that each one has proved a successful project and the range caters for a variety of interests. They are presented under four headings, reflecting the main spheres of activity of chromosomes; in division, in development, in reproduction and in evolution. By appropriate choice between or within these groups it is possible to maintain a breadth of interest from cellular to population biology, or to develop a specialization in one area.

4.2 Chromosomes in the cell

4.2.1 Chromosomes in living cells

It is possible, at least over a limited period, to observe the active phases of division in living cells without elaborate culture techniques or expensive equipment beyond perhaps a phase contrast microscope.

Mitosis

Mitosis can be most readily observed in young staminal hairs of *Tradescantia*. Staminal hairs should be removed when about 1–2 mm long from pre-meiotic buds of *Tradescantia virginiana*, 'Purple Dome', and mounted in 2% sucrose solution under a coverslip which is then ringed with vaseline.

Mitosis can be clearly observed in the absence of thick walls or large cell inclusions in the last two or three cells of the uniseriate filaments and the process will continue for several hours under these conditions.

Meiosis

Meiosis can be observed in living pollen mother cells mounted as for staminal hairs, or in grasshopper spermatocytes, which are smaller but clearer because they have no cellulose walls, mounted in 0.75% NaCl solution.

4.2.2 The duration and timing of the mitotic cycle

The cell cycle in young fern gametophytes

The simplest system in which to determine the length of the cell cycle is one in which the number of dividing cells, ideally one, is known and the number of daughter cells produced in a measured period of time can be easily determined. Such a system is provided by the uniseriate protonemal stage of the young gametophyte of certain ferns. In *Dryopteris filix-mas* and *D. pseudo-mas* for example the protonema develops from a germinated spore by repeated division of the apical cell only. Spores can be cultured floating on a liquid medium at a constant temperature between 5°C and 30°C under fluorescent light. The filamentous phase can be extended for up to 7 apical cell divisions by using low intensity white light or maintained indefinitely by growing under a red filter. A suitable medium is $MgSO_4$, 0.25 g 1^{-1}; KNO_3, 0.12 g 1^{-1}; $FeCl_3$, 0.01 g 1^{-1}; $Ca(NO_3)_2$, 1.00 g 1^{-1}; KH_2PO_4, 0.25 g 1^{-1} with 100 000 units 1^{-1} Mycostatin, a fungicide. At intervals of 24 hours or preferably less, from germination until divisions are re-orientated to form the prothallus, two separate samples of gametophytes should be removed from each of two replicate dishes

Table 4.1 Mitotic indices in root tips of *Hyacinthus orientalis* cultivar 'Roman Hyacinth'.

Stage	All	Interphase	Prophase	Metaphase	Anaphase	Telophase
Frequency	10461	9077	563	300	131	390
Mitotic index	100	86.8	5.4	2.9	1.2	3.7
Duration (hrs) assuming mean value for whole cycle = 20 hrs	20	17.36	1.08	0.58	0.24	0.74

Table 4.2 The effect of temperature on chiasma frequency in *Endymion non-scriptus*. (From Wilson, 1959.)

Temperature °C	Duration of meiosis (prophase 1 = 80% of total) (hours)	Mean chiasma frequency	Range of mean chiasma frequency in different clones	Range of chiasma frequency in different cells
0	864	17.10	16.77–18.70	15–22
5	360	16.03	15.57–16.90	13–20
10	168	15.87	15.03–16.00	12–20
15	84	15.43	14.37–15.43	11–19
20	48	15.50	14.30–15.73	11–19
25	30	14.13	13.70–15.10	11–19

with a glass rod and placed on slides and fixed in 1:1 ethanol/chloroform after removing excess medium. When all cells are colourless, mount gametophytes in lactopropionic orcein. Cell numbers (discounting colourless rhizoids on the basal cells) should be recorded for 50 individuals selected at random from each sample, and the results for the 200 individuals for each treatment at each time pooled and averaged. The graph plotted for mean cell number per protonema against time gives the division rate for the apical cells.

These cultures can be conveniently grown in dishes floating in a controlled temperature water bath, so it is a system in which the effect of temperature on division rate can be easily investigated. The division rate should be determined for a range of temperatures from c.5–30°C at $2\frac{1}{2}$°C intervals to find the minimum, optimum and maximum temperatures for cell division.

A kit for these experiments is available from Philip Harris Biological Ltd.

Mitotic index and the duration of mitotic phases

In certain circumstances, the proportion of cells in visible stages of division (the *mitotic index*) directly reflects the relative durations of those stages. In an asynchronous system it cannot provide absolute values for the duration of individual stages without additional information on the duration of the whole cell cycle (see below). Thus, a high value for the mitotic index in such a system does not mean division is rapid, merely that mitosis occupies a large proportion of the total time. A typical value is about 10%. Values for indices for all the identifiable stages of mitosis in roots of *Hyacinthus orientalis* cultivar 'Roman Hyacinth' are given in Table 4.1.

At best, this method only gives average values and it is known that there are wide variations between cells even within a single root meristem. Moreover, in equating the relative frequency of a stage with its relative duration it is assumed that it is a steady state system, with as many cells ceasing division as are formed by division (which may be approximately true for root tips over short periods), that it is completely asynchronous (which may not always be true of root tips) and that all the cells in the scored sample are at some stage of the cell cycle, none of those apparently in interphase having ceased to prepare for another division (which is almost certainly not true in root tips).

Despite these reservations, this simple technique has yielded interesting results from comparisons of different tissues within the root and shoot apex and comparisons of the same tissues at different temperatures and after different chemical treatments. As might be expected, colchicine inhibition of spindle activity has a marked effect on the indices of the various phases of division.

A measure of total cycle duration can be obtained from mitotic indices in asynchronous cell populations such as root apices if a synchronous sub-population can be identified within it. Treatment with colchicine (6 hours, 0.05%) will cause all nuclei at metaphase to become polyploid as they enter the next cell cycle, while caffeine treatment (1–2 hours, 0.1%) will induce all cells at telophase to become binucleate, and after a further period of culture (see Section 4.2.4) the affected cells can be recognized as they enter mitosis once more. The interval between treatment and the first appearance of colchicine-induced polyploid cells at metaphase or of caffeine-induced binucleate cells at telophase is equal to the duration of the shortest complete mitotic cycle in the cells concerned. However, this may not be the same as the duration in untreated cells, which can only be determined from mitotic indices when the cell population is naturally partially synchronous. Preparations by the standard technique of samples taken every two hours would then reveal peaks of mitotic activity at intervals which equal the length of the cell cycle.

CLOWES, F. A. L. (1976). The root apex. Chapter 7 in *Cell Division in Higher Plants*. Ed. M. M. Yeoman. 253–284. Academic Press, London.

LÓPEZ-SAEZ, J. F., GIMÉNEZ-MARTIN, G. and GONZÁLEZ-FERNÁNDEZ, A. (1966). Duration of the cell division cycle and its dependence on temperature. *Z. Zellforsch.*, **75**, 591–600.

LYNDON, R. F. (1976). The shoot apex. Chapter 8 in *Cell Division in Higher Plants*. Ed. M. M. Yeoman. 285–314. Academic Press, London.

4.2.3 Chiasma formation

The effect of temperature on chiasma formation and frequency

Within a certain range, temperature can have a small but detectable effect on chiasma frequency, reduced frequency usually accompanying increased localization. Outside that range, extremes of temperature frequently induce marked failure of chiasma formation and pairing, although species vary in their response. While any organism which can survive a period in a constant temperature incubator can be used, the best material is probably a clonally propagated, and thus genetically uniform, perennial plant in which meiosis normally occurs underground. In these, the meiotic cells will suffer minimum disturbance from factors other than temperature, such as lack of light. Prolonged treatment does not necessarily have the same effect as a brief 'shock' treatment at the same temperature. It is therefore necessary to ensure that at each temperature, the same phases of division have been subjected to the temperature treatment, which means that the treatment will be longer at low temperatures. Material should be placed at the experimental temperature just prior to meiosis and kept there throughout prophase until it reaches metaphase I, when it can be scored for chiasma frequency. The plants should all be kept at the same constant temperature prior to treatment. *Endymion non-scriptus* is one suitable species, with eight distinguishable bivalents and approximately two chiasmata per bivalent, and clonal material is readily available at the correct stage in the winter, about January. Results have been obtained which reveal a fall in chiasma frequency from 0°C to 25°C (Table 4.2). Natural conditions probably impose temperatures in the range 0°C to 10°C.

DOWRICK, J. (1957). The influence of temperature on meiosis. *Heredity* **11**, 37–49.

WILSON, J. Y. (1959). Temperature effect on chiasma frequency in the bluebell *Endymion non-scriptus*. *Chromosoma* **10**, 337–354.

4.2.4 The induction of chromosome mutation

Much of the research into the induction of chromosome mutation, and in particular chromosome breakage, has used *Vicia faba*, the broad bean, as experimental material. It is readily available, easily handled, and has relatively few chromosomes and these are of reasonable size and distinguishable morphology. The cultures are however susceptible to fungal infection and the following routine should be followed for all experiments to produce quantities of healthy lateral roots.

Wash the seeds of any variety, but all of the same variety and of last season's crop, for 1 minute in 1% Teepol detergent and then for 15 minutes in Domestos diluted 1:5 in water (=4% sodium hypochlorite). Rinse thoroughly and leave in tap water for 2 days. Carefully remove testa. Plant in seed pans in damp vermiculite and leave to germinate. If possible, maintain at a constant temperature. A relatively high temperature (24°C) will deter fungal growth. When the radicles are 1.5–2 cm long (2–3 days later) remove the apical 3 mm with a clean razor blade and replant. Discard any diseased or slow growing individuals. Keep the vermiculite moist but not waterlogged. After 4–7 days each plant will have several laterals about 1 cm long. These should be used in the experimental treatments, taking care to avoid mechanical damage as this suppresses mitosis.

Another common source of uniform root tips for experimental purposes is *Allium cepa*. Many roots can be obtained from a single bulb after cleaning and planting in vermiculite, aerated water, or culture solution. Other clonally propagated bulbs and corms would be equally suitable, such as *Crocus* and *Hyacinthus* but they are normally only available at certain times of the year.

Chromosome mutations of various types are frequently visible during the early phases of germination of aged seeds. Ageing can be accelerated by storage of moist but not fully imbibed dormant seeds at 40°C for about 1 week. In samples with less than 50% viability, up to 10% of dividing cells in the emerging radicle show mutations. Comparisons of progressively older roots will reveal the elimination of the more unstable mutation types.

Polyploidy can be induced in root tips by a 4–6 hour treatment with 0.05% colchicine and revealed by standard preparations of cells after 12–36 hours growth following treatment. The time taken for the first tetraploid cells to appear in mitosis is a measure of the duration of the cell cycle in the most rapidly dividing cells. Polyploid shoots, and thus ultimately polyploid plants, can be induced by treating seedling plumules or adventitious buds with 0.1–0.4% colchicine. Treatment may be more effective if the plant is totally immersed or if the colchicine is applied in cotton wool or lanolin paste. Repeated treatments at high temperatures (c. 30°C) may also help.

Chromosome breakage can be induced by immersing roots for 1 hour at 20°C in a fresh 2.5×10^{-7} M solution of either Mustine hydrochloride or maleic hydrazide (at pH 4 to 5) or for 1 hour at 15°C in a 10^{-2} M solution of 8-ethoxy-caffeine. After thorough washing in water, the material should be replanted and grown at 20°C. Preparations by the standard technique should be taken at 2 hourly intervals after treatment, preceded by colchicine treatment unless anaphase effects are to be examined, during the first 30 hours of recovery. The types, distribution and frequency of aberrations should be recorded according to a standard system. Aberrations induced by alkylating agents such as mustine hydrochloride are first seen at mitosis after a delay which is more or less equal in duration to the G_2 period (Table 2.2). The first aberrations to appear after treatment are therefore induced during the S and G_1 periods. They include sister chromatid reunions (intrachanges). Intrachanges are replaced by non-sister chromatid reunions (interchanges) after a period approximately equal to the duration of the whole mitotic cycle. This indicates that interchanges are among those aberrations induced during the G_2 period but not revealed until the next but one mitosis. In contrast, the effects of oxypurines such as 8-ethoxy-caffeine are detectable at metaphase within 3 to 4 hours of treatment, showing that in this case aberrations induced at G_2 are visible at the next division. For all treatments, examination at longer intervals over several days will reveal the selective survival of the more stable products of chromosome mutation.

EIGSTI, O. J. and DUSTIN, P. (1955). *Colchicine in Agriculture, Medicine, Biology and Chemistry*. Iowa State College Press, Ames, Iowa.

MCLEISH, J. (1953). The action of maleic hydrazide in *Vicia*. *Heredity* **6** (Suppl.), 125–47.

KIHLMAN, B. A. (1975). Root tips of *Vicia faba* for the study of the induction of chromosomal aberrations. *Mut. Res.* **31**, 401–12.

REVELL, S. H. (1953). Chromosome breakage by X-rays and radio-mimetic substances in *Vicia*. *Heredity* **6** (Suppl.), 107–24.

SAVAGE, J. R. K. (1975). Classification and relationships of induced chromosomal structural changes. *J. Med. Genet.* **12**, 103–122.

4.3 Chromosomes and development

Several important features of cell division and chromosome behaviour vary as a normal accompaniment of development (Section 2.4). Perhaps the best known are the changing 'puffs' of dipteran polytene chromosomes but these are not generally found. Of more general occurrence are controlled changes in the rate and direction of division, in the sequence of events of the mitotic cycle, in the condensation cycle of individual chromosomes and in the composition of the chromosome complement. Of these, most is known about changes in rate (Section 4.2.2), but for the remainder almost any research is likely to yield new information.

4.3.1 The orientation of mitotic division in the development of the stomatal complex of grasses

The development of the stomatal complex provides a clear example of the controlled changes in division orientation which are an essential component of development in a higher plant. The grass leaf, with its basal meristem producing files of cells with a gradient of increasing age from the bottom to the top of the leaf, provides a clear demonstration of this developmental sequence. The stomatal complex consists of two dumb-bell-shaped guard cells and two subsidiary cells. The complexes are produced in particular rows of cells formed by the basal meristem and along these rows the developmental sequence can be traced. An unequal division produces the stoma mother cell which later divides again, at right angles to the first division, to produce the two guard cells. Between these two divisions, the nuclei of the nearest cells in both the adjacent rows have moved to a point opposite the stoma mother cell and each cell has then divided unequally at right angles to the long axis of the leaf to produce a small subsidiary cell against the mother cell wall. The complex then differentiates. In other plants, particularly dicotyledons, the sequence is more difficult to follow and often more complex.

Preparations are made, for example from 3–4 day old germinated wheat seeds grown on damp filter paper in Petri dishes, by first removing the whole shoot, slitting it up the middle and then removing the basal 1 cm of the cut first leaf for fixing and staining. Epidermal strips are difficult, but whole mounts are satisfactory. The material should be treated by the standard procedure except that the material is kept intact to preserve the cell rows and perhaps eventually mounted in lacto-propionic acid without orcein to clear the preparation.

Division during this sequence may show spontaneous or induced mis-orientation and subsequent abnormal cell differentiation.

Experimental treatment of such a system might provide much needed information on the mechanism and significance of the re-orientation of division.

PICKETT-HEAPS, J. D. and NORTHCOTE, D. H. (1966). Cell division in the formation of the stomatal complex of the young leaves of wheat. *J. Cell. Sci.*, **1**, 121–8.

STEBBINS, G. L. and SHAH, S. S. (1960). Developmental studies in cell differentiation in the epidermis of monocotyledons. II, Cytological features of stomatal development in the *Gramineae. Devl. Biol.*, **2**, 477–500.

STEBBINS, G. L., SHAH, S. S., JAMIN, D. and JURA, P. (1967). Changed orientation of the mitotic spindle of stomatal guard cell divisions in *Hordeum vulgare. Am. J. Bot.*, **54**, 71–80.

4.4 Chromosomes and reproduction

Most cytological investigations are concerned sooner or later with the transmission of chromosomes through sexual reproduction from one generation to the next. This usually involves analysis of chromosome behaviour at meiosis, during gametophyte development in plants and in the products of fertilization, although the emphasis on these three stages will vary.

4.4.1 Meiosis and pollen fertility in polyploids

Investigations of pollen development in relation to meiotic behaviour in polyploids can do much to explain the effects of polyploidy on fertility, particularly if comparisons are made with related individuals at other levels of ploidy. The approach to such an investigation is indicated by the results in Table 4.3 for *Tradescantia paludosa* ($2x = 12$), *Tradescantia virginiana* ($4x = 24$) and a triploid hybrid ($3x = 18$) (Fig. 4.1). A parallel set of data for isogenic diploid, triploid and tetraploid clones would be even more instructive, particularly if a species with a naturally high chiasma frequency,

such as *Lilium auratum*, could be compared with one with a lower frequency, such as *Tulbaghia violacea*. Analysis of events on the female side and of pollination and seed set would complete the story. Under most British conditions *Tradescantia* rarely sets seed after open pollination even when most of the pollen is viable.

SIMONSEN, O. (1975). Cytogenetic investigations in diploid and autotetraploid populations of *Festuca pratensis. Hereditas*, **79**, 73–108.

SYBENGA, J. (1975). The quantitative analysis of chromosome pairing and chiasma formation based on the relative frequencies of MI configurations. VII Autotetraploids. *Chromosoma*, **50**, 211–22.

4.4.2 The inheritance of B chromosomes

The remarkable B chromosome boosting mechanisms in some plants (Section 2.4.3) provide interesting material for tracing the inheritance of chromosomes through the stages of sexual reproduction from meiosis to the developing seed. The consequence of the boosting mechanism can be seen by examining the endosperm and embryo complements after crosses between plants of known karyotypes. The frequency and distribution of B chromosomes among the progeny indicates the stage at which directed non-disjunction occurs (Fig. 2.10) and this can be confirmed by direct examination of the appropriate stage of development (Section 2.4.4). Directed non-disjunction is rarely totally precise but much remains to be learned about the factors affecting the behaviour of supernumeraries. An analysis of the effects of conditions such as temperature, genotype and the number of B chromosomes in the cell on the regularity of direct non-disjunction would be of great interest, as would a study of B chromosome transmission as revealed by a comparison of the frequency of B chromosomes in pollen and embryo sacs with the frequency in developing seeds after controlled pollination.

Table 4.3 Meiosis and pollen development in 2x, 3x and 4x *Tradescantia* (x = 6) (see Fig. 4.1). Data on chromosome behaviour during successive stages of pollen development obtained during an undergraduate class project. The values for metaphase I were obtained from 25 cells of each clone. All other values refer to the number of cells observed in each category.

	2x *Tradescantia paludosa*	3x Hybrid (*T. virginiana* × *T. brevicaulis*?)	4x *Tradescantia virginiana* cv. 'Purple Dome'
MEIOSIS **METAPHASE I:**			
Mean frequency per cell of			
Univalents	0.1	4.3	2.0
Bivalents	5.9	3.7	5.6
Trivalents		2.1	0.7
Quadrivalents			2.2
Mean chiasma frequency			
per cell	10.4	11.2	13.0
per chromosome	0.87	0.62	0.55
Chiasma distribution frequency			
Proximal	2	0	6
Median	12	15	2
Distal and terminal	246	265	317
% terminal chiasmata	86	87	97
ANAPHASE I:			
Chromosome disjunction			
6/6	20 (100%)		
6/11		2	
7/9		2	
7/10		1	
7/11		1	
8/8		3	
8/9		1	
8/10		4	
9/9		7 (35%)	
11/12			4
11/13			2
12/12			14 (70%)
TELOPHASE I:			
Cells with			
0 lagging chromosomes	46 (92%)	21 (42%)	38 (76%)
1 lagging chromosome	2	9	9
2 lagging chromosomes	2	16	3
>2 lagging chromosomes	—	4	—
UNINUCLEATE POLLEN GRAINS:			
Normal	100 (100%)	56 (56%)	87 (87%)
With one micronucleus		27	11
With two micronuclei		4	1
Empty		13	1

POLLEN GRAIN MITOSIS:

Chromosome number at pollen grain mitosis

6 (x)	50 (100%)		
7		4	
8		12	
9		22 (44%)	
10		7	
11		4	3
12 ($=2x$)			45 (90%)
13			2

BINUCLEATE POLLEN GRAINS:

Normal	100 (100%)	6	85 (85%)
With one micronucleus		13	12
With two micronuclei		6	—
Empty		75 (75%)	3

MATURE POLLEN:

Germination in culture	90%	1%	82%

Boosting mechanisms may well be more widespread among plants with B chromosomes (Section 3.4.2g) than currently realized. A plant which might be particularly well suited for investigations of this kind is *Puschkinia libanotica*. It is a diploid with two genomes of 5 large and distinguishable chromosomes together with up to 7 quite large, partially heterochromatic, B chromosomes (Fig. 4.2c) each of which can also be recognized in interphase nuclei as a chromocentre. The presence of up to four B chromosomes increases the length of the mitotic cycle and the chiasma frequency in the standard bivalents. The B chromosomes may also pair. Preliminary investigations have revealed that in plants with one B chromosome, almost half the pollen grains have two B chromosomes in the generative nucleus and none in the vegetative nucleus, as revealed by interphase chromocentres (Fig. 4.2b and c) and dividing generative cell complements. This suggests random transmission at pollen meiosis and directed non-disjunction at pollen grain mitosis. This mechanism is not uncommon in grasses but has not previously been described in the Liliaceae. Transmission in the embryo sac has not been studied. The plant is relatively cheap, easily maintained and propagated and many of the plants available from commercial sources have B chromosomes. Preparations of meiosis, pollen grain mitosis and, in germinating pollen, generative cell mitosis, are clear and not difficult to obtain at the appropriate time of year (Appendix 1). It sets seed readily, so developing embryos and endosperm are also readily available.

BARLOW, P. W. and VOSA, C. G. (1969). The chromosomes of *Puschkinia libanotica* during mitosis. *Chromosoma* **27**, 436–441).

BARLOW, P. W. and VOSA, C. G. (1970). The effect of supernumerary chromosomes on meiosis in *Puschkinia libanotica* (Liliaceae). *Chromosoma* **30**, 344–355.

JONES, R. N. (1975). B chromosome systems in flowering plant and animal species. *Int. Rev. Cytol.* **40**, 1–100.

4.5 Chromosomes and the species

The simplest approach to considering the chromosome complement in relation to the species is to describe the mitotic karyotype of a representative individual. This will provide the taxonomist with a useful additional character in the description of a species and

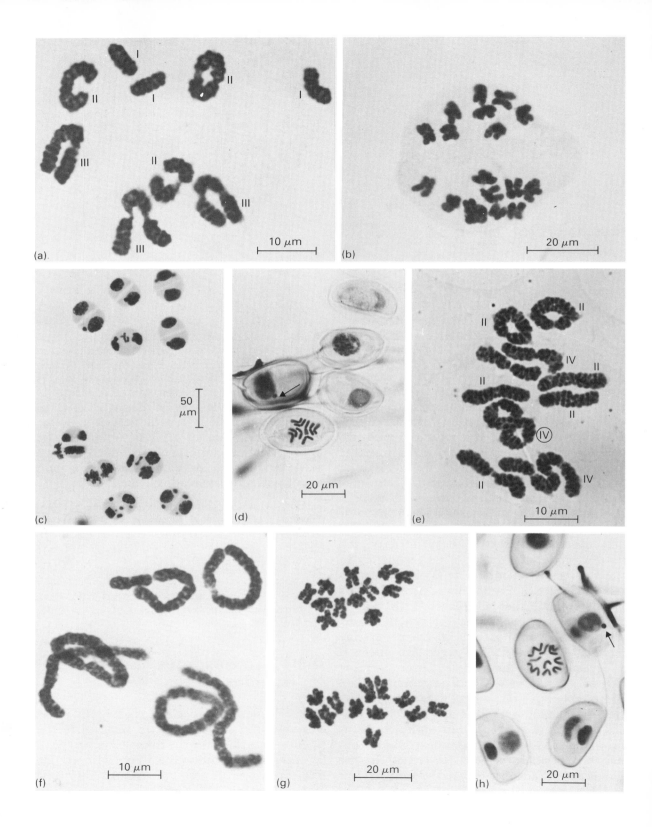

(a)

(b)

(c)

(d)

(e)

(f)

(g)

(h)

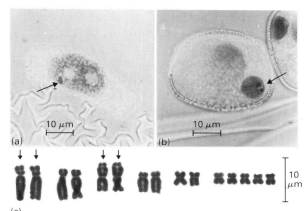

(a)   (b)

(c)

Fig. 4.2 Supernumerary B chromosomes in *Puschkinia libanotica*. **a**, Root tip cell of a plant with one B chromosome ($2n = 10 + 1B$). The interphase nucleus contains one chromocentre (arrowed). **b**, Two chromocentres in the generative nucleus (arrow) and no chromocentres in the vegetative nucleus of the pollen grains of the same plant as **a** indicates directed non-disjunction (DND) at pollen grain mitosis. **c**, Chromosome complement of a root tip cell of a plant with 5 B chromosomes. Nucleolar chromosomes arrowed. (From a preparation by Dr J. H. Timmis.)

may even reveal a situation of considerable significance. Moreover, it is surprising how many species, even in Britain, have not yet been studied adequately in this way. For example, until recently there was no detailed description of the karyotype of *Iris pseudacorus*, the Yellow Flag, even though it is a conspicuous plant with one of the largest flowers in the European flora and belongs to a genus which has received considerable attention from cytologists. Obtaining the first accurate chromosome count and description for British material made a successful student project.

DYER, A. F., ELLIS, T. H. N., LITHGOW, E., LOWTHER, S., MASON, I. and WILLIAMS, D. (1976). The karyotype of *Iris pseudacorus* L. *Trans. bot. Soc. Edinb.* **42**, 421–29.

4.5.1 Karyotype analysis in *Tulbaghia*

A more elaborate approach is to use comparisons of karyotypes to indicate relationships between individuals of distinct genotypes. Though by no means always possible, this approach is widely used by taxonomists in conjunction with other data, and has sometimes yielded unique information which has had a significant effect on classification. A useful introduction to this approach is the 'staged' investigation, using vegetative, floral and chromosomal characters, of the relationship of a number of 'unknown' plants. A successful student project involves living material of 6 labelled clones of *Tulbaghia*, which are *T. verdoornia* ($2x$), *T. violacea var. obtusa* ($2x$), *T. violacea var. violacea* ($2x$) and its isogenic tetrasomic triploid ($3x + 1$) and tetraploid ($4x$) autopolyploids, and the synthesized $2x$ hybrid, *T. verdoornia* × *T. violacea*. All are vigorous, clonally propagated perennials which are easy to maintain. The diploid species are distinct in vegetative and floral characters and have some characteristic chromosomes (Fig. 3.2d). The hybrid is morphologically intermediate, with a hybrid karyotype and evidence of structural heterozygosity at meiosis and is sterile. The *T. violacea*

Fig. 4.1 Meiosis and pollen grain mitosis in polyploid *Tradescantia* ($x = 6$) (see Table 4.3). See Fig. 3.1 for diploid *T. bracteata* ($2n = 2x = 12$). **a** to **d**: triploid hybrid, *T. virginiana* ($4x = 24$) × *T. brevicaulis* ($2x = 12$). **a**, Meiosis metaphase I, with three trivalents (III), three bivalents (II) and three univalents (I). **b**, Anaphase I with 8/10 disjunction. **c**, Interphase I showing micronuclei resulting from lagging chromosomes at anaphase. **d**, Pollen grain mitosis, with nine chromosomes. One of the other, mononucleate, pollen grains contains a micronucleus (arrow). **e** to **h**: tetraploid *T. virginiana* ($2n = 4x = 24$). **e**, Meiosis metaphase I, with one ring quadrivalent Ⓘ𝐕, two chain quadrivalents (IV), and six bivalents (II). See also Fig. 2.1. **f**, Meiosis metaphase I, with six quadrivalents, three rings and three chains. Such cells are rare in this material. **g**, Anaphase I with 12/12 disjunction. **h**, Pollen grain mitosis, with twelve chromosomes. One of the other, binucleate, pollen grains contains a micronucleus (arrow).

varieties differ markedly in floral characters but are cytologically indistinguishable. The polyploids are similar in appearance to the diploid but larger. There are sufficient characters for the student to be able to determine the relationships unaided, although of course to determine the names would require a taxonomic key.

BURBIDGE, R. B. (1978). A revision of the genus *Tulbaghia* (Liliaceae). *Notes Roy. Bot. Gard. Edinb.*, **36**, 77–103.

DYER, A. F. (1963). Allocyclic segments of chromosomes and the structural heterozygosity that they reveal. *Chromosoma*, **13**, 545–76.

VOSA, C. G. (1966). Chromosome variation in *Tulbaghia*. *Heredity*, **21**, 305–12.

VOSA, C. G. (1966). *Tulbaghia* hybrids. *Heredity*, **21**, 675–87.

VOSA, C. G. (1975). The cytotaxonomy of the genus *Tulbaghia*. *Annali di Botanica*, **34**, 47–121.

4.5.2 The cytogenetics of *Ranunculus ficaria* L

A less artificial investigation is the study of natural populations of a chromosomally polymorphic species. The Lesser Celandine has received considerable attention from cytogeneticists but still the relationships within the species are far from clear. Taxonomists recognize four morphologically similar sub-species: ssp. *fertilis* (Clapham) Lawalrée from Western Europe, spp. *calthifolius* (Reichenb.) Arcangeli from S.E. Europe and ssp. *ficariiformis* Rouy et Fouc. from the Mediterranean region, all of which produce many achenes, and ssp. *bulbifera* Lawalrée from throughout most of Europe, which typically produces bulbils in leaf axils and few achenes. Bulbil forming plants are almost always tetraploid ($4x = 32$), those without almost always diploid ($2x = 16 + 0 - 8B$). Occasional exceptions include a few tetraploid forms without bulbils and triploids with bulbils ($3x = 24$), reported from Britain, Portugal, Italy, Germany and Poland. Pentaploid and hexaploid plants have also been reported once or twice. The species is very variable and while in one population some diploids can be distinguished from some tetraploids by characters such as flower and leaf size, petal number, leaf shape and pattern, stomatal cell and nuclear volume and pollen size, there is considerable overlap between the cytotypes. The relationship between leaf characters and cytotype can vary between populations. On the basis of plant and chromosome morphology it has been previously claimed that the near sterile tetraploids are clonal autopolyploids or at least derived from chromosomally indistinguishable sexual diploids. Tetraploid variation has been attributed to many independent origins from different diploids, although some tetraploid fertility is implicated in the suggested origin of triploids by crossing between diploids and tetraploids. Cross-pollination in this species is apparently by flies and beetles. Achenes are dispersed by ants and bulbil dispersal may be by water which would account for the predominance of tetraploid populations along the sides of paths and streams. All cytotypes also reproduce vegetatively, presumably with no dispersal unless the ground is disturbed, by subterranean root tubers.

Surveys in Britain have shown that the three lower ploidy levels occur throughout the country, but the B chromosomes are restricted to diploids in the south where they may occur in up to 50% of the individuals in the population. As in Europe, the tetraploid appears to be more frequent in shady habitats and is therefore more common relative to the diploid on the east side of Britain where the species grows less often in exposed habitats. Although in coastal habitats populations appear to be exclusively diploid, the diploid and tetraploid are frequently mixed within the other populations. Triploids have now been reported in about 10 widely distributed localities, usually in populations with many tetraploids and fewer diploids, and more extensive surveys may show them to be more wide-spread. They can occur as occasional scattered individuals or form a major proportion of the population.

An investigation of a population near Edinburgh has provided a successful student project during the growing season from February to May in successive years. The population is small (10 m × 15 m) and compact, with closely packed plants of *R.*

them in this population were the reverse of those reported for other British sites. One particularly robust tetraploid form with distinctively marked leaves dominates a large part of the population and appears to be a particularly successful clone, but it is not

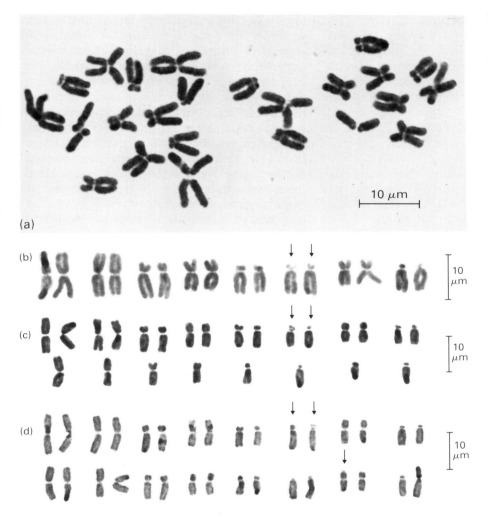

(a)

(b)

(c)

(d)

Fig. 4.3 The mitotic chromosome complements of colchicine pre-treated root tip cells of diploid (2*x*), triploid (3*x*) and tetraploid (4*x*) plants of *Ranunculus ficaria* (*x* = 8) taken from the same population. Arrows indicate chromosomes with 'satellites'. **a**, Triploid complement at metaphase. **b**, Diploid complement arranged in an idiogram as eight distinguishable pairs. **c**, Triploid complement (not the same cell as **a**). Two of the genomes appear to be very similar to the genome of diploids but the third genome is slightly different. **d**, Tetraploid complement. Two of the genomes appear very similar to the genome of diploids; the other two resemble the odd genome of the triploid apart from one heteromorphic pair, presumably the consequence of structural rearrangement.

ficaria providing the only members of the herb layer under a dense canopy of trees. A random sample on a grid system of 40 plants included 33 tetraploids, 5 diploids and two separate and phenotypically distinct triploids. Both tetraploid and diploid plants are phenotypically very variable and the few morphological features which distinguished

known whether its exclusion from part of the population reflects limited dispersal capabilities or an ecological preference. The tetraploids form the characteristic cauline bulbils and, in addition, produce some viable pollen, as demonstrated by pollen germination in culture, and ten or more achenes per flower although it is not known whether the latter are viable. The diploids produce pollen with a higher germination percentage and many achenes but the triploids are sterile. The diploids occur in small groups, perhaps as a result of limited achene dispersal. The tetraploid karyotype (Fig. 4.3d) shows structural polymorphism for the nucleolar satellites and some other small differences in chromosome morphology between the genomes which might reflect an allopolyploid origin. Two of the genomes in the triploid (Fig. 4.3a,c) and in the tetraploid resemble that of the diploid (Fig. 4.3b), and the triploid appears to be an allopolyploid hybrid between the diploid and the tetraploid.

There are at present three possible interpretations, none entirely satisfactory, of the relationships between the three cytotypes. If the $3x$ and $4x$ forms are autopolyploid and sterile clones, then each $3x$ has formed by fertilization of an unreduced gamete in a diploid while the tetraploid variability represents many recent doublings of a range of different diploid genotypes. If the tetraploid is autopolyploid but partially fertile, it must have regular bivalent or multivalent disjunction due to low chiasma frequency and/or genome differentiation since its origin a considerable time ago. Phenotypically variable populations of tetraploids could then have arisen by recombination and perhaps also by introgression with diploids involving unreduced gametes of the latter. At the same time, crosses between such tetraploids and normal reduced gametes of diploids could have produced the triploids. Finally, the possibility should not be discounted that the tetraploids are fertile segmental allopolyploids formed by doubling in diploid hybrids between two cytological forms, one of which may be now extinct, restricted to some remote part of the species range, or widespread but not recognized as being distinct within the overall variability. Such tetraploids, which may have arisen independently on several occasions, could also have produced phenotypic variability and triploids through sexual reproduction. It

may be that all three types of polyploid occur within the species range. The occasional pentaploids and hexaploids could be the consequences of fertilizations involving unreduced gametes of the triploids or tetraploids.

One curious feature is the bulbil formation of nearly all tetraploids. It is not unusual for a polyploid species to survive because of vegetative propagation, despite temporary or permanent sexual sterility, but usually the propensity for propagation is detectable in the ancestral diploid and it is developed in the surviving polyploids in response to strong selection pressures. So far however no diploid origin for bulbil formation has been found in *R. ficaria*. Either the characteristic entered the tetraploid from a second, unknown diploid, or it arose when the original near-sterile autotetraploid was formed and is responsible for its survival, or it has arisen since then and was not essential for the polyploid's survival.

It will only be possible to reveal the extent and origin of karyotype diversity in this species when more information is available. In particular, further detailed karyotype analysis and investigations of meiosis in different genotypes of the three cytotypes are required, along with detailed population analyses. Any single-population survey, however restricted, could yield new information, while a more detailed analysis of chromosome behaviour within individual plants or a collation of survey results over a wide ecological range or geographical area is almost certain to add to our understanding of the evolution of this species. In the southern part of the range, the function and inheritance of the B chromosomes in some diploids, which seem to have a boosting mechanism similar to *Crepis capillaris* and others (Sections 2.4.3, 4.4.2), present further intriguing problems.

This species is particularly suitable for student investigation. It is widespread and abundant, successful and resilient. It is easy to maintain in cultivation and easy to find in the wild. It yields clear chromosome preparations, and root tips, meiotic cells and developing pollen and endosperm can be obtained from plants in the wild and in the laboratory. It includes several of the cytological conditions described in earlier sections and offers a number of cytogenetical problems capable of solution.

BRIGGS, D. and WALTERS, S. M. (1969). Plant variation and evolution. Weidenfeld and Nicolson, World University Library.

EHRENDORFER, F. (1961). Akzessorische Chromosomen bei *Achillea*. Struktur, cytologisches Verhalten, zahlenmyssige Instabilität und Enstehung. *Chromosoma*, **11**, 523–52.

FROST, S. (1960). A new mechanism for the numerical increase of accessory chromosomes in *Crepis pannonica. Hereditas*, **46**, 497–503.

GILL, J. J. B., JONES, B. M. G., MARCHANT, C. J., MCLEISH, J. and OCKENDEN, D. J. (1972). The distribution of chromosome races of *Ranunculus ficaria* L. in the British Isles. *Ann. Bot.*, **36**, 31–47.

HEYWOOD, V. H. and WALKER, S. (1961). Morphological separation of cytological races in *Ranunculus ficaria* L. *Nature*, **189**, 604–5.

LARTER, L. N. H. (1932). Chromosome variation and behaviour in *Ranunculus* L. *J. Genet.*, **26**, 255–83.

MARCHANT, C. J. and BRIGHTON, C. A. (1971). Mitotic instability in the short arm of a heteromorphic SAT chromosome of the tetraploid *Ranunculus ficaria* L. *Chromosoma*, **34**, 1–18.

MARCHANT, C. J. and BRIGHTON, C. A. (1974). Cytological diversity and triploid frequency in a complex population of *Ranunculus ficaria. Ann. Bot.*, **38**, 7–15.

MARSDEN-JONES, E. M. (1935). *Ranunculus ficaria* L. Life history and pollination. *J. Linn Soc. Bot.*, **50**, 39–55.

MARSDEN-JONES, E. M. and TURRILL, W. B. (1952). Studies on *Ranunculus ficaria. J. Genet.*, **50**, 522–34.

METCALF, C. R. (1939). The sexual reproduction of the *Ranunculus ficaria. Ann. Bot.*, **13**, 91–103.

NEVES, B. (1942). Sobre a cariologia del *Ranunculus ficaria* L. *Bol. Soc. Brot.*, **16**, 169–81.

POGAN, E. and WCISLO, H. (1975). Studies in *Ranunculus ficaria* L. III, Karyotype analysis. *Acta Biol. Crac. Ser. Bot.*, **18**, 79–99.

RUTISHAUSER, A. and ROTHLISBERGER, E. (1966). Boosting mechanism of B chromosomes in *Crepis capillaris*. In 'Chromosomes Today', Vol. 1. (Eds. C. D. Darlington and K. R. Lewis), 28–30. Oliver & Boyd, Edinburgh.

4.6 Conclusion

Although the activities of chromosomes have been considered in the preceding pages under a number of different headings, the distinctions have been artificial ones. The synthetic activities of chromosomes during division and development and the mechanical events during mitosis and reproduction all ultimately relate to the success of the organism in its natural habitat and no single component feature can be wholly understood if considered in isolation. The objective of this book is to bring the reader to the point where the knowledge gained from the guided examination of a range of material by a variety of techniques can be readily applied to an independent investigation of the whole spectrum of interrelated chromosome activities operating within a single species in the wild. *Ranunculus ficaria* provides an excellent example of material with which to achieve this transition, making this an appropriate place to end a practical introduction to the study of chromosomes.

Appendix 1
Chromosome calendar

The reproductive phases of many animals and plants are seasonal even when somatic development is not. This is an important factor in determining the availability of material suitable for chromosome studies. In the following tables the dates given indicate when the relevant stages are naturally available or can be made available by appropriate cultural conditions. The species listed have been selected for their availability and clear karyotypes so as to represent a range of cytological stages and conditions. The uses indicated in column 1 refer only to those for which the material is best suited. For further information and additional species refer to the appropriate parts of Chapters 2 or 3.

Angiosperms

Hardy temperate plants, including those native to Great Britain, are seasonal in their growth and flowering and any possible extension of this season requires environmental manipulation by varying planting time and supplying supplementary heat and light. Those perennial angiosperms (P) which normally flower early in the season, often after undergoing meiosis below ground within a bulb, corm or rhizome, include several of the monocotyledons and dicotyledons with few, large, chromosomes which provide good material for cytological investigations. They usually suffer from the disadvantages that the plant has to be sacrificed for meiotic studies and that it is only possible to advance or delay normal development over a limited period. Some later flowering perennials (L) with meiosis above ground are more readily manipulated by splitting and re-planting under optimal conditions at any time of the year but for best results some require a period of dormancy before growth is stimulated and some still have a more or less restricted flowering season, even when vegetative growth is induced all the year round, unless an appropriate daylength regime is provided. Those annuals, biennials and perennials (S) which can be induced to flower in

the first season after seed sowing can usually be brought into flower at any time of the year if given suitable conditions.

Key to abbreviations

Uses as demonstration material (column 1):

The number(s) opposite a name refer to the chromosome characteristic(s) and activities of those listed below which can be most clearly demonstrated in that species.
1, Mitosis. 1a, Gametophyte mitosis. 1b, Endosperm mitosis. 2, Karyotype analysis. 3, Meiosis. 4, Chiasma distribution. 5, Acrocentrics. 6, Telocentrics. 7, Dispersed centromere. 8, Conspicuous nucleolar organizer. 9, Nucleolar organizer suppression in hybrid. 10, Chromocentres. 10a, Sex chromosomes. 10b, H segments. 11, Endopolyploidy. 12, Karyotype segregation during development. 13, Chromosome number. 14, Chromosome size. 15, Karyotype asymmetry. 16, Apomixis. 17, Polyploidy. 18, Aneuploidy. 19, Supernumerary chromosomes. 20, Dysploidy. 21, Structural heterozygosity. 21a, Deletion. 21b, Interchange. 21c, Inversion.

Origin and cultural type (column 2):

C = obtainable from commercial sources (see p. 84). L = later flowering perennials with meiosis above ground. NH = not hardy in Great Britain. P = early flowering perennial (*with meiosis below ground in winter). S = annual or perennial flowering in first year from seed. W = grows wild in Britain and can be sampled in moderation and with any necessary permission. (W) = grows wild in Britain but scarce and should only be sampled from stocks in cultivation.

Time of year (columns 4 to 7):

1, 2, 12 etc. = available in January, February, December, etc. AYR = available all the year round. ( ) = season extended by artificial heat and light.

Species (and uses as demonstration material)	Origin and cultural type	Chromosome number n =	Time of year			
			Sporophyte mitosis	Meiosis	Gametophyte mitosis	Endosperm
Allium cepa (1, 2, 3, 4, 8)	C, L	8	(AYR)	5–6	5–6	6
,, *cernum* (16)		8		6–7	6–7	6
,, *fistulosum* (1, 2, 3, 4, 8, 21)	C, L	8	(AYR)	4–5	4–5	4–5
,, *neapolitanum* (13)	C, L	7	(AYR)	(AYR)	(AYR)	(AYR)
,, *paradoxum* (1, 2, 8, 16)	P, W	8	2–4	3	3	
,, *sativum* (21b)	C		(AYR)	5		
,, *triquetrum* (1, 2, 3, 8, 21)	P(W)	7	2–4	3–4	3–4	4–5
,, *ursinum* (1, 2, 3, 8)	P, W	8	1–4	3–4	3–4	4–5
Bellevalia romana (1, 1a, 2, 8, 15)	C, P★	4	(10–4)	4	4	4–5
Campanula persicifolia (21b)	C, L, W	8, 16		5–7		
Crepis species (2, 13, 15, 20)	S, W	3–7	(AYR)	5–6(AYR)		
,, *capillaris* (9, 12, 19)	S, W	3	6–9(AYR)	6–9(AYR)		
,, *setosa*	S, W	4	7–9(AYR)	7–9(AYR)		
,, *foetida*	S, W	5	6–8(AYR)	6–8(AYR)		
,, *rubra* (9)	S	5	7–9(AYR)	7–9(AYR)		
,, *paludosa*	S, W	6	7–9(AYR)	7–9(AYR)		
Crocus balansae (1, 2, 3, 5, 8, 13)	C, P★	3	(10–4)	10		
Endymion non-scriptus (1, 2, 3, 8)	P★, W	8	1–4	1–2	2–3	
Fritillaria species (1, 2, 3, 4, 14)	C, P★	12	(10–4)	3–4		
Galanthus species (1b)	C, P★, (W)	12				11–4
Haemanthus albiflos (1b)	C, NH	8				8–9
,, *coccineus* (1b)	C, NH	8				8–9
,, cv. 'Koenig Albert' (1b)	C, NH					3–4
,, *multiflorus* (1b)	C, NH	9				6–7
,, *puniceus* (1b)	C, NH	8				2–3
Haplopappus gracilis (1, 2, 3, 8, 12, 13, 15, 19)	S	2	(AYR)	4(AYR)	(AYR)	
Hordeum vulgare (1, 2, 8)	C, S	7	(AYR)	(AYR)	(AYR)	(AYR)
Hyacinthus orientalis cultivars (1, 1a, 1b, 2, 3, 8, 11, 14, 15, 17, 18, 21)	C, P★	8–16	(10–4)	10		4
Ipheon uniflorum (1, 2, 3, 8, 11)	C, P	6	(10–4)	4	4	5–6
Kniphofia species (1, 2, 3)	C	6		4–6		
Lilium species (1, 1a, 1b, 2, 3, 4, 5, 11, 12, 14, 15, 21)	C	12	(10–5)	5–9		
,, *auratum*	C	12	(10–5)	8–9		
,, *martagon*	C, (W)	12	(10–5)	7		
,, *regale*	C	12	(10–5)	7		
Lolium perenne (1, 2, 8)	C, S, W	7, 14	(AYR)	(AYR)	(AYR)	(AYR)
,, *multiflorum*	C, S, W	7, 14	(AYR)	(AYR)	(AYR)	(AYR)
Luzula species (7)	L, S, W	3–38		7		
Narcissus species and cultivars (1, 2, 3, 21)	C, P★	7–14	10–4	10–12	12–5	2–5
,, *bulbocodium*	C, P★	7, 14 etc.		12	12	
,, *poeticus*	C, P★ (W)	7		11		
,, *pseudo-narcissus*	C, P★ (W)	7		10		
Nothoscordum inodorum (1, 2, 5, 13, 14, 15, 16, 20, 21)	C, L (W)	9, 10	(AYR)	4–10	5–10	5–10
Oenothera biennis (21b)	C, S	7		6–7		
Ornithogalum montanum (10, 15)	C	9	(10–4)	4–5		5
,, *pyrenaicum* (10, 15)	C, (W)	8, 16	(10–4)	5–6		
,, *umbellatum* (10, 15)	C, (W)	8, 16 etc.	(10–4)	4–5		

Paeonia species (1, 2, 3, 4, 21)	C, L	5, 10		4–5	4–5	
Paris quadrifolia (1, 3, 17)	P★, (W)	10	(10–4)		4	4–5
Primula kewensis (4x) (17)	C, NH, S	18		3		
Puschkinia libanotica (1, 2, 3, 10, 12, 13, 19)	C, P★	5	(10–4)		2	4
Ranunculus ficaria (1, 1a, 2, 3, 8, 12, 15, 17, 19)	P, W	8	2–4	3–4	3–4	3–4
Rhoeo discolor (21b)	C, NH	6	(AYR)	(AYR)	(AYR)	
Scilla sibirica (10b)	C, P★	6	(10–4)			
Secale cereale (1, 1a, 2, 3, 4, 8, 10b, 12, 19)	C, S	7	(AYR)	6(AYR)	6(AYR)	6(AYR)
Tradescantia bracteata (1, 2, 3, 4)	C, L	6	(AYR)	5–10	5–10	
,, *paludosa* (1, 2, 3, 4)	C, NH	6	(AYR)	(AYR)	(AYR)	
,, *virginiana* cultivar 'Purple Dome' (1, 1a, 2, 3, 4, 17, 19, 21c)	C, L	12	(AYR)	2–12	2–12	
Trillium species (1, 2, 3, 4, 10b, 12, 14, 15, 21c)						
,, *cernuum*	C, P★	5	(10–4)	1–3	4–5	4–6
,, *chloropetalum*	C, P★	5	(10–4)	10–11		4
,, *erectum*	C, P★	5	(10–4)	11–12	4	4–5
,, *grandiflorum*	C, P★	5	(10–4)	8–10	2–3	4–5
,, *kamtschaticum*	C, P★	5	(10–4)	12–1		4–5
,, *luteum*	C, P★	5	(10–4)	10–11	2–3	4–5
,, *ovatum*	C, P★	5	(10–4)	9–10		3–5
,, *sessile*	C, P★	5	(10–4)	10–11		3–4
Triticum aestivum (1, 17)	C, S	21	(AYR)	(AYR)	(AYR)	(AYR)
Tulbaghia; most species incl. *T. violacea* and *T. verdoornia* (1, 2, 3, 4, 8, 9, 11, 14, 17, 19, 21)	L	6	(AYR)	5–9	5–9	5–9
Tulipa species (1, 2, 3)	C, P★	12	(10–4)	9–11	2–5	5
Uvularia grandiflora (1, 2, 3)	C, P★			2	2	
Vicia species (1, 2, 14, 20)	S, W	5–8	(AYR)	5–8		
,, *faba* (1, 2, 10b, 14)	C, S	6	(AYR)			
Zea mays (1, 10, 19)	C, S	10	(AYR)	(AYR)	(AYR)	(AYR)
Zebrina pendula (1, 2, 6)	C, NH	12	(AYR)	(6–8)		

Insects

There are several species commonly found in the wild in Britain (W) or easily cultured (C) which are particularly suitable for meiotic studies.

Species		$n =$	Time of year (meiosis and associated mitoses)
Chironomus tentans (3, 13)	W	4	4–9
Chorthippus species (1, 2, 3, 4, 6, 10a)	W	8, 9	7–9 (adult)
Culex pipiens (3, 11)	W	5	4–9
Drosophila species (1, 2, 3, 11, 13, 20)	C	3–6	(AYR)
Forficula auricularia (3)	W	12	7–8
Locusta migratoria (1, 2, 3, 4, 6, 10a, 12, 19)	C	11–12	(AYR)
Myrmeleotettix maculatus (3, 10a, 19)	W	8, 9	6–9 (adult)
Periplaneta americana (3, 10a, 21b)	C, W	16, 17	(AYR)
Schistocerca gregaria (1, 2, 3, 4, 6, 10a)	C	11, 12	(AYR)
Tipula maxima (1, 2, 3, 13, 10a)	W	3, 4	3–4 (last instar)

Appendix 2
Genetic garden

For those who wish to establish an easily maintained collection of species which can be used to demonstrate most of the major features of karyotypes covered in Chapter 3, as well as the important aspects of division and development in Chapter 2, the answer is a 'Genetic Garden'. The following selection of widely available hardy perennials grown in an outdoor bed will meet many of the needs and require very little maintenance. The numbers after each name refer to the page(s) where further information and additional examples are to be found.

SPECIES LIST

Allium cepa (35, 65, 112), *A. fistulosum* (65, 111, 113), *A. neapolitanum* (111), *A. sativum* (111), *A. triquetrum* (111, 113), *A. ursinum*† (35, 65, 113).

Campanula persicifolia (87, 109, 111).

Chrysanthemum cv. 'Orange Sweetheart' (109).

Crocus aureus (113), *C. balansae* (35, 85, 113), *C. chrysanthus* (111, 113), *C. speciosus* (111), *C. sieberi* (113).

Endymion non-scriptus† 2x (2, 65, 85); 3x (87, 88, 111), *E. hispanicus* 2x (35, 65, 111); 3x (87, 88, 111).

Hyacinthus orientalis cv. 'Anne Marie' (87, 88, 110), cv. 'Blue Giant' (87, 110), cv. 'City of Haarlem' (87, 112), cv. 'Myosotis' (112), cv. 'Ostara' (110, 112), cv. 'Rosalie' (85, 87, 112), cv. 'Tubergen's Scarlet' (86, 110), cv. 'Vanguard' (35, 45, 84).

Iris histrioides (87, 112), *I. reticulata* (87, 112), *I. reticulata* cv. 'Joyce' (87, 112).

Lilium hansoni (35, 45, 84), *L. martagon* (42, 65, 111), *L.* cv. 'Marhan' (86, 88, 112).

Narcissus bulbocodium (28, 111), *N.* cv. 'Geranium' (88).

Nothoscordum inordum (= *N. fragrans*) (84, 87, 110).

Ornithogalum umbellatum (84).

Paeonia delavayi (65, 113), *P. peregrina* (113).

Puschkinia libanotica (48, 85, 123).

Ranunculus ficaria v. *fertilis*† (35, 48, 85, 113), *R. ficaria* v. *bulbifera*† (44, 112, 126).

Rumex acetosa† (28, 86, 87).

Tradescantia virginiana cv. 'Purple Dome'* (42, 65, 86, 121), *T. brevicaulis** (35, 66, 113), *T. virginiana* × *T. brevicaulis** (87, 122).

Trillium grandiflorum (28, 45, 65, 84, 109).

Tulbaghia verdoonia (2x)* (85, 111, 125), *T. violacea* v. *violacea* (2x, 3x + 1 and 4x)*, *T. violacea* v. *obtusa* (2x)* (44, 47, 66, 84, 121, 125), *T. verdoornia* × *T. violacea* (2x)* (28, 88, 110, 125).

† Available from wild populations.
* Available from Philip Harris Biological Ltd.
The remainder available from commercial sources, P. de Jager & Sons Ltd. of Marden, Kent, and Perry's of Enfield can supply many of them.

Appendix 3
Film loops and films on Chromosomes during division

The emphasis in the following films and loops is on chromosomes and nuclear division. The list does not include treatments of genetic, embryological and developmental topics which include a brief mention of chromosomes.

Instructional film loops

Colour, 8 mm, Super and Standard unless indicated. ★Super 8 only. †Standard 8 only.

Title	Duration	Catalogue no.	Distributor (sale)
Mitosis in plant cells		2001/C2★ ⎫	Eothen
Abnormal mitosis in plant cells		2001/C3★ ⎬	H.B.S.
Mitosis in animal cells		2001/C5★ ⎭	
Mitosis		XX0144† ⎫	H.B.S.
		XX0456★ ⎭	
Meiosis		XX0133† ⎫	H.B.S.
		XX0447★ ⎭	
Cell Division		†	Technicolor
'Continuity of Life' series (with teaching notes)			
Mitotic divisions – cells of onion root tip	150 sec	601R13	EFVA
		BC/263	Ealing
			Technicolor
Mitosis in animal cells – white fish embryo	130 sec	601R14	EFVA
		BC/264	Ealing
			Technicolor
Mitotic cell division – staminal hairs of *Tradescantia*	150 sec	601R15	EFVA
		BC/265	Ealing
			H.B.S.
			Technicolor
Spermatogenesis of grasshopper – meiosis in sperm mother cells	160 sec	601R18	EFVA
		BC/268	Ealing
			H.B.S.
			Technicolor
Comparison of chromosome behaviour in meiosis and mitosis	140 sec	601R19	EFVA
		BC/269	Ealing
			H.B.S.
			Technicolor
'Biology of Development' Audio-Visual Course (with tape and work book)			
Mitosis (Programme 3)		0582 270065 ⎫	Longman
Meiosis (Programme 4)		0582 270081 ⎭	

16 mm films

Title	Silent or sound	Colour or black and white	Duration (mins)	Distribution (hire)
Living cell – meiosis (1968)			14	EFVA
Living cell – mitosis (1968)			13	EFVA
Meiosis (1955)	So	Co	12	AH, BH, EFVA
Meiosis (1977)	So	Co	25	OUFL
Mitosis (1958)	So	Co	11	AH, BH, EFVA
Mitosis (1963)				EFVA
Mitosis	So	B/W	25	OUFL
Mitosis in endosperm (1957)	Si	B/W	25	BFI, FP, RMS
Mitosis and meiosis (1960)	So	Co	17	CFL, EFVA
Phase contrast microscopy of spermatocytes in the grasshopper (*Psophus stridulus*) (1936)	Si	B/W	27	BFI

Key to distributors:

AH: News and Information Bureau, Australia House, Strand, London, W.C.2.

BFI: British Film Institute, Film Library, 81 Dean Street, London, W.1.

BH: Boulton-Hawker Films Ltd, Hadleigh, Ipswich, Suffolk.

CFL: Central Film Library, Government Building, Bromyard Avenue, Acton, London, W.3.

Scottish Central Film Library, 16–17 Woodside Terrace, Charing Cross, Glasgow, C.3.

Central Film Library of Wales, 42 Park Place, Cardiff.

EFVA: Educational Foundation for Visual Aids, Foundation Film Library, Weybridge, Surrey.

Ealing: Ealing Division, Hugh Wood & Son Ltd, 23 Leman Street, London, E.1.

Eothen: Eothen Film Ltd, 107–109 Wardour Street, London, W1V 4PJ.

FP: Films of Poland, 81 Portland Place, London, W.1.

HBS: Harris Biological Supplies Ltd, Oldmixon, Weston-super-Mare, Somerset.

Longman: Promotion Co-ordinator, Room 502, Longman Group Ltd, Burnt Mill, Harlow, Essex, CM20 2JE.

OUFL: Open University Film Library in association with Guild Sound and Vision Ltd, Woodston House, Peterborough, PE2 9PZ.

RMS: Royal Microscopical Society, Tavistock House South, Tavistock Square, London, W.C.1.

Technicolor: Technicolor Ltd, Bath Road, Harmandsworth, West Drayton, Middlesex.

Index